HAPPY TOGETHER

Daily Insight
for Families
from Scripture

Pebble Press, Lethbridge, Alberta, Canada

HAPPY TOGETHER
Daily Insights for Families from Scripture
Second Edition
Copyright © 2014 Ann Norford and Bryan Norford

ISBN-10: 1500929034
ISBN-13: 978-1500929039

To Our Readers

We dedicate this book to you with our prayer that you will find in its pages guidance to the joyful and fulfilling family life you desire and God intends for you.

Thank You

To Dr. James Packer of Regent College, Vancouver for kindly contributing a foreword to our first edition and allowing for its inclusion in this second edition.

Also by Ann and Bryan Norford
War Kids: Growing Up in World War Two England

Books by Bryan Norford
Guess Who's Coming to Reign: Jesus Talks about His Return
Gone with the Spirit: Tracking the Holy Spirit through the Bible
Anointed Preaching: The Holy Spirit and the Pulpit
Getting to Know You 1: Seeking God in the Old Testament
Getting to Know You 2: Finding Christ in the New Testament
Jesus: Is He Really God? Does It Really Matter?
Prostate Cancer: My Story of Survival

Contents

.

Foreword

I t has often, and truly, been said that what you get from the Bible, God's word of revelation, old yet ever new, depends on what you bring to it and what questions you ask it. This book, which the Norfords have laid out as a year's course of practical and devotional Bible readings, centres on the quest for wisdom about sex, marriage and the family, as one very important part of the life of faith and holiness. Their comments on the chosen passages yield a wealth of wisdom on these themes, far more, I guess, than most of us ever dreamed was there.

Christianity is truth and power: truth about our Creator God and his redeeming love for us, and power from Jesus Christ through the Holy Spirit for remaking our relationships—relationships with God, with our fellow humans (neighbours), and with ourselves. All life, looked at realistically, is relationships, and all our relationships are at first out of joint, due to sin in everyone's moral and spiritual system; thus they all need redirection and some measure of reconstruction. Until the self–centredness of grab–and-exploit is dethroned, and the other–centredness of love established in its place, relationships will be consistently distorted. This includes parent–child and child–parent relationships, just as it includes relationships between spouses. For though spouses pledge themselves to each other "till death do us part," as the Anglican Prayer Book put it, they are flawed human beings like the rest of us, and need the renewing grace of our Lord Jesus Christ as much as any.

The Bible's teaching about marriage and the family starts on its opening page and continues into the pastoral letters of the New Testament. The climax of it is the revelation that the husband–wife relationship is meant to reflect the mutual covenant love of Jesus Christ the Saviour and his church, while the parent–child relationship is meant to reflect the response of Christians to God the Father, whose adopted sons and heirs they are in the spiritual royal family. This book, used as prescribed, will impart a very rich understanding of these things.

Asked after the first fifty years to characterize their married relationship, Billy and Ruth Graham described themselves as "happily incompatible." I suspect that if the Norfords were asked the same question they would give substantially the same answer; I know that my wife and I would. The Grahams coined a telling phrase for something that is in fact quite typical. Opposites attract, and marital affection grows from the sense, not just of having a lot in common, but also of being significantly different from each other, in ways that both want to explore further. When agape–love—patient, kind, forbearing, forward–looking, habitually seeking the best for the loved one—rules the roost for them both, their marriage will yield mutual gifts of joy, peace, strength and contentment in abundance, even as they grow in awareness of how unlike each other they really are. Vive la difference, say the French (and the Norfords too), and they are right; for the sense that the loved one is still a bit of a mystery adds what you might call pepper, salt and sweet sauce (pardon my pun; it's intentional) to their relationship with each other. Any pair of incompatibles who want to go deeper into happy togetherness in their marriage will do well to take the Norfords' one-year course.

Marriage in the Western world is rocky today, as much from our personal immaturity and lack of common sense as from any other cause, and there could hardly be a more strategic time for this book, with all its down–to–earthness anchored deep in God, to come on the market. The good it could do is very great, and I heartily commend it. May it have the rich, wide ministry that it deserves.

J. I. Packer
Regent College, Vancouver
January 2009

About This Book

We have reformatted this second edition of *Happy Together*, condensing the daily devotions to a page a day while retaining the basic content. We added a title, a text from the day's subject, a prayer, and shortened the paragraphs for easier reading.

Bryan roughed out the original manuscript and the singular pronoun "I" refers to him. Ann's review and critique provided constructive insights, so the work is the thoughtful product of them both.

The first week of devotions selects passages from Proverbs and Romans to set a context for the meditations that follow. The rest of the book works its way through the Bible from Genesis to Revelation reviewing all passages that have a bearing on marriage, family, and relationships.

We have provided five scriptural meditations weekly Monday to Friday. For the weekend, we have included insights about marriage or anecdotes from life that may loosely relate to meditations from the preceding week.

Thus, the weekend gives time to investigate other areas, change your routine, or simply catch up. Alternatively, exploring other noted Scriptures supporting the week's meditations may extend your grasp of each day's reading.

The devotions combine the benefits of a devotional format with incremental teaching on the subject of marriage; exploring not only what the Bible says about marriage and family, but also ideas about God himself. The more we know about his attributes, attitudes and actions, the more we will understand ourselves made in his image, and better grasp how our relationships are meant to work.

You've probably noticed that family relationships—with partners, parents, or children—can be the most rewarding and yet the most exasperating of life's experiences; the closer the relationship the greater the challenge. Some families appear to sail through life, while other families seem to stagger from crisis to crisis.

In answer to this there are hundreds of books, tapes, videos, TV shows, and counselors devoted to helping marriages succeed. Yet even the amount of help available often confuses rather than clarifies issues.

This book does not replace the many resources available to marriages, but considers a variety of family issues daily from Bible passages that can improve relationships incrementally. But some Christian approaches to marriage simply use Scripture to provide a Christian veneer to sociological ideas. In doing so, they miss the transcendent meaning of marriage.

All relationships, supremely marriage, reflect God and the relationship he has with his people. This basis for relationships provides the most effective approach to significant marriage—for both the partners' happiness, and as a meaningful contribution to family, community, and culture.

2015 will mark our sixtieth year of marriage. We recall it with joy and our family with pleasure. But we recognize our commitment to God, and more especially his faithfulness to us, has provided this gratifying outcome. Not that we have avoided mistakes or achieved a level of excellence, but consider God's design for marriage both the basis and mainstay for our union.

The stories you encounter are from life and, apart from those about us, we changed the names of people involved. The book provides a year's devotions, and you can start reading the book any time of the year as the weeks are undated.

We trust these thoughts from Scripture and almost sixty years of marriage will give you an appreciation for both the foundation and the ongoing safeguards for the relationships that are most meaningful to you—as partners or parents, single or married.

Ann and Bryan Norford,
Lethbridge, Alberta, Canada
August 2014

Beginning the Journey

You may have worked your way through the Bible before or used devotionals that give general comfort or direction for your life. But this journey is unlike any you have undertaken, directed specifically to family life. If you are married, thinking about marriage, or even living common law, this journey will identify areas of success and failure from Scripture that most of us encounter in life with our partners and children.

While the Bible has some instructions about married life from Old Testament legal requirements to New Testament guidance, it more often records stories of men and women who ran into the same joys and sorrows of life common to us all. These people may have lived up to four thousand years ago, but their problems and responses were as human and recognizable as ours—sometimes handled well, but often not.

We will learn from Jacob whose actions produced a dysfunctional family history of pain and misery, and from David whose adultery created major problems for the rest of his life. Yet both were men of great faith who fell into the same temptations we all face. Love stories from Ruth to Solomon's love song to his bride will remind us of the depth and allure of faithful love for each other.

But these stories are not just about human relationships. As we will learn from the second week's meditations, family is part of the image of God created within us. God teaches us about families from who he is, and his love and reactions to our faith and failures.

So the more we learn of him the better we will understand ourselves and find our greatest joy in our closest relationships. Join us on this adventure through the Bible: of love, failure and recovery by lovers and families just like us.

1

ANN AND BRYAN NORFORD

Wisdom for Life

Read: Proverbs 1:1-7, 20-33

**The fear of the Lord is the beginning of knowledge,
but fools despise wisdom and discipline. Proverbs 1:7.**

The day you bought a new car, you doubtless spent time in the instruction manual. The cost of the vehicle was enough to ensure you drove and maintained the car to provide long and trouble free service.

Similarly, to obtain the maximum benefit for the short lives we have; we need wisdom from our Creator. In Proverbs, we find wisdom in "the fear of the Lord" for it "is the beginning of knowledge."

The greatest challenges we face in life are our relationships to others, for the closer those relationships, the greater the chance of tension and conflict. That is in families where most of us live. How can we be sure of strong families, both for us as individuals and for a stable society?

Proverbs tells us the fear of the Lord is also the beginning of wisdom, 9:10; a fountain (or source) of life, 14:27; leads to (fullness of) life, 19:23; and even adds length to life, 10:27.

"Fear of the Lord" in this context means a reverence for our Creator's ultimate knowledge and wisdom. Today's reading carries a warning against rejecting that wisdom, for she "would have poured out my heart to you and made my thoughts known to you," if we responded to her call.

If we reject her call, wisdom will mock at our calamity when it overtakes us. Simply put, if we do not absorb his wisdom as a regular practice of life, we will be unprepared for the tough times. That wisdom can be found in God's instruction manual to us, the Bible.

Prayer: Lord, we want to live by your wisdom always. Draw us constantly to your Word to hear your voice and heed your wisdom from its timeless truth.

3

WEEK ONE: TUESDAY

Wisdom for Each Day

Read: Proverbs 3:1-10

Trust in the Lord with all your heart and lean not on your own understanding; in all your ways acknowledge him, and he will make your paths straight. Proverbs 3:5–6.

Many of you, like me, often find yourselves in circumstances or tasks for which we feel inadequate. That drives us to our knees. We recognize our need of guidance and strength, and pray earnestly about those tasks.

But we may blithely sail through those for which we are gifted or where we feel confident with little more than a perfunctory prayer. For example, when it comes to writing, I enjoy the gift that enables me to write this. But knowing that lulls me into thinking I can do this work alone using my personal resources.

However, verses 5 and 6 tell us we still need to trust God's guidance when working in our strengths. If we do, then we will not depend on our own wisdom, misuse our gifts, or take credit alone for the outcome.

Furthermore, recognizing his overall control of our destiny will lead to thankfulness to him in *all* things, for praise and gratitude to him are the primary means of maintaining allegiance to him. Neglect of these disciplines is the beginning of folly, Romans 1:18–21.

Our critical need for direction is in our family relationships. We may lack parenting skills or fail to adequately live up to the standards God requires of us, and so jeopardize a secure outcome for our family. But God is gracious to us, responding to our inadequate attempts to trust him. This gives us hope.

Prayer: Heavenly Father, direct us to acknowledge you in all areas of our life; to trust your guidance daily in our strengths as well as weaknesses.

God's Plan for Us

Read: Romans 3:21–28; Ephesians 2:1–9

God, who is rich in mercy, made us alive with Christ even when we were dead in transgressions—it is by grace you have been saved. Ephesians 2:4–5.

You must agree, there is something terribly wrong with the human race. This clearly conflicts with the image of God originally stamped upon us. But each of us is a flawed creation. Not that God's creation was originally flawed; he said it was very good, Genesis 1:31.

If we are to improve our relationships, we need to deal with our own failure to measure up first. Recognizing we have fallen short of God's creation ideal, we realize we need to be reconciled to God. This is the first step to enable us to reconcile with others.

Scripture tells us that God not only created all things well, but when man sinned God also saw the need to remedy human failure. Jesus Christ came and paid the penalty on the cross for our failure, paving the way for God to forgive and reconcile us to himself.

Today's readings remind us that upon recognition and repentance of our sinfulness, and simple faith—belief and trust in Jesus Christ's sacrifice for us—we become a new creation, 2 Corinthians 5:17–19. This is the first step in the process that allows God to restore his image in us, Ephesians 4:22–24.

As we commit ourselves to God's creation ideals, we commence a new journey of hope. We discover the wisdom of God is basic to our living as it begins to untangle the threads of life and provides joy in relationships, support through adversity, and comfort in sorrow.

Prayer: Thank you Father for making the ultimate sacrifice of your Son in our place. We repent of our sinfulness and gladly accept your offer of reconciliation.

WEEK ONE: THURSDAY

Wisdom For Our Children

Read: Proverbs 4:1–9

Wisdom is supreme; therefore get wisdom. Though it cost all you have, get understanding. Proverbs 4:7.

When Solomon gained the throne, God commended him for desiring wisdom rather than prestige, 1 Kings 3:10–12. This passage reminds us it was David who taught the young Solomon to seek after wisdom.

So Solomon taught *his* son, as his father David had taught him while "still tender and an only child of my mother."

Wisdom is often associated with grey hair, probably because most of us learn over time by our mistakes instead of learning from others. But both David and Solomon emphasized the importance of teaching children at a young age the principles of God's timeless wisdom.

Although Solomon was later seduced from the faith, he began well, recalling his father's teaching for direction. What we convey to our children may extend through succeeding generations as with David and Solomon, though our children may follow or ignore it.

What wisdom are we passing to them? Do we allow them to absorb current cultural values without comment, or assimilate a convenient pragmatism? Or are we teaching them what we consider critical for life through the wisdom of God's Word?

If we love them, we will teach them from a young age values that will hold them in good stead and provide direction for life—not only for themselves, but also for the generations that follow.

Prayer: Heavenly Father, our children are the most precious gift you have given us. Stir our hearts today and always to pass your wisdom to our children in all circumstances of life.

Wisdom Regarding Adultery

Read: Proverbs: 7:1–27

Say to wisdom, "You are my sister," and call understanding your kinsman; they will keep you from the adulteress, from the wayward wife with her seductive words. Proverbs 7:4–5.

Solomon addresses his son. He probably had other sons and daughters, but reserved his comments for the son who would likely succeed him on the throne. It's a pity Solomon did not heed his own advice—women were his downfall, 1 Kings 11:1–3.

The Bible confirms men are usually the rapists, stalkers, and voyeurs. It records the adultery of Reuben, Genesis 35:22, and David, 2 Samuel 11:2–4; the rape of David's daughter Tamar by her half brother, Amnon, 2 Samuel 13:1–19; the rape of Jacob's daughter Dinah by Shechem, Genesis 34:1–2, and the abhorrent abduction of wives by the Benjamites during Israel's anarchy, Judges 21:15–24.

As cultural restraints and personal discipline ease, men resort to animal behaviour, living by instinct rather than honour. A respectful society depends on personal discipline, and in a society that respects women, men achieve their greatest nobility.

Christianity based on biblical wisdom develops a culture that respects all human life, especially the vulnerable: women, children, the unborn, sick, and elderly. With these virtues, marriage and family become the norm and predator behaviour is stigmatized and restrained.

Marriage is the "tender trap." Women who draw their men into a faithful lifelong union and channel their husband's energy into building strong families, pay us all a valuable service.

Prayer: O Lord, assist us to remain faithful to each other as husband and wife for life, and deliver us from the destructive evil of adultery.

WEEK ONE: WEEKEND

The Source of Wisdom

I t's unnatural for me to be religious. I rely on reason rather than emotion or intuition. I easily identify with the idea of Christianity as one religion among many, or adapting one according to my personal logic.

Or, like the secularist, I could accept that some higher power brought the world into being, but life generally belies the fact that God is still involved in our sorry state. This produces a practical atheism—believing in God but living as though he does not exist.

So why am I a Christian? Those who lack the experience of a Christian home may inherit a skepticism that inoculates them from considering Christ's claims. Growing up in a Christian home gave me a view of Christianity from the inside without the disadvantage of a critical view from outside.

At ten years of age, the claims of Christ made sense. In addition his love demonstrated to me from the cross was emotionally compelling and I made a decision for him. Since that time the Bible's wisdom and authenticity has become clearer as the years advanced.

I found that the Bible carried its own authority and gave the only meaningful explanation of life as we know it. All other ideas I examined pale in comparison.

Furthermore, it is the only religion or philosophy I can find that deals effectively with the problem of evil, both its cause and its cure.

I'm sure, if I had not committed my life to Jesus Christ and the Bible's guide for life, my life and marriage would likely be in the same disarray that is prevalent today.

Oh! The grace of God

Prayer: Lord, we long for a joyful and secure home for our family. Holy Spirit, reveal to us wisdom from your Word for our marriage every day.

Families Are a Trinity

Read: Genesis 1:1–4; John 1:1–5

In the beginning God created the heavens and the earth . . . and the Spirit of God was hovering over the waters. Genesis 1:1–2.

Through [Jesus] all things were made; without him nothing was made that has been made. John 1:3.

Today's readings show all three Persons of the Trinity existed and were present at creation. If this is true, then we will find evidence of the Trinity in the world we inhabit.

There are only three dimensions: length, width, and height? Matter is made up of three forms, solid, liquid and gas as is earth's most common matter: ice, water, and steam? Even time is divided into past, present, and future.

The Trinity is also evident in us: body, mind, and spirit, and we determine actions by intellect, emotions, and will.

But the idea of male and female becoming one flesh, Genesis 2:23–24, and the child—one or more—also being part of the same flesh, mimics the trinitarian God. Clearly, the roles of human family members are only similar to the Trinity; nor does human sin exist within the Trinity.

Never-the-less, the idea of God in relationship within the Trinity prefigures the dependence we have on relationship with others. We need another person to reproduce children, for companionship and friendship.

Family relationships find their meaning in the fundamental relationship of God himself—one of love and cooperation within the Trinity, and expressed outside of himself by sacrifice for those he created.

Without these qualities, relationship is no longer companionship but simply a convenience. One disgruntled wife once expressed this by complaining: "living with my husband is more like having a room-mate!"

Prayer: Heavenly Father and Creator. Thank you for the way you made us in your image. Show me daily how to reflect that image to my family and community.

9

WEEK TWO: TUESDAY

Equality of the Sexes?

Read: Genesis 1:24–27

God created man in his own image, in the image of God he created him; male and female he created them. Genesis 1:27.

I f you are a man, you have probably growled the words "women drivers" in a derogatory manner during some traffic incident involving the opposite sex. If you are a woman, you are probably rolling your eyes at this brainless expression.

That phrase is only a symptom of the wider discussion on whether women are equal to men in the ability to handle life. Some well entrenched views on both sides of the argument claim support from Scripture.

However, contrary to some views, this passage, and others to come, show decided support for equality of the sexes. The word "man" in today's reading is generic, and includes male and female; *both* were equally created in God's image.

This is in contrast to the earlier creation of the animal world not stamped with the image of God. In fact, the Scriptures clearly show that humankind should rule the animal world mandating a level of superiority for humans.

Both the man and the woman received the order: "Let them rule over the fish of the sea and the birds of the air . . . and over all the creatures that move along the ground," giving an equal co-responsibility for nature.

Unfortunately, the word "rule" is often associated with dictatorship, but in Scripture it includes the need to care for the governed who depend on the ruler. When applied to families, it means to provide protection and provision for the weaker and dependent ones, also made in the image of God.

Prayer: Thank you Lord, for the partners you have given us. Open our eyes to the equal and opposite talents with which you have blessed each of us.

Equal Mandate

Read: Genesis 1:28

God blessed them and said to them, "Be fruitful and increase in number; fill the earth and subdue it. Rule over the fish of the sea and the birds of the air and over every living creature that moves on the ground." Genesis 1:28.

T oday's one verse reading continues God's mandate to humankind, but adds the need to subdue and rule nature. As we suggested yesterday, "subdue" is often considered to mean exploit, and the word "rule" has dictatorial connotations to it. You may know some men who consider this their right within the family.

Although some may think differently for their own benefit, "subdue" simply means to bring under control, and rulership carries a responsibility for those dependent on that rule. But note these instructions were given to both the man and woman, conferring equal responsibility for governing.

All the imperative verbs in this verse—be fruitful, increase, fill, subdue, rule—are plural in the original Hebrew, emphasizing marriage as an equal partnership. The need for co-operation in the need to multiply intensifies the equality in these commands..

But this passage also has a bearing on family in the instruction to "be fruitful and increase in number." Children were not an afterthought following the fall and impending death of Adam and Eve to ensure the human race continued.

Children were part of the original creation that God saw and considered very good. This affirms what we previously noted: families are also part of the image of the Triune God: father, mother, and child(ren) giving us a three part picture of the Trinity.

Prayer: Thank you Father, for my partner and children. Reveal to me your image in them and instill in us the understanding of dignity that equality implies.

WEEK TWO: THURSDAY

God's Provision for Us

Read: Genesis 1:29–30

I give you every seed-bearing plant on the face of the whole earth
and every tree that has fruit with seed in it.
They will be yours for food. Genesis 1:29.

A boy was asked by his teacher what he was drawing. He kept working. "I'm drawing God."

"But no–one knows what God looks like," said the teacher.

The boy looked up. "They will when I've finished!"

None of us can fully comprehend God. But the similarity between the Trinity and our families gives some insight into who he is, for the relationship within families pictures the relationship within the Trinity. Scripture also tells us that the love that exists between members of the Trinity, God extends to us.

The Bible pictures God's relationship to us as one of marriage and the child/parent relationship. God's people are referred to as his wife in the Old Testament, Hosea 1:2–3 and 3:1–3, and as the Bride of Christ, 2 Corinthians 11:2–3 and Revelation 19:7, in the New Testament.

Similarly, they are God's children in both the Old, Isaiah 49:15 and 66:13, and New Testaments, John 1:12 and 1 John 3:1. In each case, we recognize the extent of God's love, care, and guidance for his people by the human relationships we experience.

But these verses also remind us that God's love is practical. He not only gave instruction for rulership of the earth, but also provided the resources needed for it. At first, humans were vegetarian although this changed after the flood, Genesis 9:3.

That promise reminds us of Jesus' promise to provide for us as we seek to follow him, Matthew 5:31–33.

Prayer: O Lord, we thank you for your promised daily provision for us and our family. Remind us continually that all good gifts come from you.

The Sexes Created Equal

Read: Genesis 2:4–22

Then the Lord God made a woman from the rib he had taken out of the man, and he brought her to the man. Genesis 2:22.

God established the equality of men and women in the first chapters of the Bible. In particular, the image of God stamped on all men and women is the basis for treating all persons with dignity.

Even those who deny any meaningful reality beyond what is perceived by our five senses, usually see something transcendent in humanity. The Canadian Charter of Rights and Freedoms points to an indefinable sacrosanct quality in humanity, both male and female.

Many believe in the superior role of men and point to this passage as support. For instance: doesn't the female taken from the body of the male make her derived and therefore inferior? But all men since Adam have come from the female, 1 Corinthians 11:11–12. Surely, being created second gives the woman secondary status? But the animals created before Adam didn't have superior rank.

Ah, but the woman was created to be a helper. Doesn't this indicate a subservient *role* even if they are *created* equal? Sorry, it can't, for several psalms remind us that God is our helper, typically Psalms 33:20, 46:1, and he is not subservient to us. Likewise, the woman created as a helper is not a sign of subservience to the man.

Helper can mean both a supporter who is less skilled, and also one who has required superior skills, and in a good marriage this works both ways. Not only does procreation require both sexes, but the complementary skills and psychologies created in the male and female are the created ideal for raising a family.

Prayer: Heavenly Father, we are thrilled you have joined us together as partners to fulfill your mandate for our family. Give us insight to the complementary functions of our relationship.

WEEK TWO: WEEKEND

Finding Equality

Ann and I were born, raised and married in England, in a different culture to North America where we now live. It was a Christian culture—not everyone was a Christian, but most accepted and lived according to Christian values.

However, the marriage partnership was definitely patriarchal; expecting the wife to support decisions made by the husband. The decision to immigrate to Canada in the sixties was my decision, although we discussed it together.

Ann dutifully went along, although she confided later that she thought I was crazy. I had just completed my architectural training and was ready to develop a career.

On arriving in Canada, Ann noticed the independence of North American women and realized the lopsided arrangement of our marriage. With assertion on her part and bewilderment on mine, things changed.

So began a balancing of the marriage responsibility. Despite my Christian background, I had not yet come to an understanding of the relationship between husband and wife that the Bible taught, rather accepting the patriarchal version of biblical interpretation that was current—and convenient—at the time.

I could have considered that this change was belittling to my manhood. But I found that the injection of female ideas and intuition into our plans contributed to better decisions. How could I have been so ignorant of the great resources Ann brought to our marriage and blind to the guidance Scripture gave me?

The simple answer is arrogance. I believed, as the "head of the house," I always had the better and final answers to all of life's questions.

Prayer: O Lord, guard us against treating each other in inferior ways. Reveal the ways in which we each excel and complement the other.

Two Shall Be One Flesh

Read: Genesis 2:19–24

The man said, "This is now bone of my bones and flesh of my flesh; she shall be called 'woman,' for she was taken out of man." Genesis 2:22–23.

For most of my life I puzzled over the meaning of "one flesh." Because Eve came from Adam's side, both she and Adam were effectively made from the same lump of clay.

Eventually, I realized that marriage consummated by intercourse effectively constituted the "one flesh" idea. In a similar way, the sexual union between a man and wife makes the two as though they were *both* made from the same piece of soil, so becoming the same flesh.

The Greek philosopher Aristophanes, in an amusing legend on the one flesh principle, suggested human beings originally had four arms and legs, moving about in cartwheel fashion. Eventually, the gods split them in two, into the form we know today. The halves were left forever seeking their other split half. This reunification then provided the intercourse that became marriage and enabled furtherance of the human race.

Our reading indicates the marriage relationship is so strong that it breaks the natural parent/child relationship, despite the fact that the child is physically part of the flesh of the parents. This lends emphasis to the idea that the marriage relationship is not only stronger than the parent/child relationship, but that marriage creates a greater "one flesh" relationship than that of parents and child.

This one flesh status of marriage partners the Genesis writer understood and Jesus affirmed, Matthew 19:5, is the created closeness of your marriage and mine.

Prayer: Lord, what an amazing marriage relationship you have created. May we reflect that one flesh closeness in our daily lives.

WEEK THREE: TUESDAY

Broken Communion

Read: Genesis 3:1–13

The man and his wife heard the sound of the Lord God as he was walking in the garden in the cool of the day, and they hid from the Lord God among the trees of the garden. Genesis 3:8.

Why is there so much tension between us? If we were meant to live in companionship together, why is there constant friction? Today's reading shows there are good reasons: Adam and Eve's fall into sin radically altered the bond between them and their relationship with God.

They failed to make a joint decision to eat the forbidden fruit. Eve chose without consulting Adam despite the joint responsibility given to them. Equally, Adam abdicated his responsibility for Eve's welfare by participating instead of interceding for her.

By blaming Eve rather than protecting her, Adam developed antagonism between them. Eve passed blame down the line—the devil made me do it! By playing the "blame game," they both tried to absolve their guilt while effectively admitting it.

Adam and Eve's sin also interfered with communion with God. At first, that communion was close, desired by God and enjoyed by them, walking together "in the cool of the day." But their sin turned joy to fear, innocence to shame, and severed direct communion with God. Now he was the only One to steer them through the jungle of existence they had penetrated.

Self-centredness interfered with the bond between the couple, and independence from God threatened to cut off contact with him. Do similar attitude exist within our marriage? The first step to restoring the joy of our relationship is admitting our disruptive attitudes.

Prayer: Thank you for the love and forbearance you have shown to us in spite of our sin. May your love inspire the same attitudes in our marriage.

WEEK THREE: WEDNESDAY

The Bondage of Women

Read: Genesis 3:14–16

Your desire will be for your husband, and he will rule over you.
Genesis 3:16.

Adam and Eve's disobedience had consequences. For Eve, it meant pain in childbirth, and change in the relationship with her husband. God didn't impose the change, but warned her of the results of her sin.

Specifically, there was this enigmatic phrase, "Your desire will be for your husband, and he will rule over you."

Was this "desire" sexual attraction, the need of protection or a need to emulate her husband? These ideas could be included, but there is probably a more sinister meaning.

Note God's response to Cain before he killed Abel, Genesis 4:7: "It desires to have you, but you must master it." This is identical Hebrew construction as the phrase used in speaking to Eve, and domination is clearly in view.

It seems obvious from today's western culture that the battle of the sexes is one of domination, but in the natural order of things, men being physically stronger will usually continue to dominate.

But in the words to Eve there was a promise that Satan would be destroyed by a Descendant of hers in the words, "He will crush [Satan's] head." This foreshadowed the death of Jesus that restored equality and freedom for women lost at the fall.

There was no longer any difference between male and female as all human divisions were cancelled at the cross, Galatians 3:28. The recognition of equality in Christ is the cornerstone, not only of women's freedom from domination, but also of equitable treatment within the family—a restoration of creation as God intended.

Prayer: Heavenly Father, help us to better understand the freedom from conflict Jesus purchased for us at the cross.

17

WEEK THREE: THURSDAY

The Toil of Men

Read: Genesis 3:17–19

By the sweat of your brow you will eat your food. Genesis 3:19.

Men did not escape the fall without penalty. Adam learned that sin pollutes the environment as well as stressing the people involved. In Adam's case the ground would be destabilized, creating undesirable products and toil necessary to ensure intended growth.

The toil to produce provisions for life was committed to Adam; Eve would have her hands full in childbirth and child-rearing. This passage, together with yesterday's, indicates the distinctive roles that sin conferred on men and women.

These passages don't mean to deny women the possibility of pursuing fulfilling roles and service both inside and outside the family: compare the varied role of the virtuous woman, Proverbs 31:10–31.

Rather, male toil would be the primary source of food for the family, relieving women of heavy physical work. Too many women today are forced into menial tasks in order to put bread on the table, particularly those in poor families and single-mother households.

Feminism has also tended to denigrate the male role resulting in many wives underestimating the load that working husbands carry. Men's work is often unfulfilling, stressful and sometimes humiliating.

Hard physical labour or heavy mental effort drain a man of energy he would like to spend on his family. A husband's career is not always what it's cracked up to be, and he treasures his home as a retreat from the rigours of business life.

Prayer: Lord, help us understand the demands life places on our partner.

Sexual Union

Read: Genesis 3:20 to 4:2

Adam lay with his wife Eve, and she became pregnant and gave birth to Cain. Genesis 4:1.

You probably know the first verse of our reading today by its King James Version (KJV): "And Adam knew Eve his wife; and she conceived." Other translations use "had relations," "had sexual intercourse," or "lay."

The Hebrew also uses the word for "know" for various other meanings. Our reading describes man as "knowing good and evil," uses the word "know" for simple acquaintance, Exodus 1:8, as well as close relationship like that between Moses and God, Deuteronomy 34:10.

It also refers to God's knowledge of humanity and human ways—even before birth, Psalm 139:1–4. This use of the same word for many aspects of life, including sex, shows the Hebrews considered sexual intercourse as a part of the whole of life.

In contrast, our western culture today exhibits sex as an isolated event, a social recreational device like bowling or sports events. Women, however, consider intimacy as companionship, caring, cosseting; a place of protection and support for their own yearnings.

Women do not easily divorce sex from the overall events of married life. There is little fulfillment for them in sexual activity without attention to these other areas.

When husbands fail to appreciate this need in their wives, sex becomes simply a relief device for the husband, it is no longer a shared activity, and the wife feels used.

It may also signify a breakdown in close communion both men and women yearn for.

Prayer: We thank you Lord for the sexual enjoyment in marriage. May we also remember its function for the birth of children who become our primary responsibility.

19

WEEK THREE: WEEKEND

Feminism

I think all of us are aware of the rise of feminism during the last century and continuing today. It demonstrates the ongoing war of the sexes we discussed earlier this week, as women try to balance men's domination of them.

The equality promoted at creation is far from complete, even in western societies, and the effort for greater equality is a scriptural mandate. Not only is equality a part of the image of God lost at the fall, but the sacrifice of the cross restores and demands it, Galatians 3:28.

However, extreme feminism concludes that as men generally rule the world they are the cause of the world's evil. Men are a necessary evil to propagate the race, but the world would be a safer and happier place if women replaced them.

This clearly falls into the same error as male domination. Inequality in marriage cuts both ways with stories of "henpecked husbands" and women "wearing the pants" common caricatures.

Feminism errs when it distorts the God given roles of the sexes or elevates women above men. Its desire to seek equality of value and function for women in society is to be commended, but it is in the family relationships we can make the biggest difference.

A discussion between you and your partner on what equality should look like in your marriage can only enhance the relationship. In the short run it may be a source of friction as any underlying resentments are aired, but an agreement—even compromise—can only improve the companionship and enjoyment of working together.

Prayer: Heavenly Father, we are aware of our selfishness and desire for dominance. Give us hearts to serve each other as you have served us.

Children Still Choose

Read: Genesis 4:1–8

"If you do what is right, will you not be accepted? But if you do not do what is right, sin is crouching at your door; it desires to have you, but you must master it." Genesis 4:7.

Few parents escape sibling rivalry—you may recall your own, but your own children's friction frustrates you. You were not the first; Adam and Eve had the same problem but with a tragic ending.

In their case, Cain had the opportunity to be restored. He could "do what is right," or give in to his anger and let sin shape his actions. Here, even God, the perfect parent, could only give wise alternatives.

Cain retained freedom of choice as all children eventually do. In this case, Cain chose wrongly: Abel was murdered and his parents grieved. While Adam and Eve had communicated God's requirements to them both, it was no guarantee of godly children.

The cause of Cain's anger was God's refusal of his produce offering but acceptance of Abel's lamb. It was not the gift that was wrong but the attitude. Able brought the "firstborn of his flock." Cain brought an offering "in the course of time,"—perhaps uneatable moldy produce.

Rivalry between siblings may start at an early age, but parents can teach children to restore the relationships after disagreement. Bringing our best to God is evident by giving our best to each other.

What if Cain had brought an offering of his "first-fruits" to God? Probably his relationship with his brother would have remained intact and much of human history might have been less violent. Our attitudes do affect those who follow us.

Prayer: Lord, we pray that we may always give our best to you, and be an example to our children to give their best to you and each other.

21

WEEK FOUR: TUESDAY

Cain's Legacy

Read: Genesis 4:10–24

"If Cain is avenged seven times, then Lamech seventy-seven times." Genesis 4:24.

Cain was unrepentant and feared his punishment. Yet God was gracious and ensured his life was spared. But there is no indication that Cain's attitude toward God changed. Rather, those who descended from him carried the same attitude towards God and life.

His descendent Lamech, justified his violent behaviour by referring back to God's sevenfold punishment of Cain's potential killers. This is a specific example of the sin of the father repeated in succeeding generations.

Why did God allow Cain to survive? After all, later punishment for murder was death. There is no easy answer to this early example of the pervasiveness of evil and the apparent ability of some perpetrators to avoid its consequences.

What is clear is that there exists for Cain, Lamech and other violent people the freedom of conscious choice that is available to all humans; wrong choices summarize their attitude towards God and bring suffering to others.

As humankind is made in the image of God, violence against a person is violence against God, and the person responsible will face the penalty for it—often at human hands, Genesis 9:6, and if not, eventually from God himself, Exodus 20:5.

A godly life is not only more likely to be a happy one, but more important, it may provide for godly generations to come. Unfortunately the opposite is also true. What legacy are we leaving to our children and grandchildren and those who follow them?

Prayer: O Lord, we pray for our children and those who will follow us. May our example lead later generations to follow you.

The Influence of Our Legacy

Read: Genesis 4:25–26; 5:18–22

Men began to call on the name of the Lord. Genesis 4:26.

The birth of Adam's third son heralded a new beginning as "men began to call on (or proclaim) the name of the Lord." Eve's recognition that her child came from God, indicates that Adam and Eve retained some relationship with him, which they endeavoured to pass to Seth.

Seth was created in Adam's likeness. The lingering image of God was still evident, but marred by the sin that Adam and Eve had introduced into the human race. But Seth, although born with a sinful nature, sought to develop the relationship of humans with God.

Clearly the faith was handed down through many generations as Enoch "walked with God," Genesis 5:21–24.

But many of his descendents departed from God and died in the flood. They included Methuselah, Enoch's son; Even Noah's father was more concerned with God's curses than his care, Genesis 5:28–29.

Still, the faith continued down the line to Noah, who also walked with God, Genesis 6:9, and was saved from the flood.

These few verses sketch out the dilemma we all face today: desiring to reflect God's likeness, but continually distracted by our innate sinfulness, whether personally or on a community level.

Yet, like Seth, we need to maintain and demonstrate our faith to our children, although it is no guarantee they will follow our example.

But without our devoted example, it will be unlikely.

Prayer: Thank you for the examples you have given us in your Word of those who followed or departed from you. Give us grace to remain faithful for life.

Children in Our Image?

Read: Genesis 5:1-4

When Adam had lived 130 years, he had a son in his own likeness, in his own image; and he named him Seth. Genesis 5:3.

When I retired, I took a course in Philosophy at the local university. I joined a class of about a hundred, mostly young adults.

The question arose whether children were born good or evil. Considering the Bible's teaching on this subject, I volunteered that I raised three children and that my experience was that they were born evil.

I expected a sharp rebuttal, but instead received a burst of laughter from the whole class. It seemed that they recognized some truth in my assertion from their memories of childhood.

Family is God's idea. Adam and Eve were instructed to be fruitful before the fall, Genesis 1:28. Today's reading reminds us that God created man in his own image, but Adam eventually gave birth to children in *his* own likeness. What was the difference?

The cryptic comparison between God's image and Adam's image is probably a comparison. It contrasts between the perfection that God created and the fallen race that now came into being as a result of Adam's sin. David recognized in himself this tendency to sin from birth, Psalm 51:5.

The idea that children are born without inherent knowledge of good and evil is a totally secular idea. My father always held that children were the proof of the doctrine of depravity: bad behaviour came naturally; they needed teaching on how to be good.

A child growing without discipline is like trying to grow a beautiful garden without tending it. Like us, our children are born with a sinful nature.

Prayer: O Lord, give us your wisdom in raising our children to discern good from evil.

WEEK FOUR: FRIDAY

Covenant: Unconditional Accord

Read: Genesis 6:13–21

But I will establish my covenant with you, and you will enter the ark—you and your sons and your wife and your sons' wives with you. Genesis 6:18–19.

God made a covenant with Noah to save him and his family from the flood if he built and entered the ark. The astonishing feature of a covenant is its unconditional nature, not requiring conditions for its continuance like a contract.

Noah was not required to perform any deed or act to obtain the safety of the ark other than simple acceptance of the covenant signified by his entry into the ark. Conversely, he could have ignored and rejected God's covenant with the risk of judgment.

The idea of covenant is central to the Bible's message of salvation—that is God's plan to secure humankind's future with him. The plan unfolds slowly throughout the Old Testament, but commences here with a simple story of the saving of one family and animal life at a time of judgment on the earth.

A fuller extent of the covenant would become clearer to Noah after the flood. The provision of the ark for Noah and his family is a symbol of the provision for our safety from God's judgment in the death of Jesus Christ for our sin. The Old Testament amplifies God's covenant and gains its fullest expression in the New Testament's offer of salvation to all who would receive it.

Noah's faithfulness provided a shield for the whole family for the immediate future. The benefits to children of a couple that maintain faithful allegiance to God and to each other cannot be underestimated.

Prayer: Heavenly Father, help each of us to show our partner the unconditional love you have given us, that our children will feel secure in our family.

WEEK FOUR: WEEKEND

Great Expectations

I'm sure you have sought expertise from many sources to assist in childrearing. Unfortunately, many "helps" assume a perfect parent stereotype which none of us are. Few recognise parents' individual limitations, nor the gap between theory and practice.

In addition, much Christian teaching implies that every obstacle and limitation will be defeated with God's help. All these approaches produce unrealistic expectations. We can only influence, not determine our child's future. We can only determine to be a good parent, not necessarily to raise a good child.

The period of greatest influence is in the earliest years when the child is the most dependant, approximately from birth to six years of age. That influence wanes with age, decreasing until about twelve. From then on, as the child approaches adulthood the loss of influence is most acute, and gives parents the most distress.

Parents have limitations, both determined by genetics, and affected by family and cultural environment. We are constrained by our heredity and temperament. Any sickness or handicap we have and accidents that happen will affect our parenting.

School and peer pressure, family relationships, and reacting to situations will shape results. Living conditions and the birth order will establish parental effectiveness with individual children.

No wonder we need all the help we can get. Do take advantage of the helps that are available, but when we meet intractable situations, we will find that our final "help comes from the Lord, the Maker of heaven and earth," Psalm 121:2.

Prayer: Lord, we know real wisdom comes from you. Guide us by your Holy Spirit and your Word as we seek to raise our children to know you.

God Works in Families

Read: Genesis 7:1–10

"Go into the ark, you and your whole family, because I have found you righteous in this generation." Genesis 7:1–2.

God told Noah to bring his whole family into the ark. Examples of God's concern for families abound. Lot's sons-in-law and others of Lot's family were included in the escape from Sodom, although they refused to go, Genesis 19:12–14. Rahab's family was included in her escape from Jericho, Joshua 6:22–23.

The Philippian jailer's whole family was included at his conversion, Acts 16:30-33. Paul indicated that there is sanctification for an unbelieving partner for the sake of the children of the union; presumably that sanctification is for the period of childhood, 1 Corinthians 7:14.

Of course, we could argue that God saved Noah's family to ensure continuation of the human race, but the same could hardly be said of Lot or Rahab. Previously, we established the stamp of the Trinity on the family so the family is part of the image of God on humankind, confirming the importance of the family to God.

But Jesus also showed compassion for the close bond between parent and child. He raised two children to life out of sympathy for the parents, Mark 5:35–43; Luke 7:11–15.

All this illustrates that God is vitally interested in your family and looks upon them with compassion. This applies not only to parents and children, but as Lot and Rahab show, often to the extended family. As prayers for our families are always a priority, so also is God's interest in answering those prayers.

Prayer: O Lord, you know the concern and sometimes the heartbreak we experience. We release our family into your care today, and will pray your protection over them continually.

27

WEEK FIVE: TUESDAY

The Promise of the Rainbow

Read: Genesis 9:1–17

"I establish my covenant with you: Never again will all life be cut off by the waters of a flood; never again will there be a flood to destroy the earth." Genesis 9:11.

Today's reading identifies the rainbow with God's promise not to flood the earth again. This is an unconditional covenant, like the original covenant with Noah.

Myths about the rainbow have developed, particularly the pot of gold supposedly at its end. But that gold is as ephemeral as the rainbow, which is simply an image refracted through a million raindrops. It's not the rainbow that assures us the flood will not recur, but God who keeps his promise.

Under certain atmospheric conditions the rainbow displays a full circle—a reminder of the ring of gold that promises a secure marriage. But the ring, like the rainbow, is only a symbol. The promise is only as good as each partner's faithfulness to the other.

At its base, marriage is a promise of faithfulness: that each will keep their pledge to the other, particularly retaining sex within the bounds of the marriage. As God promised no more flood, so the man promises no more women—and vice versa.

God's rainbow covenant made no demands of Noah and his family; similarly, the promise made in the traditional marriage covenant is also unconditional. But we all recognize that in practice marriage becomes a scene of give and take, and that there are practical limits to human endurance.

Nonetheless, it is sobering to recall when we married that we made a covenant to remain faithful, irrespective of our partner's actions—for better or for worse.

Prayer: O Lord, especially about our marriage, lead us not into temptation, but deliver us from evil.

28

Noah's Advice

Read: Genesis 9:18–29

But Shem and Japheth took a garment and laid it across their shoulders; then they walked in backward and covered their father's nakedness. Genesis 9:23.

Nakedness has always engendered a sense of shame since Adam and Eve's sin in the Garden of Eden, Genesis 2:25; 3:7 and 10. Today's reading gives an account of Noah's moment of weakness and Ham's apparent misuse of it.

Was Ham's report to his brothers one of mirthful amusement, ridiculing his father's state? We don't know, but his brothers certainly took exception to it. Upon awaking, Noah showed the same, even greater, concern about Ham's dishonour than his brothers did.

Did Noah's blessings and curses on his sons fix their futures, or were Noah's remarks simply a prediction of the future for each of them if they continued the same course? As we have seen with Adam and Eve, God's curses on them were consequences, not necessarily judgments, of their sinful act

Perhaps we should think of outcomes and judgments as the same: natural outcomes for good or bad behaviour—although not always consistent in an unstable world. To put it another way, our lives generally go well or badly depending on whether we follow our Creator's instructions.

At the very least, Noah was giving his sons good advice, required of all parents. But the fact that children eventually make their own decisions does not release us from the responsibility: to point out the risks of ignoring our Creator's requirements.

Prayer: Father, we pray our children will seek your wisdom from your Word. Continue to instruct us as an example for them to follow.

WEEK FIVE: THURSDAY

Influence on Later Generations

Read: Genesis 10:6–20

These are the clans of Noah's sons, according to their lines of descent, within their nations. From these the nations spread out over the earth after the flood. Genesis 10:32.

This must seem a totally boring passage, mainly lists of unpronounceable names with little apparent relevance to family life. Yet we often obtain our sense of identity from those who've gone before us, particularly our parents. This list notes the influence of Ham upon his descendents.

Shem was the father of the Semitic races which included the Jews, and eventually gave birth to Jesus. But the enmity Noah predicted between Ham and Shem follows them down to the descendents of today.

We are familiar with two of Ham's sons: Mizraim (Egypt) and Canaan, Israel's idolatrous tempters from Joshua's time and for a further nine hundred years. Nimrod, verse 8, created the historic cities of Nineveh and Babylon, both of which deported and enslaved Israel.

Canaan's descendents, verses 15–19, also opposed Israel. Jezebel came from Sidon to be Israel's queen. The Philistines were Egypt's descendents, and their Arab descendents continue to oppress Israel today.

Several other nations eventually came under God's judgment for their sin; note the repetition of several nations in Genesis 15:12–19. Eventually, the Canaanites peopled Sodom and Gomorrah that God destroyed, Deuteronomy 29:23; others moved into present day Gaza.

It is unlikely that we will have the same influence in history. However, the fractious nations that descended from Ham reinforce a warning to us that our attitudes to life and God's people can significantly influence our children and the generations that follow.

Prayer: Lord, keep us aware of the influence our way of life will have on our children and later generations.

The Pain of Separation

Read: Genesis 11:27–32; 12:4–5

He took his wife Sarai . . . and the people they had acquired in Haran, and they set out for the land of Canaan. Genesis 12:5.

Ten years into our marriage, we emigrated from England to Canada with our two young daughters. My parents, together with brothers and sisters and Ann's grandmother and aunt—Ann's surrogate parents—were at the docks as we boarded our ship.

The excitement of the trip made me unmindful of the pain of parting that it brought to our families. Several years later my father told me of the lump in his throat that lasted for several days after we left with our children.

Similarly, Terah lost his son Abram, his daughter Sarai (or Sarah, Abraham's stepsister and wife, see Genesis 20:11–13) and his grandchildren as they made the journey to Canaan. But unlike our journey to Canada, Abram's journey was less of a choice and more of a response to the call of God. Abram believed God's promise that the land would be given to his descendents, even when he discovered its fulfillment was centuries away, Genesis 15:13–14.

You may feel the pain of separation as your son or daughter travels abroad to answer God's call; perhaps to hazardous lands—the world is an increasingly dangerous place. Today's communications and ease of travel may soften the blow, but you are joining in the sacrifice—perhaps less willingly—that marks the Christian call.

Our children will make their own decisions regarding life; we must prepare ourselves for the possibility for God's call and support their sacrifice with our own. And that call may be a result of our influence upon them!

Prayer: Even though it may separate us from our children, we thank you for your call on their lives and the response to follow you.

31

The Covenant Relationship

Have you noticed we often treat our family members with less respect than we treat others? Yet we have a covenantal arrangement with our marriage partners that we do not have with the population in general.

Like the promises to Noah, marriage is a covenant, not a contract. A contract is void if either party should fail to fulfill the contract requirements. Traditional wedding vows do not have conditions dependent upon which each partner remains faithful to the other. Rather, each makes a vow to the other without conditions "for better or for worse."

The greatest example is the covenants made by God to his people—the old covenant to Israel, and the new covenant to Christians—called the Old and New Testaments. These covenants are the source of assurance of faith that God will keep his promises despite lapses in maintaining our side of the covenant.

So the marriage covenant remains in force even if our partner breaks his or her vows. While there are times when a total breakdown is unavoidable, we are not obliged to break our vows in retaliation for broken promises by our partner.

The strength of a marriage is the ability to maintain our covenant vows through difficult times and always assume the possibility of reconciliation. Using God's secure covenant promises as our guide, and his forgiveness as our pattern, we make our marriages more secure, and witness to the faithfulness of God in the process.

Prayer: Heavenly Father, give us the fortitude to make our marriage covenant to each other a witness of your faithfulness to the covenants you made with us.

Faithful to the Covenant

Read: Genesis 12:1–7

"All peoples on earth will be blessed through you." Genesis 12:3.

The rainbow covenant God made with Noah, Genesis 9:9–17, simply forestalled judgment on earth similar to the deluge; it did not preclude a further judgment on a sinful earthly population. We needed a way out of our sinfulness, not judgment for it.

Today's reading begins that salvation history many of us have come to claim for ourselves. The promise to Abram was for a nation that would descend from him, a land to call their own, and a covenant of international scope that promised to bless all peoples through him.

Instead of a warning of judgment to come, it promised deliverance without conditions, except for one. This condition was not so much one of action but one of faith, confirmed by a move to a new land. Provision by God's grace and acceptance by faith, clearly enunciated in the New Testament, Ephesians 2:8, started here: Abram's belief was accepted as righteousness, Genesis 15:6.

The bride-to-be's "yes" is a confirmation of faith placed in her future husband that he will fulfill his promises to her. Her further preparations for the wedding and their future together do not earn her husband's promise. His promise is a gift of his love for her, and her actions are simply a response of faith.

In this way, the marriage covenant that we enter into reflects the relationship that Abram enjoyed with God, and we enjoy now as Abram's spiritual descendants. Or put another way, our marriages are a witness to the relationship of love that God has with us.

Prayer: Lord, we want to thank you today for your covenant guaranteeing us eternal life with you, and for the marriage covenant we have made with each other. We pray our faithfulness will encourage others.

33

WEEK SIX: TUESDAY

Abram Believed God

Read: Genesis 15:1–7

Abram believed the Lord, and he credited it to him as
righteousness. Genesis 15:6.

Ann and I came to Canada as a family of four.
Currently, our grandchildren are marrying and having
children, and we now number over twenty with more
to come. We covet all of them for the faith, which drives our
desire to pray for all of them regularly.

As you start out in marriage, it may be difficult to
visualize a large family of children, grandchildren, and
great-grandchildren that is the legacy of most of us. But we
may be responsible for a vaster legacy. Abram is reminded
of the vast family that will descend from him—as countless
as the stars in the sky, and for us as for him, it requires
many generations to accomplish.

However, the message to Abram in today's reading is
that his descendents are from God, according to God's
promise. It is a reminder that all children are a gift from
God, Psalm 127:3, even those born under adverse
circumstances. Their destruction in the womb is a rejection
of this gift and consequently a rebuff to God, and why
Christians abhor abortion.

Perhaps even Abram, watching his children and
grandchildren had doubts about their being God's gift to
him, but all children, however pleasing or disappointing,
are a gift from God. However, Abram has influenced
countless generations since, and millions of the world's
people have retained that same faith in God. Will our
descendents want to follow in our faith?

Prayer: Our Father, we desire our children and future generations
to put their faith in you as Abram did. Increase our joy in
you and in each other so they will be hungry for you and
your truth.

34

Shaping the Future

Read: Genesis 16:1–16

Hagar bore Abram a son, and Abram gave the name Ishmael to the son she had borne. Genesis 16:15.

This passage raises awkward questions. Was Abram's intercourse with Hagar a lapse of faith in God's promise for a son? In giving Sarai permission to "do with her whatever you think best," did Abram tacitly condone Sarai's treatment of Hagar? Why would God promise descendants to Ishmael like Isaac if he knew the friction it would cause? These are pictures of real life, and there are no clear answers to these questions. However, we can find clues to help us avoid similar situations.

Whatever Abram's reason for intercourse with Hagar, Ishmael's example reminds us that children from today's illicit relationships and broken marriages may carry the scars and resentment for a lifetime unless God intervenes. Today, blended families face additional challenges raising children as those that Sarai, Hagar, and Ishmael later exhibited, Genesis 21:8–9.

We can partially answer why God allowed Ishmael to become a nation by the fact that we all bear consequences of our actions. Restricting outcomes of our behaviour undermines free will, for actions without consequences have no significance. Later, as Abram sought God's blessing on Ishmael, Genesis 17:17–18, God told Abram that he would keep his promise to Ishmael because he was Abram's son equal to Isaac, Genesis 21:13.

Despite the difference in birth between Abrams's two sons, and although the covenant that brought us salvation came through Isaac, God would treat them with equal dignity. All children, irrespective of the conditions of their birth, are equal before God.

Prayer: Lord, we need your wisdom to avoid creating difficulties for our children and grandchildren, particularly by preference or favouritism for individual children.

35

WEEK SIX: THURSDAY

A Participatory Covenant

Read: Genesis 17:1–14

No longer will you be called Abram; your name will be Abraham,
for I have made you a father of many nations. Genesis 17:5.

As God changed Abram's name to Abraham, he repeated the promise that all the earth would be blessed though a Descendant of his, Genesis 18:18; 22:18. In today's reading, God restated his promise to Abraham that he would become a great nation and the land would be his. God introduces at this time a reciprocal agreement, opened by the phrases "As for me," verse 4, and "As for you," verse 9.

Until now, Abraham had been participating in the covenant by faith but with little outward sign of that participation. But God's promise remained the same—a gift of grace to Abraham, and still no requirement for Abraham to act to earn his place in God's covenant.

Rather, a sign was required that Abraham accepted the promises of God and was willing to participate in his covenant. Circumcision showed this sign, and Abraham's descendants still show this commitment in their flesh. Not to have this mark was a rejection of that partnership, and rightly denied that person membership in God's community.

Marriage is signified by the exchange of rings. Just saying "yes" is insufficient. By accepting her groom's ring, the bride outwardly expresses her faith and participation in her new husband's promises to her. The same is true of his acceptance of her ring. From that time on they both wear on their flesh the sign of the covenant they both willingly entered.

Prayer: O Lord, give us greater understanding of the idea of covenant that we have entered into with you and with each other.

Devastating Choices

Read: Genesis 19:1–11

The men inside reached out and pulled Lot back into the house and shut the door. Then they struck the men who were at the door of the house, young and old, with blindness so that they could not find the door. Genesis 19:10–11.

Lot's offer of his daughters to a mob of licentious men is outrageous; it can only be a parody of eastern hospitality. We can see nothing to excuse such obscene behaviour toward his girls. Even so, there may have been reasons.

Lot may have been paralyzed with fear, verse 9; the whole family could have been raped. Lot's actions may have been pure cowardice: he could have offered himself in place of his visitors and his daughters. But he may have gambled the intruders would not accept it as they were homosexual.

In fact, they rejected the offer of his daughters. The city of Sodom was completely homosexual: "*all* the men from *every part* of the city of Sodom—both *young* and *old*—surrounded the house" (my emphasis). So the reason for Sodom's destruction was the absolute practice of homosexuality and violence. Sin had "reached its full measure." Note the use of this clause in Genesis 15:16.

In contrast, parents who willingly give up lives for their children are countless. Both the maternal and paternal instinct to preserve the young is God-given to preserve the species he created, whether animal or human. But in addition to instinct, humans have the ability to reason. We may not sacrifice our lives for our children, but are we prepared to make other sacrifices to ensure their wellbeing?

Prayer: Father, you know love for our children is shown in the sacrifices we are willing to make for them. May we also love and honour you by similar sacrifices when necessary.

WEEK SIX: WEEKEND

Facing Reality

Wedding vows rarely take account of our fallen nature and tendency to deceive ourselves. I have included warnings in the following "Revised Version" of the traditional vows—partly tongue in cheek—placing our capricious nature in the picture.

"I now take you to be my wife (husband) according to God's holy Word; to have and to keep from this time forward. I will love, esteem and respect you, I will be faithful to you; I will encourage you to become all that God intends, for as long as we both shall live.

"Should I fail to love you, I can expect a deteriorating closeness and companionship; should I fail to esteem and respect you, you will exhibit a deteriorating personhood and dignity; should I fail to be faithful to you, our marriage and our children's future will be in jeopardy. Should I fail to encourage you to become all that God intends, you will lose your individual distinctness and our combined potential for him will be lost. Should my actions or attitudes bring our marriage to an end before death parts us, we will both experience misery, displaced children, and an enduring sense of loss.

"I make this solemn vow and covenant to you and to God."

You can refine these vows with your own words, but you get the general idea. Try reciting these vows to your partner, and sense the response in your own heart.

Prayer: Thank you Lord, for this reminder of the consequences of failing my partner. Guard our eyes and desires so we may each remain faithful to the partner you have chosen for us.

God Works With Families

Read: Genesis 19:12–16

"Do you have anyone else here—sons-in-law, sons or daughters, or anyone else in the city who belongs to you?" Genesis 19:12.

We noted earlier God shows a particular interest in families of godly men and women, even though some family members are not responsive. As the impending judgment of Sodom drew near, the angels asked Lot about his family—see the text above. The promise of safety for Lot covered not only himself but also his extended family.

Most of his family had little interest in God's warning. Lot's sons-in-law laughed at his entreaty and no one else responded. After a night of attempted persuasion, only his wife and two daughters took the warning seriously, and even then the angels had to drag them from the city.

Despite God's mercy extended to the remainder of Lot's family, they had the freedom of choice whether to leave or go. To their loss they decided to stay—they simply didn't believe what the angels had to say.

The story emphasizes the frequent disbelief that God will really judge sin. The most obstinate will ignore even predictable calamities. Old Harry Truman perished when he refused to leave his home in the path of the Mount St. Helens 1980 eruption in Washington State.

The sense of invincibility follows us all to some degree, but particularly the young. To train children in godly living from an early age will help preserve them from drunkenness, reckless driving, sexual disease, drug addiction, and other hazardous pursuits they think will not harm them.

Prayer: Heavenly Father, thank you for your certain care for those we love. Help us love and care for our families in the same way, so they will accept the way of salvation you offer so freely.

WEEK SEVEN: TUESDAY

Devastating Results

Read: Genesis 19:26–38

So both of Lot's daughters became pregnant by their father.
Genesis 19:36.

The urgency of Lot and his family's flight from Sodom prompted the angels' warning not to look back, Genesis 19:17. There was no time to stop and view the spectacular fireworks that erupted over the cities of the plain.

The death of Lot's wife was probably not just a glance to the rear, but perhaps grief and longing at the life left behind. Fear at the alarming sight transfixed her to the spot until the fallout from the destruction overtook her. Her disobedience and death had tragic results, perhaps avoidable had she lived.

It is doubtful Lot's wife would have defended his decision to live in a cave with two adult virgin daughters. But Lot didn't believe the angels' promise that he would be safe in a small neighbouring city, and he fled to the mountains, Genesis 19:21–22.

These two girls faced the cultural pressure of the time to have children. The actions of Lot's wife left them in a dilemma to which they responded improperly by incest with their father.

The resulting children generated the nations of Moab and Ammon, nations that frequently oppressed the Israelites. Lot's disbelief and his wife's disobedience resulted in tragic consequences for both their generation and descendents.

We cannot know where our actions may lead; we can only act according to the guidelines laid down for us by our Creator. But whatever our choice, the results of our choosing will surely follow.

Prayer:　O Lord, thank you, not only for the warnings, but also for the promises in your Word placed there to guide us and our families safely through this life. Give us grace to obey and choose life.

40

The Ultimate Sacrifice

Read: Genesis 22:1–19

"God himself will provide the lamb for the burnt offering, my son."
Genesis 22:8.

Today we come to a parental story of tragic potential but with a bright outcome. Whatever lapses of faith Abraham had, this story illustrates his dogged determination to establish his faith in God's promises.

The promised nations and the One who would bless the world would come through Isaac, and God was asking him to slay this childless son. The words of faith, verse 8, uttered by Abraham on his way to this crucial sacrifice are legendary. He believed God would provide an answer, without which all God's promises to him and the world would die.

But his words were also prophetic. The story of Christ's crucifixion and resurrection shines all through this event. Isaac is the willing and only son offered as a sacrifice, and symbolically received back from the dead, Hebrews 11:19.

The significance of the event caused God to repeat the covenant made with Abraham: a nation, a land (inferred by conquest) and a blessing to all nations through his offspring—"because you have obeyed me," verse 17. The irony is that Abraham's obedience to a command that would negate all God's promises became the basis of their certainty.

We can sense the darkness in Abraham's soul as he trudged up Mount Moriah, but rejoice with him at the reclamation of his son and the revitalized fellowship with God. We can also match the intensity of family life with joy in knowing the benefits that will accrue to our loved ones by our steadfast faith, Romans 8:18.

Prayer: O Lord, we pray for the faith of Abraham during life's crises and tests of faith. Help us to trust your promise when circumstances appear to be contrary.

41

WEEK SEVEN: THURSDAY

A Wife for Isaac

Read: Genesis 24:1–9

"The Lord, the God of heaven . . . promised me on oath, saying, 'To your offspring I will give this land.'" Genesis 24:7.

What father wouldn't like to find a wife of his own choosing for his son? Abraham had that ability to choose for his son Isaac and took advantage of it. Although he did not make the final choice, he made two stipulations regarding the marriage that were consistent with the covenant that he had entered into with God, and to promote Isaac's commitment to it.

He did not want Isaac to settle back in Harran, the place Abraham had left to follow God's call. The country God had promised Abraham was the best environment to keep Isaac faithful to the covenant. This is in contrast to the neglect that Isaac gave to the selection of wives for *his* sons. Esau selected wives for himself from other clans, Genesis 26:34, and Jacob—later setting out for Harran—only came back to Canaan because of God's intervention, Genesis 28:15 and 20–21.

Abraham also wanted Isaac's wife from his own clan. This wasn't racial discrimination against the Canaanites; his objection was not racial, but rather religious: it was highly idolatrous. He wanted a wife for Isaac who would continue living within the covenant to which God had called the family.

We may not be able to choose who our children will marry, but we must pray for our children, grandchildren, and the partners they will marry: that they will come to faith in Christ and those partners will keep them faithful to God and to each other.

Prayer: Lord, keep our minds alert to these critical needs: that we may pray regularly for our children, grandchildren and those they will marry.

Isaac and Rebekah

Read: Genesis 24:32–66

They called Rebekah and asked her, "Will you go with this man?"
"I will go," she said. Genesis 24:58.

In this delightful story, Abraham's servant sought God's guidance as he searched carefully for a wife for Isaac. He had met Rebekah, and in today's reading the servant is recounting his story to Laban (who later deceived Jacob) hoping Rebekah would return with him.

As the end of the story shows, the marriage had a "once upon a time" start: "so she became his wife and he loved her." Two incidents confirm these last words.

When Isaac saw his wife was barren he prayed for her, and she became pregnant, Genesis 25:21. Later while in a neighbouring country ruled by Abimelech, Isaac referred to Rebekah as his sister, fearful that as her husband, he might be killed on account of her beauty.

Abimelech became aware of their married status when he "saw Isaac caressing his wife Rebekah," Genesis 26:7–8. The caress was more than a brotherly embrace.

Here was the beginning of an "ever after" relationship, but it didn't last as the later story of Isaac and Rebekah shows. Most couples who marry expect their marriages to last, each expressing by wedding vows they want to be with the other for life.

But, as we all know, often the initial attraction and sacrificial care for each other is lost, and the marriage ends in separation, divorce, or even a continuing dysfunctional relationship.

Prayer: Lord, you know we love each other. Guard us against self-centred ambition that may destroy our marriage and lead our children astray.

WEEK SEVEN: WEEKEND:

I Believe: Therefore I Understand

To believe in order to understand goes against our natural thought process; it's easier to believe what I understand. That is the basis of our scientific age; belief depends on verification of the facts. But when it comes to spiritual things, we can provide circumstantial evidence, but final proof is not available to us.

The agnostic bases his skepticism about the existence or character of God on this issue—he cannot know for certain and has no proof of either his existence or non-existence. At least in this he is being more honest than the atheist; for absence of proof of God is not evidence he does not exist.

Jesus claimed it was the Spirit of God that provides conviction of the truth about God and the need of a Saviour, John 16:8. Paul concurred, 1 Corinthians 2:11–12. Accepting the message of Christ's sacrifice on the cross for us opens a door to a new world of understanding about God, ourselves, others, and the world around us.

Many people find the Bible dry, making little sense until becoming a Christian. But almost overnight, the Bible suddenly provides insights about themselves and all aspects of life, leading to greater interest in spiritual things.

This is simply a reflection of the need to believe in order to understand spiritual things and the deeper truths of our faith. Belief and understanding combine into an upward spiral of learning and change that rebuilds the image of God in us.

Prayer: Heavenly Father, thank you for sending your Holy Spirit to indwell each of us. May his continued presence advise and enlighten us on all activities and events throughout our lives.

Favouritism

Read: Genesis 25:19–28

Isaac, who had a taste for wild game, loved Esau, but Rebekah
loved Jacob. Genesis 25:28.

The blissful relationship of Isaac and Rebekah did not last. Today's classic story exposes the dangers of favouritism; Isaac favoured Esau, Rebekah favoured Jacob, each making the choice based on the individual temperaments that neither son could change.

Further, it would have been wrong to expect the children to compensate for the parents preferences. It is the parents' responsibility to love and provide opportunity equally, irrespective of personal inclination.

Of course, we may have favourite children. It is easy to draw a parallel with families of today. A sports oriented dad may have more difficulty relating to a studious bookworm son, than a son whose love of outdoors and involvement in sport matches his own.

Conversely, a mother may worry and fret more over a gregarious high energy risk taker than a stay-at-home child that her motherly eye can protect.

It is not natural affinities that we have with one of our children that are wrong; it is the blatant exposure of that favouritism at the expense of another child. Worse still, it was probably more than favouritism that played a role in Isaac and Rebekah's actions towards their sons. More likely, their sons were pawns in a growing resentment towards each other.

Parents who use their children against each other set both the children and themselves up for misery as the later story of Isaac and Rebekah will illustrate.

Prayer: Lord, help us to clearly show that we love each of our children equally, despite differences we may feel.

45

WEEK EIGHT: TUESDAY

A Covenant for Life

Read: Genesis 26:1–6

All nations on earth will be blessed, because Abraham obeyed me and kept my requirements, my commands, my decrees and my laws. Genesis 26:4–5.

God made his covenant with Abraham, confirming it to him twice more, Genesis 18:18; 22:18. We might consider the promise died with him, without repetition to Abraham's son Isaac—particularly the promise: "All peoples on earth will be blessed through you and your offspring."

Not only was the covenant confirmed to Isaac, it also affirmed succeeding generations would retain the promise; not only in their memory, but also in their flesh. The promise of an Offspring to bless the world remained alive for future generations.

God continually reminded Israel of the promise to the patriarchs, by referring to himself as the God of Abraham, Isaac, and Jacob, typically as in Exodus 2:24; 3:6. It was this God that appeared to Moses and led Israel out of Egyptian slavery. Thus, succeeding generations received the covenant as an enduring promise, a mainstay in times of trial and affliction.

God, whose promises are permanent, also calls us to make a covenant that our partners can rely on for a lifetime; especially through the difficult times.

Those difficult times are opportunities. We can opt out of the marriage to avoid the trouble (usually *not* the easiest way out), or we can determine to keep our covenant and resolve the problem for the strengthening of the marriage.

As a ship's captain gains his skill on rough, not calm seas, so strong marriages are built by working through the difficult times.

Prayer: Heavenly Father, your promise to us is totally reliable, but we are subject to failure. Strengthen us that our commitment to our partners will mirror yours to us.

A Necessary Deception?

Read: Genesis 27:1–17

Jacob said to his father, "I am Esau your firstborn. I have done as you told me. Please sit up and eat some of my game so that you may give me your blessing." Genesis 27:19.

Rebekah was aware of the prophecy that Jacob would lead Esau, Genesis 25:22, and probably rationalized that her subterfuge fulfilled God's will. She reminds me of a rebellious teenager who justified her behaviour by claiming she was fulfilling the prophecy that children would turn against their parents, Matthew 10:21.

But the boys were not innocent. Jacob had already obtained the birthright by sharp dealing, which Esau considered of little worth at the time, Genesis 25:29–34, although he regretted it later, Hebrews 12:16–17.

Despite losing his birthright to Jacob, Esau was quite willing to receive it from his father. Jacob also acquiesced in Rebekah's elaborate subterfuge, only questioning whether it would work.

Most children come between parents at some point to achieve their ends; even small children seem to act instinctively. The initial scenario looks quite harmless, the parents disagree on some course of action for a child, and one parent defends the child openly. The child may then despise the other parent who is then humiliated.

If this practice continues, resentment builds in the victimized parent, and self-righteousness in the other. The child develops a means of manipulating parents, and others in later life.

Always discuss affairs affecting the child privately and face the child with a united front—even if one parent does not entirely agree with the decision.

Prayer: Lord, it is too easy to think my way is the best for our children. Keep us united in guiding them.

WEEK EIGHT: THURSDAY

The Price of Deception

Read: Genesis 27:18–40

When Esau heard his father's words, he burst out with a loud and
bitter cry and said to his father, "Bless me—me too, my father!"
Genesis 27:34.

The full story of Jacob is of a "street-wise" individual who knew instinctively how to take advantage of situations. He performed his act flawlessly, even though he could not camouflage his voice. He lied consistently and convincingly, even bringing God into his deception, finally persuading his father.

In response he received Isaac's blessing, fulfilling God's prophecy about him; an example of pragmatism—the end justifies the means. It assumes God needs help to achieve his plans.

Esau showed genuine grief at his loss. Then about 80 years of age, he regretted the rashness of his youth. Unfortunately, many decisions we make in earlier years have consequences in later life, requiring the grace of God to deal with them.

Isaac's anger was the result of Rebekah and Jacob's connivance. We hear no more of Rebekah; her actions had no further significance, and Jacob's own sons gave him a life of grief.

How would the prophecy of Jacob's pre-eminence have been accomplished if Rebekah and Jacob had not intervened? Would God's purposes have been thwarted if Esau had received the blessing given to Jacob? We cannot know, but the story points out God uses our foolhardiness as well as our faithfulness to accomplish his purposes.

Without either, he will still complete his mission. But our faithfulness is more likely to bring harmony in the end as we work *with* him for the sake of our children.

Prayer: Father, we are tempted many times to intervene when our prayers seem to go unanswered. Strengthen our faith in those uncertain times. Teach us to wait on you.

Children's Rebellion

Read: Genesis 27:41 to 28:9

So Isaac called for Jacob and blessed him and commanded him: .
. . "May God Almighty bless you and make you fruitful and
increase your numbers until you become a community of peoples.
May he give you and your descendants the blessing given to
Abraham." Genesis 28:1, 3–4.

Esau had married Hittite women, not of his parent's
faith, who "were a source of grief to Isaac and
Rebekah," Genesis 26:34.

Again, Rebekah used deception to convince Isaac to
send Jacob away. Rather than telling Isaac she was afraid
for Jacob's life, she preferred to discredit Esau by using his
choice of women as an excuse to send Jacob away for a
wife in their own clan.

Isaac's anger at Jacob appears to have dissipated.
Perhaps he had come to terms with God's desire to pass his
blessing through Jacob rather that Esau; that Abraham's
blessing was meant for Jacob. In fact, God's covenant given
to Abraham passed to Isaac. Genesis 26:2–5, and was about
to be repeated to Jacob, Genesis 28:13–15.

Eventually, Esau's relationship with Jacob improved,
welcoming Jacob back to Canaan some twenty years later,
Genesis 33:4 and the two buried their father together,
Genesis 35:27–29.

As rebellious children age—especially when they have
children of their own—friction with parents begins to
soften. Hostile relations with a child can cause as much
grief as losing a child; it is ongoing, and has added
antagonism.

As we trust that time will soften our children towards
us, prayer for them will help maintain a tender attitude
towards them.

Prayer: Lord, give us practical love and patience for those
children that turn away from us and our faith in you. Hear
our fervent prayers for each of them.

WEEK EIGHT: WEEKEND

A Result of Favouritism

A family we knew had two children, a boy and a girl of which the girl was the more highly treasured. She was attractive and the parents dressed and made a fuss of her to the exclusion of attention to the boy.

He resented his sex, becoming uncertain of his identity and developing a latent homosexuality. Eventually, his confusion and humiliation drove him to suicide. We don't know if the parents ever realized their part in his death.

All children are different. We cannot always treat every child the same; effective encouragement and punishment varies from child to child. What our first child took as a warning, our second accepted as a challenge.

Birth order also has an effect on the attention that children get. First children tend to be "control freaks," often lumbered with more duties for younger siblings. Middle children often receive less attention than older and younger ones.

Siblings of a handicapped child may receive less attention. It is these children that may become the victims of inadvertent favouritism and placed at risk by seeking the notice they need elsewhere.

Attention paid individually on a regular basis to each child, especially in the earlier years, can pay dividends later on. A child that feels special to his or her parents will develop a sense of acceptance and identity that will help to shield them from the dangers outside the home.

Prayer: O Lord, raising children seems such a complicated task. We will seek you and your Word constantly for your wisdom in providing love, guidance, and discipline for the little ones you have given us.

God Chooses Jacob

Read: Genesis 28:10–22

When Jacob awoke from his sleep, he thought, "Surely the Lord is in this place, and I was not aware of it." Genesis 28:16.

You may recall the story of Jacob's ladder, but few will recall the message God gave to Jacob. The message Jacob received from God at the top of the ladder contains the promise of life from God to the world: "all peoples on earth will be blessed through you and your offspring."

The ladder and angels were only trappings to draw attention to the message. The prophecy to Jacob's mother Rebekah, Genesis 25:21–23 is fulfilled in this passage, Genesis 27:20.

Jacob, later named Israel, became the progenitor of the nation of Israel. But considering the conniving nature of Jacob, he seemed an unlikely candidate. He had little knowledge or regard for God up to the time of his deception of Isaac, talking to Isaac of "your God," Genesis 18:19.

So God chooses people based on their future faithfulness rather than their past record; consider Paul: the fierce persecutor of the Early Church.

God called Jacob's attention to his grandfather, who was chosen by God because Abraham would "direct his children and his household after him to keep the way of the Lord by doing what is right and just," Genesis 18:19.

Abraham's selection was not just a matter of personal faithfulness, but made on the basis of his future allegiance and passing the faith to his household and children. The greatest thing we can do for our children is to maintain our faithfulness to God.

Prayer: Lord, keep us committed to you, that our allegiance may be a blessing that will transfer to our children.

51

WEEK NINE: TUESDAY

Love That Lasts

Read: Genesis 29:16–20

Jacob served seven years to get Rachel, but they seemed like only a few days to him because of his love for her. Genesis 29:20.

At first glance, it's difficult to think of Jacob's love for Rachel making years appear like days. But Jacob was not counting the waiting time, but considering the price to pay for such a bride; seven years seemed like a trifle.

In contrast, Jacob may have considered seven *days* too high a price for Leah. As it happened, he was deceived into paying seven years for Leah, then placed in debt another seven years for Rachel.

Jacob was not measuring the worth of the girls so much as his love for them. So how do we measure the value of our partners? Most lovers wax eloquent on the lengths to which they will go to win their beloved. But ask that question again after a few years of marriage!

The Christian view of love is one of service; love measured by the level of service we give to our partner. Conversely, our level of selfishness measures the amount of love lost.

In the days of first love, many a lover will claim he is prepared to die for his beloved, placing the ultimate value on her. This provides a glimpse of God's love in giving his life for those he loved, Romans 5:6–8.

But Jesus not only gave his life for us, he rose again so that he could live for us. Few of us will need to die for our beloved, but to live for him or her—and that may be more drastic than dying for them.

Prayer: Heavenly Father, we thank you for the partners you have given us. May our love and service to them reflect your care for us.

Responding to Deception

Read: Genesis 29:21–35

"What is this you have done to me? I served you for Rachel, didn't I? Why have you deceived me?" Genesis 29:25.

Jacob was the arch deceiver, outwitting both his brother, Genesis 25:27–34, and father, Genesis. 27:18–24. In this passage, he met his match in Laban, who used him to marry off his two daughters, and simultaneously ensured Jacob would work for him for fourteen years without pay.

As a result of Laban's deception, Jacob was left with two wives. Both wives were unhappy, Rachel because she was barren, Leah because she was unloved.

Leah's story is heart-wrenching; she was the innocent victim in Laban's trickery. It is a journey from hope to despair, but finally finding her peace in God. The birth of her four sons tells the story of her desire and effort to earn Jacob's love.

Birth of three sons failed to bond Jacob to her, and she named her fourth son Judah—meaning praise to God—and simply left her situation with God.

Physical attraction alone will not sustain a marriage, although a critical element. The necessary relationship between love and allure will always be a mystery, some mistakenly assuming one or the other to be the "real thing." Jacob's behaviour is not blameless; he could have provided some healing of the wrong done to them both.

When someone deceives us, it's too easy to transfer our resentment and anger to our partner—the closest target. But our partner is our closest ally. To bring him or her on side to face the incident together not only strengthens us, but also strengthens the marriage.

Prayer: Lord, we know we will be deceived, perhaps by our partners. Help us to respond with healing, not harmful attitudes.

WEEK NINE: THURSDAY

Qualifications for Influence

Read: Genesis 29:31–35

"Surely my husband will love me now." Genesis 29:32.

We read again some verses from yesterday, to note that the birthright depends, not only on birth order, but also behaviour.

Laban fraudulently substituted Leah (presumably veiled and in the dark) for Rachel. Jacob married Rachel within a week, but had to work another seven years for her. The result of this deception by Laban was that "Leah was not loved." But God had pity on Leah who bore Jacob his first four children, Reuben, Simeon, Levi, and Judah, while Rachel remained barren.

These four sons of Leah's were the most significant for the nation of Israel and for us. In particular, Judah's clan became the kingly line, giving birth to the "Lion of Judah"— Jesus the Messiah and our Saviour.

But Judah was fourth in line; the elder sons lost this special birthright as a result of evil behaviour and lack of repentance. Jacob foretold their future, as well as Judah's, before his death, Genesis 49:3–12.

We don't know if Leah was alive for the actions of her sons, but Jacob was, and dismayed by their behaviour. But it is important to note that all Jacob's children—including Reuben, Simeon, and Levi—remained within the covenant that God made with their forefathers.

Our children are distinct individuals who will make their own decisions in life and may well pay the price for their foolish ones. But God is merciful, open to repentance from those who desire to reconcile with him.

Prayer: O Lord, may we not lose our place of influence because of foolish mistakes or deliberate transgression. Guard our responses and attitudes.

Adultery and Polygamy

Read: Genesis 30:1–2

[Rachel] said to Jacob, "Give me children, or I'll die!"
Genesis 30:1.

Legalization of gay marriage opens the door to other marriage relationships—in particular, acceptance of polygamy.

At the time of writing, polygamy exists in the province of British Columbia and the police do not pursue it. This is partly because to do so would provoke a challenge under the Canadian Charter of Rights and Freedoms. Approval of one alternate form of marriage reduces the defence against others.

Polygamy was practised in Old Testament times, but this and other readings indicate that it was not very satisfactory, recall Hannah and Peninah, 1 Samuel 1:1–7. Both of Jacob's wives were unhappy, Leah because she was not loved and Rachel because she was barren. While tolerated in the Old Testament, polygamy was illicit by New Testament times when Jesus restated the creation ideal of one man and one woman, Matthew 19:4–6.

Polygamy may not yet be a serious issue, but adultery is rampant and repeats all the problems of polygamy—humiliation, jealousy and possible abandonment. The problem, unfortunately, is not restricted to the married partners. It has its effect on the children.

Hagar's child Ishmael copied the scorn of his mother, Genesis 16:3–4; 21:8–9, and rival children from David's wives turned to violence and murder. Similarly, children in adulterous homes often suffer lifelong trauma, and may develop habits of their adulterous parents in adult life.

The greatest security we can give children is a home that is secure in its created parental relationships—where both parents love and respect each other.

Prayer: Heavenly Father, guard our marriage relationship so we may remain faithful to each other as you are faithful to us.

WEEK NINE: WEEKEND

Jacob and Charles

The story of Jacob and his wives has a remarkable counterpart in modern history. Prince Charles, youthful heir to the British throne, fell in love with attractive Camilla Shand, but failed to propose to her as she was not royal material.

While Charles was absent in the navy, Camilla married another friend. At twenty-eight years of age Charles met Diana Spencer, sixteen, of suitable royal heritage and later married her. The relationship between Charles and Diana, despite the fairytale romance, was akin to Jacob and Leah. Camilla remained Charles' first love as Rachel did to Jacob.

Camilla divorced her husband in 1995, but had already resumed her relationship with Charles. Diana, sick with bulimia and consumed by jealousy, attempted suicide several times. She tried finding comfort in affairs of her own, which ended with Diana's death in the Paris subway.

Charles faced a dilemma. As future head of the Church of England, he could not marry a divorced woman and the relationship continued in stagnant fashion. Eventually, a compromise allowed Charles and Camilla to wed after thirty-four years of courtship.

It is easy to look on these relationships as typical unfaithful behaviour, with blame to be scattered liberally over all the participants. But what different outcome might there have been for both Jacob and Charles had there been no outside interference?

The pressures of friends and family, however well meaning, can be disastrous for a marriage. We should seek advice from those we trust, but resist unsolicited "advice" from others regarding our relationships. Only then can we be sure that our commitments are our own and take responsibility for the outcomes.

Prayer: Lord, lead us to those who will give godly advice in our difficult decisions, especially as we choose our relationships.

Dangers of Manipulation

Read: Genesis 30:3–13

"Here is Bilhah, my maidservant. Sleep with her so that she can bear children for me and that through her I too can build a family." Genesis 30:3.

Jacob and Rachel followed the example of Abraham and Sarah, and Rebekah and Isaac. These were not faithful believers simply fulfilling God's direction, but using a faithless manipulation to achieve what they considered a godly result.

It frequently led to undesirable results—our world still labours under the consequences four thousand years later. Perhaps Jacob considered Rachel the primary wife for continuation of God's covenant. If God wasn't providing a child to Rachel, then Jacob would help.

Even today, the cutting of ethical corners is acceptable if it yields good results. This may be as simple as tax evasion to support a Christian organization. Joseph Fletcher, an early proponent of situational ethics, coined the phrase "therapeutic adultery"; adultery offering solace to a needy woman.

For the "Christian" manipulator, the end justifies questionable means to achieve some spurious "spiritual" progress.

The children born to Rachel through her maid had unremarkable lives and descendants. The children born later to Rachel herself had specific roles to play. Joseph saved the family from extinction as ruler of Egypt.

Benjamin's descendants remained loyal to the kingly line of Judah when Israel split a thousand years later. This underlines the necessity of living godly ethical lives if we are to make a mark for God's glory—even if it appears to be a losing proposition in the short term.

Prayer: Lord, it's too easy to try to fulfill your will our own way when prayer appears to be unanswered. Give us patience to allow you to work out your purposes in your own time.

WEEK TEN: TUESDAY

Game Playing

Read: Genesis 30:14–16

"You must sleep with me," [Leah] said. "I have hired you with my son's mandrakes." So he slept with her that night. Genesis 30:16.

Y ou may have heard frequent accusations against the patriarchal system of the Old Testament that it exploited women as chattels. There is no doubt the system had its failings as much as any society.

But this event tells a different story. The wives of the patriarchs had their own household of servants and freedom of action. Abraham conceded to Sarah's wishes regarding a son, and to deal with a scornful Hagar as she chose, Genesis 16:1–6. Rebekah had sufficient freedom to deceive Isaac, Genesis 27:5–10.

But today's reading is illuminating and even a little humorous. The belief that mandrakes increased fertility prompted Rachel to bargain for Leah's mandrakes; Rachel wanted them for an occasion of intimacy with Jacob in hope of breaking her barrenness.

She agreed for Leah to sleep with Jacob that night in exchange for the mandrakes. Both women assumed Jacob would simply acquiesce in their scheme; the wives obviously had control over who slept with Jacob and when.

A wider reading of Jacob and his wives' story shows the home was not happy. The wives were fierce rivals for offspring, and resorted to manipulation to achieve their ends; unsurprising with Jacob's previous history of deceit.

But patriarchal or not, our culture abounds with manipulation and game-playing to ensure reasonable co-existence by some marriage partners. We have probably resorted to them ourselves at times, but isn't true marriage more than simply co-existing?

Prayer: Dear Lord, sometimes we don't even know how manipulative we are; the habit is so ingrained within us. Holy Spirit, show us our sin and lead us to repentance.

Deception

Read: Genesis 31:22–42

Laban said to Jacob, "What have you done? You've deceived me, and you've carried off my daughters like captives in war. Why did you run off secretly and deceive me? Genesis 31:26–27.

After twenty years working for Laban, Jacob decided to leave. This was not easy; Laban had manipulated him to stay several times, and had manpower enough to force Jacob to stay. Jacob, himself a deceiver, had met his match.

This story emphasizes the way habits of parents rub off on their children. Jacob's deception of Isaac repeated the deception by both Abraham, Genesis 12:10–13; 20:1–2, and Isaac, Genesis 26:7, and encouraged Rachel to deceive her father about his household gods.

If Jacob had a desire to be "just like my dad" he certainly achieved it. Not only did Jacob copy his father and grandfather's mistakes, his wives followed his example. In addition, Rachel—with Leah's agreement—justified her behaviour based on her father's deceit, Genesis 31:14–16.

In our culture some practice manipulation on a grand scale by posing as victims when accused, thus placing blame for their behaviour on others. Our children must see our willingness to own our actions, if they are to become responsible members of society.

Undesirable actions by others may provoke us. But the mature Christian is to recognize and channel anger and frustration into positive responses, those that address injustice in ethically valid and spiritually acceptable ways. We want our children to live lives that they control, not to be victims of the whims of others.

Prayer: Heavenly Father, it's too easy to blame others for our faults and mistakes. Help us to be honest with ourselves and others.

WEEK TEN: THURSDAY

A Guarded Reunion

Read: Genesis 32:1–31

So Jacob was left alone, and a man wrestled with him till daybreak. Genesis 32:24.

The rivalry between Isaac and Rebekah caused Jacob and Esau's separation for twenty years. But the sons also were responsible for their behaviour. Jacob assimilated the example of Rebekah's conniving and Esau accepted the offer of Isaac's blessing to which he was no longer entitled.

Now, as Jacob returned home, he still faced Esau's threat of death, and feared the four hundred men Esau had with him. But Jacob prayed and met with God; these encounters giving him hope. While his elaborate preparations to meet a hostile Esau reflect on Jacob's old ways, his meetings with God tempered his approach. He made what preparations he could to reduce the probable hostility of the meeting, but his faith was in God as he met Esau.

Esau also reconsidered. The years—and perhaps a maturing faith—had softened his attitude and he was overwhelmed to meet Jacob. But the brothers remained estranged, Jacob refusing Esau's offer of company and help. The only other recorded meeting of the two was at their father Isaac's funeral.

Much later, the nations of Israel and Edom—the descendants of Jacob and Esau—became enemies. Obadiah, 8–14, warned Edom of judgment for their cruel treatment of Israel. It should remind us the treatment of our children can have consequences well beyond our generation.

Prayer: Dear Lord, guide our children to avoid the mistakes we make. Give us the courage to be honest with our children and admit our errors.

Restored Communion with God

Read: Genesis 35:1–15

"Let us go up to Bethel, where I will build an altar to God, who answered me in the day of my distress and who has been with me wherever I have gone." Genesis 35:3.

The patriarchs are so named because they were the fathers of the covenant people—for Israel and for Christians—not because families were subservient to them.

Additionally, they were not just fathers of a family but leaders of a great clan, and so had responsibilities for their descendants and employees. The greater the following, the greater the duty to lead by example and even direction when necessary.

In this chapter, Jacob as head of the family clan considered it time to make fresh allegiance to God. He made this decision unilaterally, but his entire household went along with his decision.

Some of the household may have been from other nations with other gods—perhaps persuading some of Jacob's own family to worship them. Presumably the earrings and other ornaments had idolatrous significance, unlike the simple adornments of today.

Jacob returned to Bethel, where God had met him as he fled from Esau. It was the place where he originally met God, but now became a place of communion with God for the rest of his life.

With the best of intentions, decisions and safeguards, we will frequently make the wrong decisions or fail to uphold our own standards.

A return to the place of communion with God on a regular basis is the only way to maintain stability and steadiness in family life, particularly during difficult and fractious times.

Prayer: Heavenly Father, draw us into your presence and Word regularly to receive strength and wisdom needed to retain loving relationships with our family.

A Story of Restoration

Angie and Gary were not Christians when they married. Angie was gentle and kindly but hankered after the freedom she had before marriage.

Following the feminist view that self-fulfillment was her right, she left her marriage and joined a gregarious, adventurous single friend Barb. Together, they sought the fulfillment that feminist ideology promised. Gary, still not a Christian, raised their two daughters alone.

Eventually, both Angie and Barb became Christians and joined a church. As Angie grew in her understanding of Christian life, she realized she needed to restore her relationship with her husband. She wasn't sure whether she still loved him, but sought his agreement to return to the marriage.

He had not wanted the separation and the two were reunited. Angie continued her church attendance and involvement, while Gary took an intellectual view against the claims of Christianity. But Gary saw a change in his wife and became sympathetic to the Christian faith.

Eventually another child was born and Angie was hospitalized during the birth. By this time, Gary wanted his two daughters to continue attending church, and took them to church himself.

The wisdom of the Christian faith gradually made sense to Gary, and on Angie's return, she reunited to a Christian husband. Despite her misgivings, Angie had returned to raise their family together, reflecting her relationship with Christ by her example of faithfulness to Gary.

Prayer: O Lord, if my partner is not a Christian, help me to extend the wisdom and fragrance of Christ to him or her.

The Destructiveness of Greed

Read: Genesis 34:1–21

Three days later, while all of them were still in pain, two of Jacob's sons, Simeon and Levi, Dinah's brothers, took their swords and attacked the unsuspecting city, killing every male. Genesis 34:25.

Today we step back to a longer reading of violence and subterfuge on the part of both the Shechemites and Jacob's sons. Particularly, the cruel actions of Simeon and Levi eliminated them from leadership of Israel, Genesis 49:5–7.

The rape of Dinah would have been unacceptable even in the permissive nature of today's western culture, but was equivalent to treason in Jacob's time. The family had a right to be furious at the rape.

We would be right in thinking that the offer of marriage was a reasonable offer of conciliation which Jacob's family appeared to accept. But as the story unfolds, both sides had ulterior motives.

Then, as verse 27 records, at least some of the other sons were complicit in the slaughter as they took the Shechemite families and their goods for themselves.

Dinah's rape is serious enough in itself, but the evidence points to the streak of selfish greed in both parties, which underlies much of the violence and misery of human history. But beyond that, the story points to the violent nature of Jacob's sons and prepares us for their treatment of Joseph later.

We are all subject to the same temptations, not necessarily to the point of violence, but frequently to compromise in our human duty and for Christians to the neglect of our commitment to God's calling on our lives.

Does our relationship with our partner or children suffer because of our unwillingness to put them first?

Prayer: Heavenly Father, we are very conscious of our selfish nature. Strengthen us to serve our family unselfishly.

WEEK ELEVEN: TUESDAY

Favouritism Continues

Read: Genesis 37:2–11

And [his brothers] hated [Joseph] all the more because of his dream and what he had said. Genesis 37:8.

Children tend to assimilate parents' habits. Jacob is a prime example, repeating the favouritism of his parents. Even before the events of today's reading, there was an evident estrangement of Leah's sons from Jacob. After Simeon and Levi's massacre of the men of Shechem, both showed no remorse and rejected their father's rebuke, Genesis 34:30–31.

Jacob's favouritism of the child Joseph was probably already evident. Clearly old habits die hard; Jacob had not learned from the pain of his mother's favouritism of him. It seems Jacob not only resented the fact that Leah had children while Rachel could not, but his special treatment of Joseph conveyed to his other sons they were second class.

At seventeen years of age, Joseph was not above exploiting his special status. Although the dreams were not of his making, his use of them seems short-sighted. His assertion of future power over his brothers enraged them and even his father rebuked him. Just because the dreams were true did not justify their humiliating use. Consider the response had Mary freely rumoured her promise of the birth of Jesus.

However, Jacob's rebuke was also out of place. He had already fostered the favouritism that Joseph used against his brothers, and was unaware of the impending tragedy he had unleashed. Showing favouritism among children has serious consequences. It will give a favoured child a false sense of importance, while impeding a disfavoured child's development. As we will see, given the right circumstances it can even be dangerous.

Prayer: Lord, the children you gave us are all equal in your sight. Help us treat them accordingly, even if we do have favourites.

Dangers of Favouritism

Read: Genesis 37:12–30

"Here comes that dreamer!" they said to each other. "Come now, let's kill him and throw him into one of these cisterns and say that a ferocious animal devoured him. Then we'll see what comes of his dreams." Genesis 37:19–20.

The danger of Jacob's favouritism becomes real in today's reading. Only Reuben and Judah of the four eldest boys come out with any sense of responsibility for Joseph, the others were quite happy to dispose of him.

Particularly, Simeon and Levi, the second and third sons, maintained their violent streak from Shechem. Neither the slaying of their own brother, nor the imminent grief of their father eclipsed the anger shared by the six younger sons. Eventually they compromised and sold Joseph as a slave.

Were these actions necessary to ensure Joseph was able to assist the family later during a famine? God certainly used these circumstances to bring about that outcome, Genesis 45:5–8. But to justify the brothers' actions based on the outcome means God would have to justify their actions.

The end rarely justifies the means, and those who participate in such schemes are accountable for their actions. Even Judas was accountable for his actions: "The Son of Man will go as it has been decreed. But woe to that man who betrays him," Luke 22:22.

Newscasts routinely report violence and death as a result of anger or jealousy in family relationships. We can never know the adversity and dangers we pose to our children—and even beyond them—by playing favourites.

Prayer: Heavenly Father, forgive us and release us from the jealousies that we have entertained, so we will not infect those who come after us.

65

WEEK ELEVEN: THURSDAY

Favouritism Returns Pain

Read: Genesis 37:31–35

All his sons and daughters came to comfort him, but he refused to be comforted. "No," he said, "in mourning will I go down to the grave to my son." Genesis 37:35.

We can imagine what effect the loss of Joseph had on Jacob. But remember Jacob's misery was partly his own making. While we have dwelt on the effect of favouritism on children, it can also come back to haunt the parents. Obviously, we can go back to Jacob's favouritism as partly the cause of his loss, but there are other pointers in the text to show how other actions came home to roost.

Jacob knew the brothers were minding their sheep near Shechem, Genesis 37:12–14. This of course was a place they had to leave in fear following Simeon's and Levi's massacre in Shechem, Genesis 42:36. Recalling the Shechem incident made him fearful for his sons and prompted him to send Joseph to ensure their safety.

As it happened, Joseph was in far greater danger from his brothers than they were from the Shechemites. The final irony in this story is that the brothers deceived Jacob with a goat, as he himself deceived *his* father Isaac with a goat.

Jacob still seemed unaware that his actions had precipitated events. He refused to be comforted, and held the brothers' guilt over them for another twenty years. If ever there was a dysfunctional family, this was it. When Jacob claimed that his years had "been few and difficult," Genesis 47:9, much was of his own making. Favouritism not only hurts children, it can return pain to the parents also.

Prayer: Father, show us any adversity we may be suffering that results from our earlier foolish actions. Please forgive us.

Lingering Resentments

Read: Genesis 42:1–5

*Jacob did not send Benjamin, Joseph's brother, with the others,
because he was afraid that harm might come to him.*
Genesis 42:4.

Some years passed, and Jacob was still very much in control. In particular, Benjamin replaced Joseph as Jacob's favourite. But guilt replaced the jealous anger the sons had over Jacob's first favourite Joseph.

Rosanne once said in her TV show: "It's a pity to waste all that guilt." Jacob now used his ongoing grief and his sons' guilt to manipulate and dominate them, and drove the message home with his favour to Benjamin. The result was a family of disoriented adult children who "looked at each other," unsure of how to act without their father's direction.

Jacob, self-centred as ever, refused to let Benjamin out of his sight, and would not trust him to the brothers for a lengthy journey to Egypt. He was partly right. If he blamed the brothers for Joseph's disappearance, how can he know whether he can trust them a second time?

This is a classic example that both sides of a dispute generally carry some blame. The boys' confession of their bitter secret and Jacob's admission of his favouritism might heal the rift. Life is too short to let barriers between ourselves and those we love remain for long. For Jacob and his sons it lasted over twenty years. We all face that possibility as long as we harbour unresolved issues.

Prayer: Father, are we harbouring buried jealousies that cloud and judge our relationships? Please reveal our hidden resentments so we can be restore our relationships.

ANN AND BRYAN NORFORD

WEEK ELEVEN: WEEKEND

Real People

A recent television advertisement had two angels discussing a third angel's wings: "They look so perky they can't be real!"

We may comment the same of people that "are so perfect they can't be real!" This is certainly not the case for the characters we have been reading about in recent days; a factor supporting their reality is their natural human conduct.

Abraham, the hero of faith in God, falls into deception concerning Sarah twice to ensure his own safety. Isaac also follows his father's example. Isaac and Rebekah descend into partisan favouritism over their sons.

Jacob's sons, reflecting the radical nature of youth, dispense with Joseph with callous disregard for the consequences. Jacob retreats into stubborn self-pitying grief to punish his sons at the loss of Joseph. Yet with advancing years, the brothers' attitude to both Joseph and Benjamin softens, even if earlier fears tend to dog them to the end of the story.

It is often the erratic behaviour of these characters that betrays their humanness. With some honest thought, we can see ourselves in them.

But the stories of these men bear witness to the basic premise of the narrative: God has control over the events of our lives and uses them for his purposes. And his purposes were—and still are—to reconcile with us, who are spiritual descendents of this all too human family. And Jesus Christ accomplished this by his coming to earth.

Prayer: Heavenly Father, it's the admission of our failures and sinfulness that makes us real. Help us choose transparency over hypocrisy.

68

Revenge or Reconciliation

Read: Genesis 42:6–17

Although Joseph recognized his brothers, they did not recognize him. Then he remembered his dreams about them.
Genesis 42:8–9.

Joseph appears very harsh with his brothers; probably reasonable—anyone treated like Joseph might seek revenge. In a complete reversal of that event, he now had control of the situation. How was he going to use his advantage? Would he turn them into slaves as they had once made him? Perhaps to give him time to consider his options, he incarcerated them for three days.

Yet when he first saw his brothers, his memory was not of their treatment of him, but his dream about them as a youth. The dream was coming true as they bowed to the ground before him. His true feelings for them were not in his words to them, but in his actions for them behind the scenes.

He wept as they confessed their sin against him, Genesis 42:24; he returned their money, not willing to take it from his own family, paid for the grain himself, Genesis 43:23, and then provided for their return journey, Genesis 42:25.

Some family feuds date back to childhood, each party continually responding in kind to the ongoing provocation perceived or received. While some of Joseph's actions become clear later, concern for his family, in Canaan determined his later actions.

Prayer and thought about our responses can provide us with options to act in the interests of our family relationships—even if they are not returned.

Prayer: Dear Lord, we confess we have harboured ill will towards other members of our family. Help us to act with wisdom and concern for them even when provoked.

WEEK TWELVE: TUESDAY

Unresolved Conflict Creates Fear

Read: Genesis 42:18–28

They said to one another, "Surely we are being punished because of our brother. We saw how distressed he was when he pleaded with us for his life, but we would not listen; that's why this distress has come upon us." Genesis 42:21.

The treatment of Joseph in his teen years continued to weigh on the brothers' consciences. We may wonder if they considered other calamities before that time as God's judgment on them.

Certainly, the idea that Benjamin would be a pawn in the dealings with this Egyptian would trigger thoughts of their treatment of Joseph, and would further inflame Jacob's simmering resentment against them. Their dilemma seemed intractable as they became the pawns themselves in a long distance silent dialog between Joseph and Jacob.

As the premier official of the country, Joseph was responsible for its security and the treatment of aliens, so his attitude towards his brothers appeared reasonable. He skillfully used the admission of a younger brother as an opportunity for proof of their claim to be "honest men, not spies," Genesis 42:10.

But he had a personal motive: he wanted to protect this youngest brother from Joseph's own fate. As long as the family needed food, Benjamin's life would be safe as a guarantee for further provisions.

The sins of the past come to haunt us as we grow older, and like Joseph's brothers, we may view calamity as punishment for earlier failures. It may take adversity to bring us to a point of confession.

In this sense, misfortune can be a blessing, bringing us face to face with the truth about ourselves, and family friction may give us the pain we need.

Prayer: Lord, help us to be honest with ourselves when facing adversity; even if it may be a result of our own actions. Give us grace to seek forgiveness and be thankful for your provision.

Prepared to Sacrifice

Read: Genesis 42:29 to 43:14

Then Judah said to Israel his father, "If I do not bring him back to you and set him here before you, I will bear the blame before you all my life." Genesis 43:8–10.

Today's reading shows partly why Reuben, the oldest, lost the leadership of the clan. He made an irresponsible and ineffective plea for the release of Benjamin. His timing was poor; there was no pressure to return as long as they had food.

Then to offer the life of his own sons for Benjamin's may sound high-minded at first, but is hardly likely to reassure Jacob; someone who would sacrifice his own sons' lives could hardly be trusted with some-one else's son.

Judah, on the other hand let the matter rest until the food was gone. His assertion that "we could have gone and returned twice" indicates how much time had elapsed. But of greater importance, Judah was willing to take complete responsibility for Benjamin himself, placing his own life on the line.

So Judah is beginning to wrest the leadership of the clan from Jacob's self-obsessive one. Jacob is less concerned with the family—note his easy acceptance of the loss of Simeon—than his own comfort. Judah's leadership does not simply capitulate to Jacob, but uses timing and circumstances to persuade Jacob to let Benjamin go.

But Judah's concern is sacrificial; he is willing to sacrifice himself if necessary to serve Jacob's ends as well as ensure the continued well being of the whole family. The pattern of Jesus' own sacrifice for us sets the pattern; we must be prepared to sacrifice if we are to repair broken relationships.

Prayer: Lord, reveal to us where our sacrifice can alleviate a rift of relationship in family and friends.

WEEK TWELVE: THURSDAY

A Revealing Decision

Read: Genesis 44:1–17

The cup was found in Benjamin's sack. At this, they tore their clothes. Genesis 44:12–13.

From the brothers' point of view this chapter is hard to read. Joseph's treatment of the brothers seems unnecessarily harsh.

But he was delighted at seeing Benjamin and treated the other brothers favourably revealing his concern for their father. His return of Simeon to them and his private weeping, all suggests a deep love and care for the whole family, Genesis 43:26–30.

So why did he use trickery, placing Benjamin—as it seemed to the brothers—in jeopardy? Here was the final test. Benjamin was the favourite son that had replaced Joseph. How would the brothers treat him when in peril? That would indicate their state of heart towards a favourite son. Would it be different from their treatment of Joseph?

The placing of his cup in Benjamin's sack would ensure the brothers made a decisive choice for themselves or Benjamin. Joseph further clarified the choice by offering to allow the brothers to return without Benjamin.

Joseph did not allow sentimental attachment to draw him into their dysfunctional relationship. To do so would compromise his ability to care for them.

We often receive testing regarding our relationships, mostly in small things; less so in major confrontations. And those tests are more often in family relationships. We see our families the most and they are the closest to us.

Are we willing to make the sacrifices necessary to maintain our relationship, and are our attitudes improving over time?

Prayer: Our Father, please give us the strength to confront where necessary, but always to deal in love for the well-being of those dependent on us.

Eloquent Love

Read: Genesis 44:18 to 45:2

"Please let your servant remain here as my lord's slave in place of the boy, and let the boy return with his brothers." Genesis 44:33.

Today's reading clinches Judah's position as leader among the brothers. His eloquent intervention on behalf of Benjamin is moving. It is both courageous and sacrificial. Judah assumes that he faces possible death just for speaking out; Joseph has power of life and death over the whole kingdom.

But unknown to Judah, using his father as defence of his position is the most telling argument, and his obvious concern for the well being of his father reaches Joseph's heart.

The distraught pleading of Judah accomplished three things. It clearly established his leadership based on sacrificial concern for Benjamin and his father. It satisfied Joseph that the brothers had changed hearts towards their father and his favourites, undermining Joseph's subterfuge and provoking his emotional outburst.

Finally, it satisfied Joseph's desire for true repentance: an admission of wrong doing and a change in behaviour.

The basis for reconciliation was set. Judah's honesty and Joseph's care for the family provided the environment in which they could reunite.

If these two basics are present, any family split can be healed. But it requires all parties to come to that agreement.

In the meantime, it is incumbent upon us to maintain our integrity until others come to that point. Remember, Joseph waited many years to meet his family, and even then it was more than a year before the final reconciliation took place.

Prayer: Lord, impart to us your wisdom and patience in the difficult family situations we face, as you did to Joseph.

Forgiveness

The characteristic that causes us to stumble the most is forgiveness. Yet it is the foremost quality of grace, demonstrated by the grace extended to us by God through the sacrifice of his Son, Jesus Christ.

I'm sure all of us have heard sermons on this subject urging forgiveness to those who have wronged us; for God's grace shown to us requires us to extend the same to others, 2 Peter 3:9.

What is also likely is that most sermons we heard failed to indicate that repentance is a condition for forgiveness. God's forgiveness, available to all, has to be accepted.

We recognized our sinfulness before God, repented of it and sought his forgiveness. In Jesus' parable of the servants, they both acknowledged the debt and need to their debtors, Matthew 18:21–35. It is not possible to receive forgiveness where there is no acknowledgement of guilt.

But does this allow us to deny forgiveness and maintain bitterness and anger toward those who refuse to listen to our complaint? Hardly, for God has offered forgiveness whether we accept or reject it.

If we are to preserve our fellowship with God, it is also necessary for us to forgive in our hearts, Matthew 6:12–14. Retained bitterness skews our thinking and damages our health. We need to deal with the conflict within ourselves, irrespective of outside acceptance.

Generally, we are really sorry if we have hurt our partners. However, if my partner is unwilling to acknowledge sin against me, he or she will bear the consequences of that denial, but I am responsible for the state of my own heart, James 2:13.

Prayer: Dear Lord, it is so hard sometimes to forgive, especially when wronged by someone close to us. Strengthen our resolve to follow your example and reflect your grace.

Reunion

Read: Genesis 45:3–15

God sent me ahead of you to preserve for you a remnant on earth and to save your lives by a great deliverance. Genesis 45:7.

We have had several reunions with our family of children and grandchildren. It becomes more difficult as they all marry and have lives of their own. But the reunion of Joseph and his brothers exceeds all others in its intensity and shock.

Joseph's command for all his attendants to leave must have raised the brother's terror in the presence of this man. What was he planning? Joseph's revelation, blurted out with little forethought of its impact created a first response of fear and bewilderment.

Knowing Joseph's real identity increased their alarm. Now they feared not just a foreign tyrant but an abused brother.

Joseph explained himself again, more calmly. This time he dismissed their fear of revenge by stating his belief that: "It was not you that sent me here but God." Once the shock had subsided, "his brothers talked with him." As he wept over his brothers, especially Benjamin, he revealed his real care for them.

The adversity God allows in our lives is not meaningless. We know why God allowed it in Josephs' life, but reasons for our own adversity are not always obvious; probably much of it will remain unknown this side of eternity.

Particularly, family splits seem meaningless which only adds to the pain. Are you able to trust God with it and wait for the explanation? Joseph waited over twenty years.

Prayer: O Lord, we yearn for the joy of Joseph's reunion with his brothers. Give us the same joy as we endeavour by your strength to repair our relationships.

75

WEEK THIRTEEN: TUESDAY

The Long Wait

Read: Genesis 45:16–28

When he saw the carts Joseph had sent to carry him back, the spirit of their father Jacob revived. Genesis 45:27.

Pharaoh and his court, impressed with Joseph's integrity, were pleased at Joseph's reunion with his brothers.

At Pharaoh's insistence, Joseph sent the brothers back with the good news: the whole family was to move to Egypt, to live on the best of the land. They would have food throughout the remaining five years of famine. Pharaoh also provided carts for transportation of the family back to Egypt and provisions for the journey.

The brothers' disclosure of Joseph's position in Egypt upon their return was too much for Jacob. Jacob is the Old Testament's doubting Thomas. His years of sullen and obstinate refusal to be comforted had blunted his faith. Why should he believe his sons now?

But there was one fact of evidence that eventually convinced him. As Thomas was able to see Christ's scars from the crucifixion and believe, so Jacob's spirit revived on seeing the carts from Egypt.

As the years go by it's easy to lose confidence that change will happen. Our tendency to criticize Jacob belies our own reduction of faith over time. Jacob had over twenty years to lose heart that he would never see Joseph again. Can we sustain faith for that length of time? Prayer for a loved one will never go unanswered.

George Muller, the great English philanthropist who provided for the orphans of Britain, firmly believed in prayer, often praying food into his orphanages for mealtimes. He prayed that a close friend would become a Christian. That prayer was answered—but not until after Muller's death.

Prayer: O Father, give us faith to trust you when circumstances seem against answered prayers for our families.

God's Promises are Sure

Read: Genesis 46:1–7

"I will go down to Egypt with you, and I will surely bring you back again. And Joseph's own hand will close your eyes."
Genesis 46:4.

It's too easy to dwell on the foolish mistakes Jacob made and his obstinacy in refusing comfort for the loss of Joseph for so long. If we are not careful, we can allow it to overshadow both the overarching faithfulness of Jacob to God and the grace of God towards Jacob.

I sometimes wonder if Jacob's continuous mourning over Joseph was a subconscious belief that he was not dead and that he would see him again. However that may be, after his reunion with Joseph he worshipped at Beersheba and Jacob's life returned to the fellowship with God he had experienced earlier in life.

Perhaps we should see those intervening years as a long test of faith, where Jacob responded badly at times, yet never renounced his faith. In this light it is easier to see ourselves, often failing under pressure, yet retaining that basic awareness that ultimately our lives are under his control.

The mystics speak of the "long night of the soul," those periods when all we have believed and trusted for seems impossible. We all experience this to some degree, but some of us to the limits of our endurance, the experience lasting for years. The times of estrangement or conflict with our close family can be the greatest trial, occasionally provoking inappropriate response from us.

But God's words to Jacob can encourage us; God had not forgotten or left him. God will one day speak to your heart again as he spoke to Jacob.

Prayer: Heavenly Father, we too often lose heart and question your control of our lives. We thank you for your grace and strength given to us at those times.

WEEK THIRTEEN: THURSDAY

The Past Catches Up

Read: Genesis 49:1–12

The sceptre will not depart from Judah, nor the ruler's staff from between his feet, until he comes to whom it belongs and the obedience of the nations is his. Genesis 49:10.

As his life came to a close, Jacob called his sons together to predict "what will happen to you in days to come." The history of his four eldest sons caught up with them.

Reuben lost his place as firstborn because of his adultery with Bilhah, Rachel's maidservant, Genesis 35:22. There is no record of his repentance for this act. Simeon and Levi lost their inheritance because of the slaughter of the Shechemites and display of arrogance rather than regret at this episode, Genesis 34:30–31.

Simeon had no land apportioned to him but rented space from Judah, Joshua 19:9. Levi's descendants also had no inheritance in the land as they became priests for the emerging nation.

It is also true that Judah himself committed adultery with his daughter-in-law, an incestuous relationship. But the full story shows his repentance of the wrong he had done to her, provoking her subterfuge, Genesis 38:24–26. Forgiveness as a response to repentance is a common theme through Scripture.

In addition, Judah's wisdom and concern for his family ensured his leadership of the clan. So Jacob set him apart as the leader of his brothers, and as the progenitor of the kingship to come—first to David and eventually to Jesus.

Our personal growth and position depends on integrity that can also provide influence with our families. Our children often indicate—and probably overrate—our stable example of faith as an influence in adherence to their faith. Dedication to faith is caught as well as taught.

Prayer: Lord, give us perseverance of faith as an example of your faithfulness to those who follow us.

Joseph's Last Words

Read: Genesis 50:15–21

"You intended to harm me, but God intended it for good to accomplish what is now being done, the saving of many lives."
Genesis 50:20.

Old fears, like old habits, die hard. After Joseph's generous spirit towards them, his brothers still feared reprisal from him. Their actions tell us more about them than about Joseph. Did Joseph really harbour a secret desire for revenge? Unlikely.

What is more probable, they could not conceive of themselves acting in such a magnanimous way, and so denied it to Joseph. In approaching Joseph they betrayed their character by resorting to subterfuge against possible retaliation by Joseph—even hiding behind a messenger with their story.

Joseph, true to his nature, wept when he received the message. His response was consistent with his understanding of God's providence. He repeated his earlier assertion that God allowed his adversity in order to save the family. He was not "in the place of God" to bring judgment on his brothers for their actions. But he laid blame squarely where it was due: "You intended to harm me."

We are responsible for our actions, good or bad, even if God uses them for his purposes. He will use our actions based on faith, but it is comforting to know that he can also overrule actions that are less than faithful.

Because family relationships are usually close they are more likely to give rise to friction. When they do, we may respond badly. But we mustn't fall into the trap of thinking that others cannot respond better than us; accept genuine offers of reconciliation gladly.

Prayer: Heavenly Father, we are comforted, and gratefully praise you that you pick up the broken pieces of our lives.

WEEK THIRTEEN: WEEKEND

Spiritual Warfare

In areas of the world where there is little or no government, gangs lead an existence based on killing, rape and pillage. The connection with Satan's work is obvious.

Satan also exploits the dark side of despotic rulers like Hitler, Stalin, Mussolini, Idi Amin, Milosovich and others. He also uses the parasites on legitimate society who make their living and fortunes by defrauding and devastating the innocent.

Less obvious to us, at times we allow our dark passions to overwhelm our better judgement and give Satan a foothold, Ephesians 4:25–32. Acting out of anger, resentment, bitterness or rivalry, placing the well-being of others in jeopardy, we aid Satan in his plans.

When we visualize worldwide the slander and malice practiced by normally "decent" people, we may realize the extent of Satan's resources and the enormous damage done by loose talk.

We all want our children to be beacons of light in so much darkness. They will not achieve this naturally; the Bible recognizes the natural bent of human beings toward sin, and the need for discipline.

Discipline is not just conforming to a code of conduct or staying away from the "bad guys." We impose discipline on our small children in hope they will eventually develop their own internal discipline of thoughts, words and actions in all situations.

This is more difficult without their commitment to Christ to provide clear direction on acceptable motives and actions. So training children in the way they should go is not only spiritual work, it is also spiritual warfare.

Prayer: O Lord, we desperately need your wisdom to raise our children to know and honour you. As we pray continually, help us to see this as a priority for them and the world they will inhabit.

Egypt's "Abortion" Program

Read: Exodus 1:8–21

The midwives, however, feared God and did not do what the king of Egypt had told them to do; they let the boys live. Exodus 1:17.

I'm sure the Egyptians would have preferred abortion to infanticide, but they could not abort without knowing the child's sex. Thus, the midwives were told to kill male children "on the delivery stool"; the closest thing to abortion.

It appears that the midwives excuse for not killing the male children—that Hebrew women were more vigorous than their Egyptian counterparts and "give birth before the midwives arrive,"—maintained male births and the Hebrew nation continued to flourish.

Developing nations, where the birthrate is high, commonly practise population control by abortion—often pressured by wealthier nations. But abortion in developed countries reduces the birthrate to well below the replacement rate of 2.4 live births per couple. Quebec leads the way with a birthrate of only 1.4.

China and India have a disproportionate male population due to abortion or infanticide of females as male children are preferred. This shortage of marriageable women leads to bartering and kidnapping girls for marriage.

Birth is simply a growing event in life, like puberty, the first sexual experience, and sickness. Thus there is only a fine line between abortion and infanticide, the latter growing in western nations.

Killing children is the most heinous of crimes and those who prey on children are the worst pariahs of society. The unborn are the most defenseless of all, yet they are often disposed of with the least regret. In the "Christian" west, we cannot point too many fingers at the king of Egypt.

Prayer: Lord, may we ever stand against the slaughter of those, who like us, are created in your image.

WEEK FOURTEEN: TUESDAY

Facing Abortion

Read: Exodus 1:22 to 2:10

Pharaoh gave this order to all his people: "Every boy that is born you must throw into the Nile, but let every girl live." Exodus 1:22.

Once Pharaoh realized that the Hebrew midwives failed to kill male children at birth, he went the next step, ordering his own people to kill all newborn Hebrew males. We do not know at what age male children were exempt from this decree, but it is likely that in a country as widespread as Egypt observance would be erratic.

Communications were not good, local governors might apply the law unevenly, and bonds between local Egyptians and Hebrews would likely save many boys.

The story of Moses and Pharaoh's daughter shows destroying a fetus can be a relatively objective procedure for a surgeon, but once the baby is born, seen, and held, killing is much more difficult for the average person.

Sending hardened soldiers to do the job, as Herod did in attempting to kill the infant Jesus, is far more effective than expecting caring adults to do the same.

Abortion is like divorce: the "one flesh" basis of marriage makes divorce seem like tearing flesh from flesh. So the physical procedure of abortion mirrors divorce and much the same turmoil and pain involves a decision to abort. While some use abortion as a method of contraception, for most women it is a very difficult decision, and compassion and help should be the Christian response to that dilemma.

You may face this decision in your own family. How will you respond?

Prayer: Heavenly Father, if our daughter becomes pregnant, help us to respond appropriately with compassion and grace as you have treated us.

Discouragement

Read: Exodus 5:19–23; 6:9–12

"Ever since I went to Pharaoh to speak in your name, he has brought trouble upon this people, and you have not rescued your people at all." Exodus 5:22–23.

Discouragement is debilitating, for it undermines resolve, action and even faith. In this passage even the great Moses questioned God. His previous approach to Pharaoh to release the Israelites from bondage had backfired, creating extra onerous conditions for them. The Israelites were understandably cynical.

In turn, Moses became skeptical, complaining that God had not rescued Israel as promised, and arguing that if his own countrymen wouldn't listen to him, then why should Pharaoh?

We easily fall prey to the same discouragement when our prayers seem unanswered, or rational arguments preclude a meaningful answer. It is particularly true of intractable problems; especially conflict within the family. Moses made two errors that we easily fall into.

First, Moses assumed that freeing Israel was God's only purpose. Later Moses received another reason for the delayed promise: God would demonstrate to Pharaoh a power greater than his own, Exodus 7:3–5.

Second, we easily forget God has ways of fulfilling his promises outside our limited understanding. For the women approaching the tomb the first Easter morning, the stone in front of the tomb was an insurmountable problem—they couldn't move it themselves. But due to God's intervention the stone was not a problem.

God still removes stones: obstructions that seem immoveable to us; even the conflict or rebellion within our own families.

Prayer: Lord, we believe we can trust you when circumstances suggest otherwise. Strengthen our faith in those difficult times.

WEEK FOURTEEN: THURSDAY

Protection, Provision, Purpose

Read: Exodus 6:6–8

"I will bring you to the land I swore with uplifted hand to give to Abraham, to Isaac and to Jacob." Exodus 6:8.

Today's reading describes how God demonstrated his love for Israel; it illustrates some principles we can use to establish affirming relationships.

God promised three things to the Israelites: freedom from the Egyptians, a land of their own, and they would be his people.

Freedom from oppression in Egypt meant protection from their enemies, not only in Egypt, but throughout life. A land of their own would provide for the necessities of life.

These terms depended on Israel's faithfulness to him; their frequent loss of protection and provision is a sad commentary on that relationship.

Finally, and most importantly, he gave them purpose for life: they would be his people to represent him to the world, Deuteronomy 4:5–8.

Our basic responsibility for our children is to protect and provide for them, a natural and legal requirement. Many consider this the end of their responsibilities.

However, the greater need is to give children a sense of purpose. Without it, life will become a meaningless existence with no direction, resulting in boredom and risky activities.

We find purpose for life in pursuing the will of God. As parents, our primary service to God is to the family he gave us. And that service includes developing a desire for a relationship with God through Jesus Christ in our children.

Prayer: Father, our children are most important to us. Thank you for reminding us of the need to give them significant purpose through a life in Christ.

The Egyptian Firstborns Die

Read: Exodus 12:1–13

"On that same night I will pass through Egypt and strike down every firstborn—both men and animals—and I will bring judgment on all the gods of Egypt. I am the Lord." Exodus 12:12.

In an ironic reversal of Pharaoh's earlier attempt to destroy male Hebrew children, Moses predicted the death of the firstborn throughout Egypt, *except* for the Hebrews.

Now the Egyptians felt the agony of loss of children that they had brought upon the Hebrews. This would be the final episode to persuade Pharaoh to let the Hebrews leave Egypt. Moses had given Pharaoh plenty of warning, Exodus 11:4–8.

The episode of plagues that preceded this latest warning was a sign of God's supremacy over Egypt and Pharaoh. Failure of the plagues to gain the Hebrews' release was not a sign of God's weakness, but of his power and patience, Exodus 7:1–5. For the period of the plagues, Pharaoh was living by the grace of God.

What is true on a national basis is also true personally. We do not have the influence over a nation as Pharaoh did, but we do have influence over those closest to us. When we fail them, we may not cause the havoc that Pharaoh did, but our sin is the same; it differs only by degree.

This is true of both parents and children, for children also have responsibility. We all live by the grace and patience of God and can avoid much of the trauma associated with life by conforming to God's requirements for us.

Prayer: O Lord God, we know you hold all things in your hands by your mighty power. Thank you that you guide us through life with patience and grace. Cause us to listen to the voice of your Holy Spirit through your Word and enjoy your presence.

85

WEEK FOURTEEN: WEEKEND

Bondage

The Israelites lived in the state of bondage for an extended time before their release under Moses. Too many women worldwide, and to a lesser extent men, live in a state of marital bondage or sexual slavery, with rarely any escape in undeveloped nations.

Even in western nations, circumstances often prevent leaving a difficult situation: threat by a partner, lack of financial alternatives or ignorance of the options available.

For children, the problem is worse. A child will remain in a hostile environment unless someone else is aware of a problem. Unfortunately, during the early years a child will think the situation normal.

The common denominator in all these situations is apparent hopelessness. But the story of the exodus is one that brought hope—although delayed—to the Israelites in their bondage.

If you are currently in a situation like this, Israel's story suggests two thoughts. First, God was aware of their cries for deliverance long before his intervention.

Deliverance delayed is not deliverance denied, but a time for recognition that God is with his children during their distress, which provides a period of strengthening faith, James 1:2–3. Our faith under stress is as much a witness to him as his deliverance.

But second, God will come to our aid in surprising ways and often at unexpected times. His presence in distress and the anticipation of his deliverance is the hope all Christians share.

Prayer: O Lord, you know the difficulty I face, my daily pain, and an uncertain future. You are my deliverer, and I wait for you to release me.

Redemption

Read: Exodus 13:1–16

"Consecrate to me every firstborn male. The first offspring of every womb among the Israelites belongs to me, whether man or animal." Exodus 13:2.

The Passover event, sparing the firstborn Hebrew children, became an ongoing celebration that Jews still practice. Because God spared the firstborn of both Hebrew animals and humans, Scripture claims they belong to God.

It is an eastern practice that if someone saves another's life, the one saved belongs to the saver. The saved life is now for the service and benefit of the one who saved it; this idea is implicit in today's reading.

Thus the life of the firstborn belongs to God. So the firstborn animals were sacrificed to him and firstborn humans were redeemed by the sacrifice of an animal in place of the human. This continuing memorial to the Passover was a teaching tool to the children that followed.

Jesus himself, being the firstborn, was also redeemed in this way, Luke 2:22–24. Later Jesus identified his shed blood with that of the lamb sacrificed for the firstborn at the original Passover in the memorial cup of wine, Luke 22:20.

In the same way, the blood that Jesus shed redeemed us and our children. Our remembrance of the Last Supper, celebrated as the Lord's Table or Communion, is not only a constant reminder of our place of allegiance to him, but is also a teaching tool for our children.

Further, it is a reminder that both children and his own people are precious to him, and he does not take the death of either lightly, Psalm 116:15, Matthew 18:2–6.

Prayer: Lord Jesus, thank you for shedding your blood for our redemption. Let our allegiance to you by taking communion be evident to our children.

WEEK FIFTEEN: TUESDAY

Love God

Read: Exodus 20:1–8

And God spoke all these words: "I am the Lord your God."
Exodus 20:1–2.

The Ten Commandments comprise two "tables," the first four commandments deal with our relationship to God, the remaining six with our relationship to one another.

While most people may give qualified agreement to much of the last six, they would ignore the first four as irrelevant to their lives. Yet all history mostly builds around religious concerns, indicating an implanted desire in all humans for a connection to their Creator.

These Commandments have been the cornerstone of western law for centuries. It is only in the last century or so that "enlightenment" has managed to dispose of God as necessary to life and develop the secular view that religion is a superstitious fantasy of personal choice.

It has left us with an affluent but empty existence. However, if God is real and a vital part of life as the Bible reveals, then any life without him is a lie. The foundation for decisions is then unstable and life becomes precarious, without any real meaning or direction.

Men once believed that the sun rotated around the earth and we still tend to believe life revolves around us. But God is the real centre of our lives, and the first four commandments define our relationship to him.

If life is uncertain without God, then our marriages without him are uncertain also. God, not ourselves or our children, needs to be the centre of our families for secure marriages, children, and society.

Prayer: Lord God, we want you to be the centre of our family. May your Spirit keep our hearts focused on you throughout our family life.

A Jealous God

Read: Exodus 20:4–6

"[I] am a jealous God, punishing the children for the sin of the fathers . . . but showing love to a thousand [generations] of those who love me and keep my commandments." Exodus 20:5–6.

Today we revisit some verses from yesterday. This and parallel passages, Exodus 34:7; Numbers 14:18; Deuteronomy 5:9–10, are often taken to mean that children will suffer punishment for their father's sins.

This idea is not limited to our time, as Ezekiel had to do battle with it a thousand years later. He condemned the saying of the time: "The fathers eat sour grapes, and the children's teeth are set on edge," Ezekiel 18:1–4. God avowed the soul that sins will be punished, not the son for the father or vice versa.

Other Scriptures clarify the meaning that God will punish those children that *continue* in their father's sins. Stories of the kings of Israel demonstrate this commencing with Jeroboam, son of Nebat.

His sinful behaviour became the standard which measured the behaviour of succeeding kings. About a dozen successive kings of Israel are accused of following the sins of Jeroboam,1 Kings 16:25–26; 22:51–52; 2 Kings 3:1–3, and others.

But today's emphasis is not the punishment that sinning generations receive, but the blessing of God on a thousand generations that love and obey him. Parents exert an immense influence on the spiritual formation of following generations.

Teaching is a critical element in this process, but parents who demonstrate their allegiance to God in every area of life are essential. The greatest gift we can give to our children is our own consistent and faithful commitment to God and his Word.

Prayer: O God, it is our desire to be faithful to you, but especially to pass a practical faith to our children. Give us power and grace be a meaningful example to them daily.

WEEK FIFTEEN: THURSDAY

Parents to be Honoured

Read: Exodus 20:12

"Honour your father and your mother, so that you may live long in the land the Lord your God is giving you." Exodus 20:12.

We have spent time on parents' responsibilities. But the Bible also teaches the responsibility of children toward parents: children are to honour their parents.

This commandment is the only one that attaches a promise, see Deuteronomy 5:16, Ephesians 6:1–3. It is the reverse side of our frequent assertion that faithful parents pass God's blessing on to the children.

If children take advantage of this promise by honouring their parents the likelihood of long and enjoyable life increases. Most children who rebel against parents' principles early in life come to an understanding of their parent's wisdom later.

Of course there are parents who are failures and the children suffer greatly as a result. But even those parents should be honoured by giving them dignity and respect while rejecting their actions.

But how do parents cope in an age of so many rebellious children? Most parents maintain a love for their children often in the face of arrogant and cruel treatment that adversely affects everyone.

Parents are not in the place of judge, but responsible parents will take the necessary steps for the welfare of their children. However, children have the responsibility emphasized by the requirement that a rebellious son could be put to death, Deuteronomy 21:18–21.

Prayer: Heavenly Father, we may be parents, but we are also children. Cause us to honour our parents during the years they have left.

Love Your Neighbour

Read: Exodus 20:12–17

"You shall not . . ." Exodus 20:13–17.

Those who reject God's involvement as unprovable and understand life only on what the five senses observe, still recognize humanity as transcendent, having a value beyond detection by the senses. There appears to be no apparent reason to make this claim other than personal identification: what I desire all others must desire also.

This mindset has given rise to generally accepted basic human rights—life, liberty and property—advanced by all "civilized" nations as the basis for law. These rights closely mirror the last six commandments, demonstrating their universality.

Jesus' command to love your neighbour, Matthew 22:37–40 encapsulates these six commandments, in the same way the command to love God covers the first four.

However, adultery, that is, consensual sex outside marriage, is not considered a violation of the person, it is the first to be questioned and rejected. Although there is no western law against adultery, it was once the only grounds for divorce, following scriptural guidelines.

But God who was intimately concerned with the welfare of his creation, and who knew the havoc wreaked by indiscriminate sexual union included the commandment against adultery. The Bible enforced the prohibition of adultery with severe penalties, indicating how serious God considered it.

Do we identify our partner also as our neighbour and consider them with the same seriousness, or are we influenced by the sexual laxity of our culture?

Prayer: O Lord, we know the seductive influence of adultery. Keep our eyes and heart focused on our faithfulness to each other and on you.

91

WEEK FIFTEEN: WEEKEND

Honoured Parents

Ann's parents failed to provide an adequate home for their children due to mental illnesses. The home was well known in the neighbourhood for its critically dysfunctional nature, and the authorities frequently took the children away.

Ann's aunt repeatedly provided required clothing, and neighbours would bring food for the children. Inside the home there was barely enough disreputable furniture for needs. Her mother's worst periods of bi-polar extremes often destroyed even that.

Ann's three brothers—all from different fathers—spent most of their childhood in institutions. Ann finally went to live with her grandmother during her teen years.

These appalling conditions did not lessen Ann's love for her parents. During her teen years, when her mother would return home after her frequent stays in the local mental hospital, Ann would attempt to restore normality in the home with donated furniture and equipment.

Even knowing the destructive behaviour would repeat itself, she determined to alleviate the home conditions— simply because they were her parents. Even during our early married years Ann used items from our growing home to rebuild her shattered childhood home.

Ann feared for our own children's safety—for a period we lived close to the mental institution that often housed her mother—and she kept the doors locked. But she kept ongoing contact with her parents, ensuring their well-being as she was able.

She honoured her parents in this way until their deaths, seeking to follow God's greater imperative more than her natural responses.

Prayer: Lord, we thank you for the examples of those who've gone before us. Help us to be the same example to those who follow us.

Protection for Women

Read: Exodus 21:7–11

If he does not provide her with these three things, she is to go free, without any payment of money. Exodus 21:11.

The Israelite community was not egalitarian despite personal safeguards under Mosaic Law. There were the poor and rich as well as masters and slaves.

Slavery was not today's notion of chattel property, but similar to indentured servants with rights of their own. In particular, where a man needed to sell his daughter due to poverty, the conditions of sale were meant to provide social protection against exploitation, although she might be exposed to physical and mental abuse as today's wives are.

Should she not please her master, her father could buy her back. If she was to marry the master's son, she had all the rights of a daughter in the family. If the son chose a second wife, all the needs of the first wife were to be met, or she was freed without obligation.

We might not consider these sufficient standards today, but the degree of protection was probably advanced for societies before 1,000 B.C. Additional Hebrew women's rights were set out elsewhere.

These passages give evidence of God's concern for women, particularly daughters, so we can be encouraged that God cares for our daughters. Despite feminist rhetoric to the contrary, girls are more vulnerable than boys.

When it comes to their adult relationships, how are our daughters going to fare? A stable home implants acceptable behaviours during growing years, but when our beloved girls pass from our influence, we can be sure that they continue in God's care.

Prayer: O Lord, we seek your continued protection on our daughters as they move into adult relationships. Grant that our influence will assist them in making wise choices.

93

WEEK SIXTEEN: TUESDAY

The Nature of God

Read: Exodus 34:1–14, 28

"The Lord, the Lord, the compassionate and gracious God, slow to
anger, abounding in love and faithfulness, maintaining love to
thousands, and forgiving wickedness, rebellion and sin. Yet he
does not leave the guilty unpunished. Exodus 34:6–7.

The Law—the Ten Commandments—was carved into
two tablets of stone. The first Moses smashed in
anger, Exodus 32:19, and in today's reading God
commanded Moses to replace them.

But God also revealed his nature: compassion, grace,
patience, love, faithfulness, forgiveness, and justice. He
juxtaposed his nature against the Ten Commandments as
an indication of how he would administer them.

Of the seven characteristics, the first six could only
work in Israel's favour, the last affording judgment if those
others did not keep Israel in fellowship.

That ratio also works for us. He is the kind of God we
need. Those of us who have entered into the New Covenant
desire to respond to God's requirements of us, so we may
enjoy the benefits of that relationship. But we need to live
in his covenant of grace and forgiveness because of our
constant failure to live up to his standards.

You probably noticed those characteristics of God are
human as well; all of us experience them in our
relationships. They are part of the image of God originally
inscribed on our souls, and their growth should be
evidence of our transformation to Christ-likeness.

That evidence should show first in our closest
relationships, expressing compassion, grace, patience, love,
faithfulness, forgiveness, and justice to our partners and
children.

Prayer: O Lord, we rejoice in your nature that deals with us in
grace and patience, and has drawn us to you. Guide us
to deal with others, especially our family, in the same
way.

Judgment or Grace?

Read: Leviticus 10:1–20

"Among those who approach me I will show myself holy; in the sight of all the people I will be honoured." Leviticus 10:3.

This passage may appear confusing, but the details are relatively unimportant; it is the behaviour of Aaron and his children that is helpful to us. Both pairs of sons, Nadab and Abihu, and also Eleazar and Ithamar, failed to perform their duties correctly. Yet the outcome for each pair was different.

The tribe of Levi provided the priesthood and Aaron, a descendant of Levi, became the chief priest of the emerging nation. Aaron consecrated and informed all sons of the duties for the priesthood, Leviticus 8:1–36

Nadab and Abihu deliberately disregarded the instruction they had been given. They took their duties lightly, perhaps fooling around and amusing themselves with the sacred implements and procedures. The judgment from God was immediate and swift on their arrogance and scorn.

Yet Moses faulted Aaron's other two sons, Eleazar and Ithamar, for carrying out the duties incorrectly. Following their brothers disaster, it seems unlikely they would deliberately abuse the requirements for office. The later brothers' error may have been a mistake or an error in judgment; even Aaron admitted he made mistakes in the past.

Aaron interceded for them, and hearing Aaron's plea, Moses, "was satisfied." We live in this period, between Christ's advents, of God's amazing grace. We must always take the opportunities available to us to intercede for our family members.

Prayer: O God, your grace is amazing, more than we deserve. May we take full advantage of the privilege of prayer for our families as well as ourselves.

WEEK SIXTEEN: THURSDAY

Sexual Prohibitions

Read: Leviticus 18:1–21

"You must not do as they do in the land of Canaan, where I am bringing you. Do not follow their practices." Leviticus 18:3.

The loosening of sexual morals since the nineteen sixties has produced a spate of alternative lifestyles previously stigmatized in the west for centuries. Breach the basic limitation of sexual relations between a man and wife, and there is no specific point at which sex can be easily restricted.

If sex outside of marriage is an acceptable recreation, why not sex between other relationships. Currently, access to a variety of sexual preferences, including pedophilia and incest, is available on the web.

Our reading today is the well known passage that sets out unacceptable sexual practices including homosexuality and bestiality. It also includes in the same passage a prohibition of offering children to Molech—the sacrifice of children to appease the god.

The use of children for sexual satisfaction is little different and Jesus' clear teaching on the need to protect children places those who abuse children before the eventual judgment of God. The trafficking in children for sexual uses is common in many eastern countries, with children, especially girls, commonly sold into sexual slavery for the economic needs of the family.

Recall the sin of Sodom, where all the men practised a violent gay lifestyle, Genesis 19:4. There is an infectious nature about alternative sexual lifestyles that threatens the basic stabilizing unit of society. Christians are not immune; the need of prayer for God's protection of all our families is essential.

Prayer: O Lord, our children are so vulnerable to the excesses of our culture. We too are susceptible to temptation. Guard our reading and viewing we beseech you.

Polluting the Land

Read: Leviticus 18:22–28

Even the land was defiled; so I punished it for its sin, and the land vomited out its inhabitants. Leviticus 18:25.

Western culture now considers homosexuality a normal sexual lifestyle, and this Scripture passage joins several others forbidding it. But homosexuality is one of many forbidden sexual unions.

In spite of that, Christians preach disagreement with gay sex while soft-pedaling the practice of other forbidden sexual unions. Outcry against one and silence on others is tacit approval of the latter.

Yesterday's reading prohibited sexual union with "any close relative," Leviticus 18:6. Most countries prohibit these liaisons because defective genes combining in close relatives often produce defective children. Scripture shows its wisdom in this regard early in human history.

But current western culture rejects other prohibitions on the basis that they do not pose the same threat. However, there are other threats from illicit sexual unions; promiscuous sex—gay or straight—furthers the spread of sexually transmitted diseases (STDs), especially AIDS.

Committed families are the first line of defence against the dangers of illicit sex. Living by the scriptural rule of one man and one woman for life provides the containment of our sexuality and avoids STD infection. To berate gays without the same censure for illicit straight sex is hypocritical, but worse, leads to considering other hazardous sexual liaisons acceptable.

Never assume any relationship outside of marriage is safe—from discredit and disease for us, from transmission of disease to our partners and children, and from heartache and misery for the whole family.

Prayer: Dear Lord, preserve us from sexual sin that is disastrous for us, and particularly for our children.

WEEK SIXTEEN: WEEKEND

Sexuality

Today's western culture is highly sexualized. It pervades TV, movies, advertising, the internet and most forms of communication. Variant sexual behaviours are culturally accepted. Recreation has become the main function of sex, even acceptable among teens.

Pornography abounds, especially on the internet, including child sex and incest which has a widening audience. Currently, there are only two limits on sexual behaviour: rape and pedophilia.

Little of this is news, but it has not always been the case. During the first half of the last century social acceptance was restricted to heterosexuality, primarily within marriage. Other sexual preferences existed in private and underground.

Christianity was the ethical source which pervaded western culture. Society was safer, less traumatized, and adrift than it is today. Today's culture considers these restrictions archaic, bigoted, and intolerable.

But the current situation provides some advantages. First, Christian morality stands out in sharp contrast to the surrounding culture and as such is an important witness to our faith. Our marriages should be a faithful witness to our beliefs.

Second, Christians must now view those of opposing views differently. In the past we wrongly considered them a negligible fringe in society. Now they face us as real people needing the grace and compassion God has bestowed on us.

We all practise unacceptable behaviour before God; it is called sin and puts all of us in need of a Saviour.

Prayer: Heavenly Father, we need the heart of compassion for all; the love you demonstrated by sending your Son to die for us. We have all disobeyed your commands; we are all in need of your grace and forgiveness.

Prostitution

Read: Leviticus 19:29–37

"Keep all my decrees and all my laws and follow them. I am the Lord." Leviticus 19:37.

There were probably as many unprincipled people in Israel as in our society. This passage deals with those who abuse people and laws without conscience. Several times the author reinforces the commands by his authority: "the Lord" or "the Lord your God."

Here, verse 29 concerns us, for it deals with a corrupt father who might "sell" his daughter. An earlier reading provided an honourable way in which a father could provide for his family; today's reading clearly prohibits prostitution as a father's option.

Civilized cultures rightly stigmatize prostitution, although our western culture has attempted to clean its image—"prostitute" is now "sex trade worker."

But prostitution by any name dehumanizes women whose lives tend to risk abuse and murder. In many parts of Canada, numbers of prostitutes just disappear or are murdered.

Unfortunately, many of the girls in the trade have little choice. Modern day slavery across national boundaries and poverty forces many into it; some nations allow the selling of daughters into prostitution who are then abused by "sex tourists."

Drug addicted girls pay for their habit by selling themselves, and others are rebellious teens who fall afoul of criminal elements in society. Today's passage reminds us that prostitution is often the leading edge of other evils.

While we need to be aware of dangers for our children, our home should be a haven, not a fortress.

Prayer: Dear Lord, help us maintain a balance between love and discipline that will guide our children through dangerous waters.

WEEK SEVENTEEN: TUESDAY

Sexual Equality

Read: Numbers 27:1–11

"If a man dies and leaves no son, turn his inheritance over to his daughter." Numbers 27:8.

W^e have previously noted that at first glance, the Bible appears to favour a patriarchal family system where the father is the autocratic head of the clan. Because the clans were large—they included servants, maidservants and herders—the need for some form of governance was necessary.

So someone took responsibility for the safety and prosperity of the clan, and the patriarchal system supplied that need. When the father died it passed to the eldest son. However, the women were not chattels of the men; they also had rights.

Earlier meditations provided examples of women asserting their rights in the early days of Scripture. Sarah had freedom to deal with her servants as she pleased, and in one case Abraham was encouraged to allow this by God himself, Genesis 16:6; 21:11–12.

The story of Leah's mandrakes is a classic. In return for Leah's mandrakes—believed to enhance fertility—Rachel allowed Leah to sleep with Jacob that night, Genesis 30:14–16. Apparently, Jacob had little say in the matter.

Zelophehad had no sons, and his girls needed inheritance laws to continue the family line and property. Moses asked the Lord for guidance, and received clear instruction: "If a man dies and has no son, give his inheritance to his daughter." This meant that the eldest daughter also took responsibility for leading her clan.

Our sons and daughters are equal before God. Let's ensure our marital relationship demonstrates this to our children.

Prayer: Heavenly Father, we learned not to play favourites with our children. May we not play favourites according to their sex.

Dominance or Security

Read: Numbers 30:1–16

"When a man makes a vow to the Lord or takes an oath to obligate himself by a pledge, he must not break his word but must do everything he said." Numbers 30:2.

This passage suggests that a father or husband had complete discretion to monitor and approve any vow that a daughter or wife made.

The concept assumed that the woman in each case was unable to make an intelligent decision, or that the man could force the woman's decisions according to his own capricious desires.

This arrangement would not be acceptable today, but probably was not then either.

Israelite society was patriarchal, which meant that as head of the household, the father was also responsible for its welfare. Thus, his oversight of his wife's decisions was to ensure that it was for the wellbeing of the household.

But he could not make his decision on a whim, nor change his mind whenever he wished. If a demand was perverse, women in that society were not voiceless.

Most women today enjoy the idea of security within the marriage bond. Where a husband's first desire is for his wife's wellbeing, a woman is foolish to step outside that safeguard, especially with children. However, she retains the right to leave an abusive situation.

Husbands will give account for love and service to their wives, serving them "just as Christ does the church," Ephesians 5:29. In the same way, women will give account for frivolous rejection of the God given support of a good husband.

Prayer: Lord, we thank you for the partners you have given us. Help us to treat them with the same love and respect you have shown us.

101

WEEK SEVENTEEN: THURSDAY

Obedient Faith

Read: Deuteronomy 5:1–21

"Hear, O Israel, the decrees and laws I declare in your hearing today. Learn them and be sure to follow them." Deuteronomy 5:1.

We noted earlier God's covenants with men were without conditions. However, this list—the Ten Commandments—looks like a list of contractual obligations.

The problem of obedient faith in God's covenant is not limited to Old Testament law but frequently queried by Christians. If we are saved by grace alone, through faith alone, and are no longer under the law, what's to prevent us from sinning?

Throughout the centuries, groups have lived without moral law on this reasoning. But almost instinctively, we realize there is something wrong with this outlook.

Although we live by grace, we still keep the Ten Commandments. Here are some reasons why. First, as God's people we are witnesses to a moral and just God and so should reflect who he is, Deuteronomy 4:5–8. Further, to indulge in sin is to contradict the rebuilding of the lost image of God in us, Romans 8:29.

But of greater importance, obedience is a response of participation in God's covenant, whether Israel in the Old Testament or ourselves under the New. Sin may not nullify God's covenant with us; but we miss the blessings and fellowship the covenant provides.

Similarly, our response to our partner's promise of faithfulness is less about maintaining a pact and more about enjoying the relationship. We can live under the same roof while ignoring or reneging on our covenant promises, and so lose the companionship it affords. But that is hardly a marriage.

Prayer: Lord, we recall we married for better or worse. Help us to choose your ways which are higher than ours, and honour the covenant by living joyfully together.

Abundant Grace

Read: Deuteronomy 5:8–10

". . . showing love to a thousand [generations] of those who love me and keep my commandments." Deuteronomy 5:10.

God is a God of abundance. At the spring of the year when blossoms and seeds appear on the trees, there are far more than necessary to propagate the species. The same is true of animal life without human interference. Waters teem with fish, and insects proliferate at an alarming pace without predators.

Today's passage reminds us that while God judges three or four generations that follow in their father's sins, he blesses a thousand generations of those who love him.

These are all a measure of the grace of God. He gives far more than is necessary. Even those sinful generations that return to him can find acceptance, for grace is far more abundant than the sin it covers, Romans 5:20.

In particular, as today's reading shows, the Ten Commandments record his love for a thousand generations. How encouraging to realize the document that reveals our sin is also the one that contains this all encompassing promise.

The passage also notes God's jealousy. Jealousy out of control can do terrible things; violence and even murder. But jealousy is a God-given characteristic to maintain fidelity; the anger at deception is a tool intended to bring the offender to repentance.

It is God's jealousy that continually calls us to repentance and condemns rebellion. We have a right to jealously guard, not only our marriages, but also our children, that they, like us, may continue to enjoy the grace of God.

Prayer: O Lord, we thank you for your abundant grace that has drawn us into your family.

God Has No Grandchildren

A bumper sticker reads: "If I'd known grandchildren were so much fun I would have had them first." With grandchildren we have no parental responsibility and can send them home when we're tired.

But to be a grandchild of God is a vulnerable place. My commitment to God when I was ten years old was a meaningful decision. But my father's conviction of *his* faith bolstered *my* assurance of faith. He clearly expressed his belief and confidently preached it.

As long as confidence in some-one else is our assurance of faith, we are God's grandchildren. If we rely on some-one else's belief, our own faith may falter and our confidence might fail.

Jacob is a prime example. Early in life, his confidence was in the God of his father Isaac: he referred to "the Lord *your* God" in Genesis 27:20. But later he met God at Bethel and the Lord became *his* God. For the rest of his life, his personal relationship with God—tenuous at times—became his mainstay.

Joseph came to that place much earlier in life. He lost all contact with his family and those who knew God. His adversity drove him to seek God for himself.

There is nothing wrong with leaning on others during a time of incubation and maturing of our faith. But a systematic knowledge of God's Word, and experience of God's involvement in our lives, will make our faith our own. Then we are able to "give the reason for the hope that you have," 1 Peter 3:15. Where are you on this journey?

Prayer: Heavenly Father, thank you for making us your children. Strengthen our intimacy with you as we seek your will and your ways.

Passing Faith to our Children

Read: Deuteronomy 6:1–9; 20–25

The Lord commanded us to obey all these decrees and to fear the Lord our God, so that we might always prosper and be kept alive. Deuteronomy 6:24.

This passage follows the recall of Israel's history and the Ten Commandments we read earlier. The commandments were basic directives given by Moses prior to entering the Promised Land.

That the instruction to teach children is the first to follow signifies its importance. Christianity is always one generation away from extinction, and our children's welfare and prosperity is dependent on our allegiance to God.

The reading explains two things about teaching children. First, teaching is done in everyday life settings: "when you sit at home and when you walk along the road, when you lie down and when you get up." Teaching is not confined to religious places or environments. If teaching is a purely religious experience, it implies a faith divorced from life.

Second, religious events are opportunities to explain our faith to children. Special times in our church calendar explain what God has done for us and why we believe.

Should we really, "bind scriptures on our hands and foreheads and write them on our doorframes"? While ultra religious Jews take this literally, it certainly means Scriptures should condition how we live and think.

It is not the observances that we fulfil, as important as these may be, but it is the way we live, the spiritual dynamic that we bring to every part of our lives and homes that will influence our children the most.

Prayer: Heavenly Father, grant that our children my see that all parts of our lives are governed by your Word to us.

WEEK EIGHTEEN: TUESDAY

Rebellion

Read: Deuteronomy 7:1–11

He is the faithful God, keeping his covenant of love to a thousand
generations of those who love him and keep his commands.
Deuteronomy 7:9.

God is a covenant keeping God, but those who fail to participate in his covenant will miss its benefits. God warned Israel not to become ensnared with the same practices that brought judgment on Canaan.

This was a time of judgment for the Canaanites and their allied nations, see Genesis 15:12-21, and for Israel to stay within the covenant God had made.

However, it was not only Israel's obedience that would keep them in the covenant; but also God's love that maintained his covenant with them, despite their smallness as a nation and their disobedience, Deuteronomy. 9:4–6.

These verses indicate the nation of Israel continually rebelled against him and his requirements set up for their benefit. The sobering truth is that Israel would suffer the same consequences as the other nations if they did not abide in God's covenant.

It is a reminder of those fractious teen years when so many young people rebel against parents' instructions given for their benefit. Yet parents' love for the children never abates.

A teen will reap the rewards of a rebellious lifestyle, either under the law or in growing health or addiction problems.

As with God, a child's unruliness highlights a parent's love. The child is not loved for achievement, good looks, or even good behaviour, but is simply loved for his or her own sake. Love does not need a reason beyond itself.

Prayer: Lord, we pray for your Holy Spirit to enlighten our children to the truth, and also to equip us to live the truth before them.

Care for Widow and Orphan

Read: Deuteronomy 10:17–22

He defends the cause of the fatherless and the widow, and loves the alien, giving him food and clothing. Deuteronomy 10:18.

Jesus recognized a variety of sources of singleness. Some are born not to marry, some become single by the actions of others, and others choose not to marry, Matthew 19:11–12. The disciples suggested maintaining a faithful marriage was so difficult that singleness was a preferable option.

The tragedy of our time is the number of persons who have become single because of that difficulty. A single mother—or father—mirrors the widow, and needs similar care. As with today's passage, Scripture states God's concern for widows and orphans many times, providing for their sustenance, and accusing those who ignore their plight, Deuteronomy 27:19.

Our culture continues to devalue the family and trumpets easy divorce. Apart from the pain of divorce, the drive for women's independence has led many women to a life of unnecessary hardship, leaving many unmarried mothers to fend for themselves and the children without the benefit of married companionship and support.

We must recognize the deluding false messages encouraging marriage break-up before accusing those that fail. Some marriages break up because of intolerable abuse, but those that end simply due to dissatisfaction could have endured to the benefit of both partners and children.

While the biblical mandate for faithful marriage may be demanding and resolving marriage conflict challenging, its rewards are incalculable.

Prayer: O Lord, we pray for our family members who are going through marriage difficulties. Enlighten them to the hindrances blocking their relationship and the rewards of maintaining it.

107

WEEK EIGHTEEN: THURSDAY:

Grace to the Unbeliever

Read: Deuteronomy 13:6-11

Do not yield to him or listen to him. Show him no pity. Do not spare him or shield him. Deuteronomy 13:8.

The punishments mandated for apostasy must seem grossly overdone by today's standards. Western society generally disagrees with the death penalty for murder, and would consider it intolerable as a penalty for religious disagreement. To execute that penalty on members of one's own family only deepens the revulsion.

So the question remains, how can we understand this passage in today's terms?

First, the standard for abandoning the true God is supreme. To deny God as the one and only true God was not only an offence against him, but also a basic lie about the world. The same lie today generates increasing decay of our western society.

We may have difficulty with the punishment this passage requires, but we must not take lightly the seriousness of the sin that the punishment measures.

Second, we need to respond in the spirit of grace ushered in by Jesus Christ who was "full of grace and truth," John 1:14–17. The grace extended to us we must extend to others, even those who deny the truth—in particular those in our own families.

A couple was concerned about visiting a daughter whose husband was an unbeliever. We suggested their presence there was probably sufficient intimidation for him, as he almost certainly knew their stand for the truth.

If he was willing to receive them, their responsibility was to love and enjoy him as part of the family, and extend to him Christian grace.

Prayer: Lord, help us recognize the foolishness and destructive consequences in wandering from you, but to be willing to extend your love and grace to those who have wandered.

Rape and Adultery

Read: Deuteronomy 22:13-29

If a man is found sleeping with another man's wife, both the man who slept with her and the woman must die. You must purge the evil from Israel. Deuteronomy 22:22.

Because the Israelites lived in a patriarchal society, many of the regulations concerning women were for protection. A woman who displeased her husband received a divorce certificate to avoid later charges of adultery, Deuteronomy 24:1. Jesus later indicated that the reason for divorce could not be trivial, Matthew 19:8–9.

Similarly in this passage, although adultery by either sex was prohibited, there was protection given for a woman who was raped.

While the regulations seem primitive compared with our laws today, there was an attempt to ascertain whether the union was consensual.

If the union took place in the country, the law took the woman's word for rape, for there was no-one to hear a cry of distress. But if the intercourse occurred in the city and she did not cry out, the union was considered consensual. In cases where rape was confirmed, marriage to the girl was mandated and there was no possibility of divorce.

Despite all this, the penalty for adultery was death. As with apostasy previously discussed, Deuteronomy 13:6-11, the response seems totally out of all proportion to the offence—especially in today's social climate that accepts all sexual liaisons. Yet as we have discussed elsewhere, adultery is a form of apostasy.

The marriage bond is a picture of God's relationship to his people, and adultery is a lie suggesting God is unfaithful to his people.

Prayer: Dear Lord, it's too easy to have a superficial view of sin, especially adultery in today's social climate. Grant us your view of the evil of sexual permissiveness.

WEEK EIGHTEEN: WEEKEND

Introducing Joshua

Next week we will consider passages from Joshua. This book records the Israelites entry into the "Promised Land" and the wars necessary to conquer the land. These stories find their counterpart in the current situation in Palestine, with the constant threat from her neighbours to "push Israel into the sea," and Israel's response.

So it is not possible to read Joshua without emotions evoked by the current crisis, both for and against Israel, colouring attitudes to Joshua's campaigns conducted some 3500 years ago. But whatever our feelings regarding Israel, methods of war reported in Joshua would repulse most of us by today's rules of engagement.

But that was a time when war to acquire fertile land and resources from elsewhere was a predominant means of national economy. An aside in the Old Testament sheds light on this: "In the spring, at the time when kings go off to war . . . ," 2 Samuel 11:1.

But the warlike ambitions of those nations are similar to today's continually erupting warfare. Part of the value of Joshua—as with much of the Bible—is the reporting of actual history, whatever our response to it.

But the warfare that we read about in Scripture is also symptomatic of individual lives and relationships. The attitudes and actions of nations are similar to family life; the foolishness, deceptions, and failures of Israel recorded in Joshua can be helpful in analyzing our own lives.

After all, the dark side of our individual natures is no different in essence from that of nations, and is the motivating force behind all conflict—personal or worldwide.

Prayer: Our Father, help us to see our poor attitudes are as destructive as armed conflict.

110

The Bill of Divorcement

Read: Deuteronomy 24:1–5

For one year he is to be free to stay at home and bring happiness to the wife he has married. Deuteronomy 24:5.

The law provided for the protection and status of women. Without a bill of divorcement the wife of a prior marriage faced charges of adultery if she remarried. The only purpose of divorce was to allow the option to remarry.

But if a partner committed adultery, divorce was not mandated. Breaking faith can be devastating and recovery usually needs a period of time, but the option to reconcile is less destructive and a more satisfying outcome in the long term.

Not all marriages were happy. The first verses of chapter 24 indicate that divorce was permissible if a man's wife is "displeasing to him because he finds something indecent about her." This did not mean burning the toast, an interpretation favoured by the Pharisees who reckoned a man could "divorce his wife for any and every reason," Matthew 19:3.

Divorce was only valid if he "finds something indecent about her." But there were two cases when a Hebrew man could not divorce his wife at all: if a man's claim that his new wife was not a virgin failed, or if he was obliged to marry a virgin he had raped.

The first year of marriage is the honeymoon period, and the last verse of our reading attests to this. In Hebrew culture barrenness brought shame. A year at home before going to war provided opportunity for the wife to be pregnant and happy, as well as ensuring a growing population.

Prayer: Heavenly Father, we are all too frail and easily led astray. Guide us to a resolution that honours you if our marriage falls on difficult times.

WEEK NINETEEN: TUESDAY

Life in the Covenant

Read: Deuteronomy 30:11–20

Now choose life, so that you and your children may live.
Deuteronomy 30:19.

When we buy a car we are careful where we drive it. Some vehicles are meant for rougher terrain than others, but most of us have vehicles that are built for highway use, not mountaineering. We sense a great freedom in taking to the highway, and in North America the places we can take our car are almost limitless.

But there is one condition—we must stay on the road. Drive across a muddy field and we soon find our freedom strictly curtailed.

Chapters 28 to 30 set out the terms of the covenant Israel should keep if they wanted to enjoy the benefits of it. Opting out did not nullify the covenant, it continued to remain in force, but to reject it meant living in a heathen wilderness and losing the freedom the covenant offered.

Similarly, enjoying the fruits of our covenant with God means staying on his "highways." If we take off across a "muddy field," we will eventually bear the consequences of it.

Making a marriage work is not just a matter of common sense, it is a God given covenant and as such requires adherence to the rules of the covenant just as for any natural law.

As many have found, a God informed, love centred marriage is not only a source of companionship and personal dignity, but also a place of great emotional freedom. But if a partner breaks faith with the covenant, conflict and bitterness will restrict that freedom.

Prayer: Lord, we desire to stay in covenant with you and with each other. Doing so will bring us the greatest happiness and honour you.

Be Strong and Courageous

Read: Joshua 1:1–9

"Be strong and courageous. Do not be terrified; do not be discouraged, for the Lord your God will be with you wherever you go." Joshua 1:9.

Today's reading stands out as one of the great motivational passages of all time, particularly for the Christian community. Unfortunately, some distort it to mean Christians will always be prosperous and successful, and most of us realize that is not so, compare Hebrews 11:32–40. So how can God's encouragement to Joshua help us in our relational dilemmas?

In practice, Joshua failed on some counts and the conquest was never completed, and Israel experienced an unstable peace. Like Joshua, we are not always able to fully maintain our faith in difficult times. But two instructions pertain directly to us as well as Joshua.

First, dwell in the "Book of the Law," the Bible, and "meditate on it day and night." Many Christians live mediocre lives because the Bible is not their foundation. Second is the promise that "the Lord your God will be with you wherever you go." Success is not totally up to us; he guides our circumstances—often in spite of us.

If you are facing the prospect of marriage—joyfully, but perhaps with some trepidation, or already in a marriage that you consider unsuccessful—the instruction and promise given to Joshua is the key to maintaining faith. After all, success is not necessarily measured by personal effort, but in remaining "strong and courageous" in our trust in God for all the situations of life.

Prayer: O Lord, we treasure your promises. Give us the strength of faith to believe in your guidance when circumstances appear to deny it.

WEEK NINETEEN: THURSDAY

Renewing the Covenant

Read: Joshua 8:30–35

Joshua read all the words of the law—the blessings and the curses—just as it is written in the Book of the Law. Joshua 8:34.

Joshua fulfilled the command given by Moses to repeat the terms of the covenant to Israel when they reached the Promised Land, Deuteronomy 11:29.

Why was this necessary? After all, the land they now occupied was one of the promises given to Abraham and his son and grandson.

Because continued enjoyment of this land depended on their active response of trust in God's covenant, a reminder of the terms of the covenant as they entered the land was appropriate.

This was not the last time that Israel renewed the covenant; it was always a corrective measure when Israel wandered from God. Further, the people of Israel faced a daunting future. They faced many battles to settle the land.

Remembering God's promises and his presence with them was a critical encouragement as they faced uncertainties ahead. Equally important was the recitation of the curses, a reminder of the dangers of forsaking him.

Recalling the marriage covenant, many couples renew wedding vows at special anniversaries, reminding themselves of the blessings their marriages have brought, and pledging to stay faithful.

But continuing to enjoy that partnership, means staying faithful to the terms of the marriage covenant as Israel needed to stay faithful to God's covenant. Perhaps we should also recall the pitfalls that face marriage and the wretchedness they could bring.

Prayer: Heavenly Father, today we want to recall and renew our marriage covenant with each other. Help us to keep our promises, and guide us through any current areas of conflict we may have.

Seduction

Read: Joshua 9:1–16

The men of Israel sampled their provisions but did not inquire of the Lord. Joshua 9:14.

Israel failed to maintain part of the covenant regarding their entry into Canaan, the so-called "Promised Land." Their mandate was to destroy the inhabitants of the land, and not to make treaties with them, Deuteronomy 7:1–6. What went wrong and how can we learn to avoid the similar traps in our marriages?

Joshua knew the right question: where did they come from? But he failed to discern the veiled response in their first evasion to his question: "We are your servants."

Further, he failed to seek God's wisdom: they "did not enquire of the Lord." They also succumbed to pressure; in three days the truth revealed itself.

Perhaps an underlying cause was a desire by Joshua to be deceived. He had already fought several battles and faced many more. This would be one less fight with a readymade excuse to avoid it.

We deceive ourselves the easiest, and when it comes to fidelity our guard falters easily; working or other legitimate liaison with the opposite sex may mask a hidden desire to be seduced.

Seduction is a form of deception, rarely fulfilling its promise, usually ending in misery. Seduction inevitably includes lies, misrepresentation, and inconsistencies and also a demand for immediate gratification.

In contrast, a talk with God—that simple act of prayer—will often interfere with plans to respond to seduction. Or conversely, the desire may interfere with our prayer.

Prayer: O Lord, help us to recognize deception, even to uncover the desire to be deceived within ourselves.

WEEK NINETEEN: WEEKEND

Avoiding Pitfalls

Some of you may be old enough to remember drive-in movie theatres. It was a great place to take a girl and make out. There, many a girl was compromised in the back seat of a car. Of course, the act didn't just suddenly occur at the drive-in; the decision to go there already initiated the action.

Frequent news broadcasts report injuries and killings from late night fights at bars and nightclubs. Avoid vulnerable risky situations in the first place.

Scripture provides guidance to receive the best from life, and warns of pitfalls to avoid. However, avoiding life's pitfalls is not always simply a matter of will power. A lifestyle that excludes risky settings may be necessary.

Some jobs provide challenging settings: travel requiring overnight lodgings, lonely shift work, or close working liaisons with the opposite sex. All these may compromise fidelity and some have chosen to change jobs accordingly.

The above examples are perfectly legitimate activities, frequently without suitable alternatives. But here are some suggestions for reducing the risk. Attend church regularly, join activities with groups, increase the activities with your partner, and avoid times apart from your partner that provide contact with the opposite sex.

Changes like this may require sacrifice, particularly where the activity is legitimate. But the sacrifice will be worth more than the price paid if it avoids future infidelity and the resulting conflict and pain.

Prayer: O Lord, guard our hearts and vision in this seductive culture. Give us the strength to make changes necessary to maintain our fidelity to each other.

A Place of Refuge

Read: Joshua 20:1–9

Any of the Israelites or any alien living among them who killed
someone accidentally could flee to these designated cities.
Joshua 20:9.

What a great idea: cities of refuge. For the Jews of Joshua's time, cities of refuge provided protection for those who had committed crimes by accident, especially killing someone, until a hearing by an impartial court. How many times have you wished for a place of refuge from the storms of life?

A few years ago, hurricane Katrina devastated New Orleans and much of Mississippi and Louisiana. For the first week there was no refuge for thousands of displaced persons until they moved out of the chaos to cities of refuge like Baton Rouge, Houston, and others.

The inability to state clearly the problem facing us hampers our understanding. We may have poor communication skills, be too emotionally involved to see things rationally, or even fearful of expressing ourselves. So where is our city of refuge in times of torment?

First, it is the Word of God, not a means of escape, but a source of instruction to clarify our distorted thinking. As a complement to that, God has provided us with a community of faith to support us in time of need.

To seek help is not to admit failure, but rather to find objective thinking for our dilemma. A Christian counselor with good analytical skills can help us state our case plainly. That is half the battle to resolving it.

Prayer: O Lord, you know the pressure I am under, and I thank you that you are my place of refuge. Help me to trust you even when circumstances appear against me.

WEEK TWENTY: TUESDAY

We Will Serve the Lord

Read: Joshua 24:14–27

The people said to Joshua, "We will serve the Lord our God and obey him." Joshua 24:24.

Two repetitions of the covenant bracket most of Joshua's campaign. An earlier reading noted the recall of the covenant at the early stages of the campaign and today we read Joshua's final review of the covenant before his death.

We also noted the habit of some to renew wedding vows at special anniversaries. Perhaps the vow renewal should take place not only at times of celebration, but also at the difficult times of marriage as well.

Joshua was a realist. He gave the Israelites the opportunity to opt out of the covenant while asserting his own determination to remain within it. Despite agreement that God was their benefactor and an assertion to serve the Lord—repeated three times in verses 18, 21 and 24—Joshua knew that they would fail to do so; he had his own experience to go by.

The notion that man is essentially good, and will improve himself using an enlightened view of humankind unfettered by religious—particularly Christian—dogma, is continually proved wrong by history; Joshua had it right all along.

We all aspire to the fairy tale romance. The story of Prince Charles and Princess Diana had all the trappings of a fairy tale romance—royalty, beauty, riches and adulation. It failed because they believed happiness existed outside the marriage.

Recognizing moral frailty within our own marriages may be the first step to avoiding the failure it could bring.

Prayer: O Lord, we are so aware of our tendency to wander from you. Seal our hearts for yourself we pray.

WEEK TWENTY: WEDNESDAY

Cycles of Rebellion

Read: Judges 2:6–19

After that whole generation had been gathered to their fathers, another generation grew up, who knew neither the Lord nor what he had done for Israel. Judges 2:10.

Today's reading is a summary of the book of Judges. Israel's cycles of rebellion against God, brought repeated oppression from surrounding nations. Each time Israel cried for deliverance, God provided judges to release them from bondage, but despite God's continued deliverances, these cycles eventually deteriorated into anarchy, Judges 17:6; 18:1; 19:1; 21:25.

The book clearly demonstrates the perversity of human nature and its repeated tendency to seek independence from God to its own detriment. It is this tendency that Joshua recognized and warned against. Independence, from God or our partner, threatens to undermine both relationships.

Restrictions placed on independence from our partner are to ensure ongoing joyful companionship. They may seem irksome, but they prevent us from responding to gratification from sources outside the relationship. Investment in interdependence with our partner will ensure future happiness in the relationship.

Our unnatural desire for independence from God is the great threat to our marriages. Even those who are not Christians can gain marital stability from adherence to godly requirements.

Unfortunately the reverse is also true; there are Christian couples that lose out because they seek the security of their marriages in the wrong places—money, illicit love, acquisitions and so on. The true security for marriage is first in maintaining our covenant with God, which in turn draws us to maintain our covenant with each other, Malachi 2:10–15.

Prayer: Heavenly Father, keep us close to you that we might also remain close to our partners.

119

WEEK TWENTY: THURSDAY

Rash Decisions

Read: Judges 11:29–40

"Oh! My daughter! You have made me miserable and wretched,
because I have made a vow to the Lord that I cannot break."
Judges 11:35.

This passage, often referred to as Jephthah's rash vow, highlights two important aspects of parenthood: love for our children never fades, and the foolishness of decisions made during emotional turmoil.

Tonya was having major problems with her sixteen year old son sparked by marital problems. After a weekend away with her husband to mend their marriage, she returned home to find a wild party had ransacked the house, smashed contents, and consumed liquor.

She angrily accused him of all the heartache and costs her son created by this incident and previous abusive, destructive behaviour. She would report him to the police and ordered him out of the house. But the immediate emotional crisis subsided and she thought more clearly.

She felt God's urging to follow her son, and caught up with him as he dejectedly wandered the streets. His cockiness had evaporated, and his misery showed. She kindly invited him into the car and he broke down in sorrowful repentance for his actions. He knew she still loved him.

Jephthah made his vow in a moment of emotional turmoil, but never considered the possible outcomes. It ended in wretchedness and his daughter bewailed her virginity.

However, we may still find that opportunity to use our love as a motivation to try to reunite with a wayward child.

Prayer: O Lord, we yearn for our children to be united with you and with us. Keep us from rash decisions in our desire to persuade their allegiance to you.

God Uses Rebellion

Read: Judges 14:1–18

[Samson] said to his father and mother, "I have seen a Philistine woman in Timnah; now get her for me as my wife." Judges 14:2.

If there ever was a stormy relationship, it was between Samson and his chosen women; first his wife, and later Delilah.

Samson did everything wrong: ignoring his parents' advice, choosing Philistine women, consorting with Philistine prostitutes, Judges 16:1–4, and always acting in angry and vicious revenge.

Yet our reading tells us that God had a plan for Israel in all this confusion and he was using Samson to confront the Philistines who were ruling Israel. This raises two questions.

First, if God was using Samson in his violent and rebellious life, did this mean that God condoned, perhaps even precipitated, Samson's actions?

The answer reveals God's ability to control events in the most adverse circumstances. God's foreknowledge of Samson's lifestyle enabled him to use it for his purposes, without denying Samson's freedom of will or subsequent guilt.

Second, how should his parents have reacted? The previous chapter shows their devotion to God and early awareness of Samson's role for Israel. But Samson's willfulness caused them to question that knowledge. Perhaps this was a case for his parents to trust God with the big picture.

Have you cause to question the purpose of your life because events are contrary to your expectations? Scripture makes it clear that you can trust him with your life, even when your closest relationships fail. God can still use for his advantage even the most rebellious and angry.

Prayer: Lord. It's our desire to for you to use us willingly to establish your kingdom on earth.

WEEK TWENTY: WEEKEND

Anarchy

We have seen in this week's readings that anarchy is simply a result of everyone seeking his or her own way. It does not necessarily mean the rule of armed thugs, although that is one form of anarchy. Where everyone conforms to their own set of rules within a "civilized" society can create anarchy.

Western culture has largely thrown off the restraints of Christian values and lives on a smorgasbord of religions and spirituality—including secularism—that provides a glut of conflicting lifestyles. Where these lifestyles reflect the fulfillment of personal desires, they undermine the cohesiveness of society and increase friction within it.

The time of the judges following Joshua's time is similar to today's western culture. As worship of God waned, so a variety of other religions and religious experiences took its place. Even individual households maintained their own priest and religion, Judges 17:1-5; clear examples of personally concocted spirituality. This process, then and now, provides religions of convenience that validate any chosen lifestyle.

With so many options and the diverse advice they offer, marriage partners may develop a disruptive anarchy within themselves. A marriage built on these shifting sands will not stand against the winds of change.

The answer to anarchy is truth. A stable society cannot survive without the influence of transcendent values. Recognizing and practising the truth revealed to us in Scripture will provide lasting stable guidance for all of life and beyond.

Prayer: Heavenly Father, grant us the ability to see beyond the world's conflicting values and keep our eyes upon your truth.

Love is Blind

Read: Judges 16:4–21

He awoke from his sleep and thought, "I'll go out as before and shake myself free." But he did not know that the Lord had left him. Judges 16:20.

Today's story of Samson recalls the story of Patrick, a Canadian, who, on the rebound from divorce met a "Christian" girl on the internet in California. He fell for her, although she had a criminal record and two children from previous relationships.

He spent money on a leased apartment, teeth reconstruction and a car for her. He purchased the car in Ontario, taxed and insured it and drove it down to California for her—a great example of blind love.

He heard very little from her afterwards, except calls for money. A good friend helped him realize the truth of the situation and Patrick had recently met a local Christian girl prepared to marry him.

He phoned the girl's landlord saying he would no longer pay the rent as the lease was up. He and his friend flew to California, "stole" the car back—he still had keys and proof of purchase—and drove it home. It still had Ontario plates on it.

I doubt Samson thought cutting his hair would make any difference to his strength. He couldn't be that foolish; he had previous experiences of Delilah's deception. Samson's blindness was in thinking his strength was his own.

He lost his strength when, in allowing his hair to be cut, he broke his vows and the Lord left him. The Lord returned Samson's strength as his hair grew back and he committed himself again to God's purposes.

Prayer: Lord, help us remember the gifts you have given us are yours for your use, and if we misuse them we may lose them.

123

Quiet Determined Faith

Read: Ruth 1:1–22

Where you go I will go, and where you stay I will stay. Your people will be my people and your God my God. Ruth 1:16.

The story of Ruth is a different kind of love story; it is one of God's guidance in arranged marriage. Ruth, a remarkable woman with quiet determination and devotion, married Naomi's son, accepted his faith, and adopted his family as her own.

When all the men of Naomi's family had died, Ruth determined to travel to Judah with her mother-in-law. Naomi assumed that Ruth's reason in following her was for a new husband based on the tradition of "levirate" marriage.

Levirate marriage plays a big part in Ruth's story. The custom required the brother, or near male relative of a deceased, childless husband to marry the widow, raise children to the dead man and ensure his lineage.

But Ruth stayed with Naomi, not for another husband, but for Naomi's faith, people, and God. Ruth became an ancestor of Jesus Christ.

Our current culture tends to despise mothers-in-law, so it is refreshing to see Ruth's devotion to hers. But the in-law relationship is a two way street. A parent who believes her son- or daughter-in-law is not good enough for her child is courting rejection for herself. A daughter will be torn between her parent and husband.

It also hinders the grandchild relationship, often denying the grandparents the joy of being a part of their grandchildren's lives. Although not recognized in our western culture, lineage is important, and a child with good extended family relationships forms a secure identity.

Prayer: Heavenly Father, as you are a wise parent to your creation, grant us wisdom when our children begin to choose their life's partners.

God Leads "By Chance"

Read: Ruth 2:1 to 3:6

As it turned out, she found herself working in a field belonging to Boaz, who was from the clan of Elimelech. Ruth 2:3.

Ruth lived in the times of the judges, Ruth 1:1, not a good time to be alive, for "in those days Israel had no king, everyone did as he saw fit," Judges 21:25. These dangerous conditions were prevalent in Ruth's time: Boaz told his men not to touch her, and Naomi warns Ruth of harm if she gleans in another's field.

This new girl in his field, and her care for Naomi, impressed Boaz. He invited Ruth to share his water, bread and grain, ensured extra grain left for her to glean, and invited her to remain in his fields until the end of harvest.

Naomi's interest was far more practical. Under levirate law we discussed yesterday, Boaz was a relative who could marry Ruth and raise offspring to keep both dead husbands' heritage alive.

Naomi gave Ruth instructions to make contact with Boaz and seek his agreement to marry her as this would maintain the husbands' heritage. Her approach has cultural overtones that we may not fully understand, but her request for him to cover her with the corner of his garment was a symbolic request for him to fulfill his levirate marriage duty.

The initial contact between the two was by chance: "As it turned out, she found herself working in a field belonging to Boaz." Yet there is little left to chance for those who choose to live godly lives. Whether arranged or by choice, God will provide a life partner with whom both can fulfill God's desires for their lives.

Prayer: O God, we long for you to lead us as you led Ruth. We commit ourselves to you today as she did.

WEEK TWENTY-ONE: THURSDAY

A Woman Requests Marriage

Read: Ruth 3:7–18

"I am your servant Ruth," she said. "Spread the corner of your garment over me, since you are a kinsman-redeemer." Ruth 3:9.

The meeting at the grain pile was open to allegations of impropriety, particularly in that culture.

However, there is some scriptural indication that there was a cultural form behind Ruth's request to Boaz: "Spread the corner of your garment over me, since you are a kinsman-redeemer." The same terminology is used of God as he prepared to look after the emerging nation of Israel, eventually leading to their "marriage," Ezekiel 16:8. A later meditation will review that passage.

There is a sense that this was an arranged marriage, although not forced: Ruth had the choice to respond to the idea. It is clear from the book and this passage that Ruth's foremost concern was the family she had adopted without reservation earlier.

This attitude was obviously well suited to marriage and the demands that would be placed upon her by others— husband, children and those who might become dependent upon her.

Boaz was an older man, and would have been attracted to this younger woman. But his response was solicitous, considering her approach a kindness. He wanted to ensure her safety in his fields, and now didn't want her roaming dangerous streets at night.

He was also concerned for her reputation advising an early return home to avoid scandal. He graciously agreed to consider her request for marriage and gave her grain for the family.

The attitudes of these two had the makings of a good marriage.

Prayer: Dear Lord, we marvel at the way you guided Ruth and Boaz. We pray for the same guidance for our children as they decide to marry.

Unlikely Ancestors of Jesus

Read: Ruth 4:1–22

"May the Lord make the woman who is coming into your home like Rachel and Leah, who together built up the house of Israel." Ruth 4:11.

B oaz' intention was clear: he was anxious to marry Ruth, but there was an obstacle. Another man, a closer relative of Ruth than Boaz, had the prior right to "acquire" her along with Elimelech's land.

However this closer relative was more concerned with maintaining his own blood line than that of his relative Elimelech. Had he married Ruth, that marriage based on personal interest would probably have been precarious. But his negative response left Boaz free to marry Ruth, and together they became the ancestors of David and eventually of Jesus.

There are some interesting sidelights to this story. There are four women, apart from Mary, mentioned in the lineage of Jesus. Two are foreigners, Ruth and Rahab, Rahab being Boaz' mother—more likely an ancestor as Rahab and David are separated by several hundred years—Matthew 1:5. It is unlikely that Rahab would have been included were she not the Rahab from Jericho, Joshua 6:22–25.

Even more surprising, the other women are Tamar, Genesis 28:34, and Bathsheba, 2 Samuel 11:3–4, both involved in adulterous relationships but included in Jesus' ancestry, Matthew 1:3 and 6.

As Ruth became part of the lineage of Jesus, so we also enter God's family by a decision to commit our lives to Naomi's God. This gives God the opportunity to guide our lives, including the provision of marriage partners.

Prayer: Heavenly Father, sin did not disallow women from entering your bloodline. Thank you for your grace in receiving us into your family.

127

WEEK TWENTY-ONE: WEEKEND

Stable Marriages

I recall a counseling professor once stating there are three kinds of marriages: stable good marriages, unstable bad marriages, but also bad marriages that are stable. The last is perhaps surprising.

Yet if we think of those we know, we can probably think of couples in the last category; the later years of Isaac and Rebekah are an example. Despite a difficult relationship, the two needed each other for maintaining identity even in a combative relationship. Unequal, but complementary relationships will stay married, even if they are unhappy.

It was always a mystery to Ann and me why her parents stayed together. The head doctor of the local psychiatric hospital identified both as psychologically challenged.

Ann's mother, with an extreme form of bipolar disorder, frequently destroyed the family home. Ann's father was a paranoid schizophrenic, aware of other men, yet he remained faithful to his wife. It seems she needed someone to dominate and he required the level of acceptance he received within the relationship.

Ann, as the firstborn and only girl, became the mother of the family who desperately tried to bring order out of chaos and keep her younger brothers out of trouble.

She complained to her father for giving her mother his paycheck, which was immediately squandered in the pub. Ann often sat on the pub steps asking customers to tell her mother to come home.

But the marriage survived until death parted them.

Prayer: O Lord, give us insight to see where our marriage is one of convenience. Help us to reflect your love by making our marriage one of service to each other.

Childlessness

Read: 1 Samuel 1:1–20

"In the course of time Hannah conceived and gave birth to a son. She named him Samuel, saying, "Because I asked the Lord for him." 1 Samuel 1:20.

This is a story of both heartbreak and joy. We noted earlier with Jacob, two wives are not a good idea. Abraham also faced the dilemma in the dispute between Sarah and Hagar.

It was true with Elkanah and his two wives. Childlessness was tragedy enough for Hannah in that culture, but doubly so when derided by her rival wife Peninnah.

The two women had opposite motives. Peninnah had little time for the religious life, taunting Hannah at the annual trip to Shiloh for sacrifice. In marked contrast, Hannah could have been bitter for her barrenness and the continual mocking from Peninnah.

Rather, in her misery, she recognized that God was her only hope for change and drew closer to him instead. She prayed silently, knowing that God hears the prayers of the heart. She left with the sense that God heard her prayers, "and ate something, and her face was no longer downcast."

Leaving our burdens at the foot of the cross will have that effect upon us. The inability to have children is frequent today, and distress for many. But knowing God is in control of our lives and he will provide children, or reasons for withholding them in his time, can be a great comfort during a time of uncertainty.

God does hear our prayers, and in Hannah's case gave her a son. But it was many years before God answered her prayers.

Prayer: O God, help us, or those we know, bear the pain of childlessness, and trust you to answer our prayers in your time.

WEEK TWENTY-TWO: TUESDAY

Losing a Child

Read: 1 Samuel 1:21–28

"So now I give him to the Lord. For his whole life he will be given over to the Lord." And [Samuel] worshiped the Lord there.
1 Samuel 1:28.

Hannah did an amazing thing. After giving birth to her longed for son she gave him up for service in the tabernacle. It was certainly within her character to give thanks for the son, but to give up that which was dearest to her heart was a major sacrifice.

The firstborn belonged to God and required redeeming by animal sacrifice. But Hannah acted closer to the letter of the law and gave Samuel up for service to the Lord. She would see him once a year when making the pilgrimage for sacrifice.

For a few years after his birth, Hannah weaned Samuel. It was also a time of instruction. Hannah probably told him about his birth as an answer to prayer, and prepared him for his service in the tabernacle. Her instruction included the knowledge of God and his requirements. As a result, Samuel, though still a child, worshipped God as he took up his duties.

Samuel grew to be the most devout and effective prophet of Israel's history. Hannah's sacrifice gave Israel a period of rare stability.

Parents often lose children. Some die early; others go into missionary service like Samuel and live in distant and often dangerous lands. The loss of a child is probably the greatest human tragedy, yet many recognize God's call in this loss.

You may make this supreme sacrifice, perhaps even unwillingly. Whatever your response to a call of this magnitude, it underlines for us the huge sacrifice of God's own Son made willingly for us.

Prayer: Dear God, we're not sure we could have the faith of Hannah. Help us to trust you if ever we are asked to make a similar sacrifice.

130

Sacrifice Has Its Purpose

Read: 1 Samuel 2:12–26

Samuel was ministering before the Lord—a boy wearing a linen
ephod. 1 Samuel 2:18.

Solomon built the first temple some 80 or so years
later. Samuel probably lived in a tent, sleeping on a
mat, and daily carrying out simple duties. He would
probably open the "Tent of Meeting" in the mornings,
watch Eli and his sons performing their necessary rituals
and serve them.

Hannah had more children, three boys and two girls.
She came yearly for the annual sacrifice and visited Samuel,
providing him with new clothes and ritual garments as he
grew. Eventually he would perform tabernacle
responsibilities himself, accepting and directing the
sacrifices of those who came for cleansing.

Eli blessed Hannah for giving Samuel to the Lord.
Samuel was an obvious asset, and he would replace his
disappointing sons. Those sons exploited their position for
personal benefits—forcing supplicants to give them
sacrificial food and sexually exploiting the serving women.

Eli asked his sons a rhetorical question. Who will
intercede for you when you sin against the Lord? Eli's sons
were intercessors for the people before God; but as the
sons sinned against God there was no other intercessor for
them before God.

Eventually, Eli's sons died as prophesied, 1 Samuel
4:17. Samuel now became the intercessor for the people to
replace Eli's sons. In this regard he prefigured Jesus Christ
who has since come and revealed himself to us. He is now
the One who intercedes before the Father for us and for our
children.

Prayer: O Lord, it is our desire to serve you, even if that results in
sacrifice. Help us to rejoice in the knowledge that your
will is being done and you are being glorified.

WEEK TWENTY-TWO: THURSDAY

Keeping Faith

Read: 1 Samuel 8:1–9

[The Israelites] said to him, "You are old, and your sons do not walk in your ways; now appoint a king to lead us, such as all the other nations have." 1 Samuel 8:5.

Samuel was a prophet, but also acted as the last in a long line of judges that ruled Israel. The Israelites became impatient with their differences from the surrounding nations; they wanted a king to rule over them like those nations.

Israel's differences were purposely designed as a witness to the living God, Deuteronomy 4:5–8. Samuel had given a lifetime of faithful service to Israel, but God comforted Samuel. It was not him they were rejecting; they didn't want God to reign over them.

As Israel's fellowship with God lessened, God became less attractive to Israel and the "grass appeared greener next door."

Novelty wears off. Temporal things, which seem so attractive to start, never eventually satisfy. This needn't be true of relationships with living creatures, as they constantly provide spontaneity and freshness in the relationship.

However, the relationship deepens by constant and meaningful intimacy. Without this interaction, a partner begins to appear less attractive and someone outside the relationship could fill the void.

Of course, the failure that created loss of attraction in the first relationship will probably repeat itself in the next— the grass was not really greener next door after all.

Prayer: O Lord, how could we fail to see your beauty and grace, leave you, and seek our fulfillment elsewhere? We know there is no greater satisfaction for our lives and marriages beyond what you have given of yourself and in the partners you have provided.

The Only Source of Satisfaction

Read: 1 Samuel 8:10–21

"No!" [the people] said. "We want a king over us. Then we will be like all the other nations." 1 Samuel 8:19–20.

Israel should have observed the adage: "be careful what you ask for; you may get it!" Despite the warnings from Samuel, Israel clamoured for a king and God obliged. What is of greater mystery is why God would agree to their request when it was not his original design?

Perhaps it was simply an accommodation to human sinfulness, similar to his permission for divorce. Maybe if God had not allowed it, Israel's insistence would have created a final, irreversible separation from God.

God's overall mastery of events meant that he was able to fulfill his desires, not only in spite of Israel's defection, but through it. God used Israel's desire for a king to provide for a lineage that will return the kingship to God in the person of King Jesus upon his final ascension to the throne of David. An earthly king for Israel would not provide for their ultimate needs, any more than surrounding nations found satisfaction in their kings.

Similarly, our partners are God's means of providing for our companionship and physical satisfaction. Thus he directly participates in marriage by serving us through our partners. But that relationship is finite, built on fallible people with limited abilities.

To expect that relationship to fill all our needs is foolish and irresponsible. There are some needs only God can supply and to lean on our partners for those is unreasonable—as was Israel's belief that a human king would bring them ultimate satisfaction and security.

Prayer: O God, show us from your Word and by your Spirit that you only are the final one to satisfy our hearts.

WEEK TWENTY-TWO: WEEKEND

Child Discipline

The child Samuel must seem too good to be true, although I'm sure that he had his moments. My father put children and animals together in one category—he couldn't stand the disobedience of either.

He was strict, and although I had bodily evidence of that quite rarely, he acted on the mantra of the day: "Children should be seen and not heard."

This is a far cry from the attitude towards children today, when allowing children to "express themselves" results in spoiled brats who rule their households by tantrums.

My study window overlooks a busy intersection with crosswalks, no signals, and lengthy sections of sidewalks approach it. Every school day, a mother, with her own and several other young children, needs to cross both streets to reach the elementary school.

The older children, seven or eight years of age ride bikes, younger ones walk or run, while a preschool toddler furiously peddles his small plastic tricycle to keep up. In addition, the mother often pushes a stroller.

What intrigues me is that while she walks at a steady pace, the children happily range forward and backward on their bikes, with no apparent concern from the mother. But they always stop and wait short of the intersection. When she arrives, she shepherds them across the streets, but once across, the children range ahead freely again.

Her control of the children is not by keeping them on a short leash, but by instilled obedience. As long as they live within her rules, the children are free to enjoy being themselves for the journey. Doesn't this give *us* some guidance about where to find *our* freedom?

Prayer: Lord, obedience to you provides the safest route through life. Help us develop our own internal discipline.

Dangers of Leadership

Read: 1 Samuel 10:1–27

Samuel took a flask of oil and poured it on Saul's head and kissed him, saying, "Has not the Lord anointed you leader over his inheritance?" 1 Samuel 10:1.

This passage tells us a lot about Saul and his fitness for king. God appointed him and Samuel anointed him. God's Spirit filled him with power and God promised to support his decisions. He was discreet, keeping his private anointing secret, 1 Samuel 9:27 to 10:1.

Saul, while taller than all other contenders, showed humility, embarrassed at his kingship on public display. He was magnanimous to those who opposed his kingship, 1 Samuel 11:12–13, and showed prowess in battle,1 Samuel 18:7.

Yet the remaining chapters of first Samuel show Saul descending into an increasingly sour, despondent, and violent disposition, erratic and vindictive. We explore this change later, but all the advantages he had for success were no insurance against failure in the future.

Saul may have considered authority from God gave him unlimited freedom of action. The gift of the Holy Spirit probably gave him a sense of superiority—others were less favoured of God—which in turn undermined his humility.

Our personal spirituality can either make or break a marriage. If I entertain the notion that I am spiritually superior to my partner, I will develop personal arrogance, believing I have a God given mandate to dictate the conduct of the relationship.

This loss of humility between partners and before God can be disastrous to a marriage, as Saul's developing arrogance was to his kingship.

Prayer: O Lord, it is only by your grace that you accept us. Keep us from pride in the favour you show us.

135

WEEK TWENTY-THREE: TUESDAY

Faith in Hard Times

Read: 1 Samuel 13:5–14

"The Lord has sought out a man after his own heart and appointed him leader of his people, because you have not kept the Lord's command." 1 Samuel 13:14.

Saul's three thousand men were vastly outnumbered by the Philistines; Saul had a right to be concerned. His men were "quaking with fear," many had already deserted his army—hiding or even joining the Philistines, 1 Samuel 14:21–22.

He sought the Lord's favour. He waited the time allotted for Samuel's arrival but he had not come. So Saul took matters into his own hands. He offered the required sacrifices in place of Samuel.

Now, the priestly and prophetic ministries were separate from the king. Samuel was responsible before God for these and Saul for kingly duties. The voice of God which bound Saul came through the prophet. Saul was to wait for Samuel, who would come and make the required sacrifices.

Saul's actions fell short on two counts: he deliberately disobeyed a direct command from God through the prophet Samuel, but worse, he showed a lack of trust in the promise of God to support him, 1 Samuel 10:7.

Under the New Covenant, the Spirit of God indwells each Christian giving assurance of God's promises to us, Ephesians 1:13–14. Whether we trust those promises is up to us, and there are times of pressure when we may doubt God's control in our situation.

It is then that we are likely to take matters into our own hands, and compound it by contravening a non-negotiable feature of the covenant. Acting like this cost Saul and his children the kingship.

Prayer: O Lord, it's so easy to turn to our own devices when difficulties arise. Help us to simply maintain our trust and wait for you at those times.

Is He a Loving God?

Read: 1 Samuel 15:1–9

"Attack the Amalekites and totally destroy everything that belongs to them. Do not spare them; put to death men and women, children and infants, cattle and sheep, camels and donkeys." 1 Samuel 15:3.

The instructions in today's reading were clear: completely wipe out the Amalekite clan, people and animals. We find these requirements horrific, and easily react against them. How can we reconcile requirements like this with the loving God the Bible maintains?

This question has been debated for centuries, and we are unlikely to find a satisfactory solution within a few thoughts. But the Bible does give us some direction.

Ask the question: what would heaven be like if everyone made it there on their own terms? The answer is simple: it would be a copy of earth as it is now. It only takes one cancer cell to destroy the body, and only one sin could destroy heaven.

God's judgment is simply a separation of good and evil; the place of the former is heaven and the latter place is hell. When humans refuse to renounce their sin, they go to the latter place with it.

The eventual judgment of God is an important concept—and one of comfort knowing there will be a penalty for injustice. The man who abuses, neglects or abandons his wife or children will face a day of reckoning. Often we may not find justice for ourselves, but God has told us that he will ensure justice is done, Deuteronomy 32:35, Romans 12:19.

But there is escape from the wrath of God as we recognize our sinfulness and avail ourselves of the forgiveness in Jesus Christ.

Prayer: Heavenly Father, thank you for rescuing us from your judgment by forgiving our sin and calling us into your family.

137

WEEK TWENTY-THREE: THURSDAY

Obedience Better than Sacrifice

Read: 1 Samuel 15:10–29

To obey is better than sacrifice, and to heed is better than the fat of rams. 1 Samuel 15:22.

Despite another opportunity, Saul had not learned his lesson and confirmed his habit of giving excuses for failure. He tried to keep the plunder a secret claiming "I have carried out the Lord's instructions." Unfortunately the animals prompted Samuel's sarcastic reply: "What then is this bleating of sheep in my ears? What is this lowing of cattle that I hear?"

At this point Saul compounded his deception, by giving a spiritual rationale for his actions: they had "spared the best of the sheep and cattle to sacrifice to the Lord your God."

Jesus condemned the same rationalization used by the leading Jews, who deflected money to themselves that could have been used for needy parents, by labeling it "a gift dedicated to the Lord," Mark 7:10–13. The Christian man who leaves his non-believing wife for a Christian girl so they can be "one in the Lord" is no different.

Unfortunately, rationalization of our bad behaviour is so common as to be almost unnoticeable. Frequently, on discovery of our poor conduct, our first reaction is to find excuses. Often it is simply to blame someone or something else, or else to point to some good that was in view.

In particular, for a husband or wife to claim some spiritual reason for poor attitudes or actions to his or her partner is the most offensive.

Fulfilling our obligations to our family is our first duty to God; if we fail our family, we oppose God.

Prayer: Lord, help us to be constantly aware of our need to follow your instruction and remember they are the best for us in the end.

Sin and Mental Instability

Read: 1 Samuel 16:14–23

Now the Spirit of the Lord had departed from Saul, and an evil spirit from the Lord tormented him. 1 Samuel 16:14.

I n today's reading, we see the Spirit of God coming upon David as he was anointed king, but departing from Saul as a result of his earlier attempts to cover his sin. Worse, "an evil spirit from the LORD tormented him."

This last phrase often raises the question of whether evil comes from God. The Bible always maintains that God is not the creator of evil, but the provider of choice. Evil comes into being when a choice is made to oppose God.

The phrase "from the LORD" confirms God's mastery over the forces of evil; they operate only with his permission, not from his weakness. Remember our spiritual warfare is against real spiritual forces, Ephesians 6:12, and rebellion against God opens the way for spiritual evil to influence our lives. But we also find the Spirit of God, through David's influence, could restrain the evil spirit in Saul.

We cannot be sure whether Saul's increasingly dark moods were spiritually influenced or were a deepening psychosis. Probably the former was the trigger for the latter.

What we do know is that moodiness in a marriage will only escalate if not dealt with, and is a potently destructive force. If it has a spiritual cause, as with Saul, it will require reconciliation—both with God and the partner and others that have suffered from it.

Prayer: Father, help each of us to keep short accounts of those things that disturb us, and lessen the injury our bad attitudes might cause to ourselves as well as others.

WEEK TWENTY-THREE: WEEKEND

A Story of Recovery

Saul's foolishness need not have been the end of his career, for Samuel's rebuke could have led to repentance and restoration rather than rebellion.

Todd's experience is an example. He followed his father and became a pastor; married, had two children and with a church to pastor, he seemed set for life.

However, friction set in to the marriage and he became angry, and his wife left him. He took steps to deal with his anger, but his wife was unresponsive and divorce followed.

This is devastating for anyone, but for a minister it was a double blow; it deprived him of his calling as well. So began a long and painful process of restoration.

In addition to loss of family and job, he risked the loss of faith as well. His desired devotion to God had led him into adversity, not a sense of achievement. Did this mean that all his work for God was meaningless? Could he trust God to order his life in the future? Would he be able to work for God again?

There were redeeming features to his life. Many had benefited from his ministry during the better years. He had married couples and followed their lives in the latter years, retaining many friendships. With his background, he was able to find work with handicapped people, a means of restoring his sense of worth as well as assisting others.

But above all, he never lost his faith, and with the help of good friends and partners in ministry he was able to experience and receive the grace of God for restoration.

Prayer: O Lord, you know all things. Keep us honest with you, even when we have failed. Forgive and restore us we pray.

Living with Bitterness

Read: 1 Samuel 18:5–16

When Saul saw how successful he was, he was afraid of him. But all Israel and Judah loved David, because he led them in their campaigns. 1 Samuel 18:15–16.

We discussed the problem of escalating negative emotions if they are not dealt with. Even David's Spirit inspired playing became insufficient to check Saul's increasingly black moods.

Fuelled by jealousy of David's successes, Israel's love for David and resentment at the Lord's presence with David, Saul spent the rest of his life trying to kill him. Occasional brief periods of regret at his conduct were never sufficient to change his course of action.

Saul, with such promise and potential, wasted his whole life with jealousy and resentment. It happens frequently, needlessly; a life paralyzed by bitterness, hatred, anger, or guilt, leaving a legacy of broken lives and injured people in its wake.

Worse, this unnatural way of living can seem normal to its practitioners, often with cynical pleasure derived in holding others in the same misery. And what about those dependent on them: husband, wife, or children that live in the shadow of that misery—or worse, carry on the same legacy?

Are you going down this road yourself, and is this how you intend to finish your life? But it's not how we start out or even where we are now that's important. It's far more vital how we finish.

Wouldn't you rather leave as Paul did saying: "I have fought the good fight, I have finished the race, I have kept the faith," 2 Timothy 4:7. It's not too late.

Prayer: Lord, let me see myself as you see me with whatever is hindering my service for you and the happiness of my family. Give me grace to seek the help I need from Christian counselors and finish the race well.

WEEK TWENTY-FOUR: TUESDAY

To Lie or Not to Lie

Read: 1 Samuel 18:20–27; 19:8–17

Michal took an idol and laid it on the bed, covering it with a garment and putting some goats' hair at the head. When Saul sent the men to capture David, Michal said, "He is ill." 1 Samuel 19:13–14.

David, though still a youth and despite amazing prowess in battle, remained remarkably humble. At first David rejected the possibility of marrying the king's daughter because of his lowly background, but the eventual marriage to Michal appeared to be happy. Michal loved David, and in today's story willingly deceived her father to save David's life.

The choice of saving David or deceiving Saul was not a difficult one for Michal and seems fairly clear to us. Those who were hiding Jews from the German Gestapo lied when asked if there were Jews in the house. You may also recall the lies of Rahab denying she was hiding the Israelite spies, Joshua 2:3–5.

These examples suggest that on occasion telling the truth aids evil. But how do we arrive at that decision? The Hebrew understanding of truth gives some guidance. The Hebrew word for truth, emet, has a wider meaning: it is not a mechanical recitation of the facts. It also carries the idea of faithfulness, as a lover promises to be "true" to his beloved.

This definition makes truth relational; communicating what gives the greatest benefit for the one we love. By withholding that which may be hurtful or harmful we express our faithfulness to them.

I recall one dear lady accused of gossiping about someone. Her justification was: "It is the truth!" Truth it may have been, but it was hardly a faithful act to her sister in Christ.

Prayer: O Lord, in those times when we have to make painful choices, guide us in making the choice that is faithful to you and those we love.

142

Loss of Faith

Read: 1 Samuel 21:1–15

That day David fled from Saul and went to Achish king of Gath.
1 Samuel 21:10.

In this story David fled for his life from Saul, and finished up among Israel' enemies, the Philistines, and sought refuge with King Achish of Gath. The story records David's lies to the priest of God, subterfuge as a madman before Achish, and David's eventual escape back to Judah.

David appears to have lost faith in God's protection and his promise of the throne as he fled from Saul. Yet, if there is any grading of sin, David chose the lesser evil. In his fear of Saul and lapse of faith, he chose to flee rather than harm Saul.

David's too human story reminds us of our own weakness of faith and probable lapses from it altogether.

For those of us facing a continually difficult home life, times of disillusionment lead to questioning God's involvement in our life and marriage. In these times of despair we may lose faith for a time, which adds guilt to the burden.

David's story of his failure of faith, reminds us of three things. Even in times of failure God looks on the heart, 1 Samuel 16:7—often stressed beyond limits—and remains faithful to us. Further, during those times God will often preserve us from mistakes that may cause greater distress later. And finally, there is always hope in God for a time at which he will release us from our adversity.

Prayer: O Lord, it's too easy for our faith to falter under stress. We thank you for your enduring grace to us in our weakness.

143

WEEK TWENTY-FOUR: THURSDAY

Loyalty

Read: 1 Samuel 24:1–22

[Saul] wept aloud. "You are more righteous than I," he said. "You have treated me well, but I have treated you badly." 1 Samuel 24:16–17.

For about fifteen years after David was anointed king, he lived mostly in fear of Saul's desire to kill him. He spent a short time in Saul's court; the remainder he spent as a fugitive in desert strongholds, or on the move.

Saul's erratic behaviour drove others from him who joined David and became loyal to him. Suddenly, David and his men had opportunity to kill Saul.

David was fiercely loyal to Saul despite the danger to his life. Despite an opportunity and his men's exhortation, David refused to kill Saul and even regretted cutting off part of his cloak.

David recognized God's anointing of Saul as king; God placed Saul on the throne, and God was the only one with authority to remove him. David would wait for God's timing for his turn as anointed king of Israel.

If you believed that marriage to your partner was God's plan for you, then your partner still remains God's choice. If he or she has reneged on the covenant made with you, or worse, wandered away from allegiance to God, it doesn't change that relationship.

Most know the real truth of their position even in denial in much the same way that Saul (at least temporarily) recognized the truth of David's claims.

Reconciliation depends largely on maintaining faithfulness to the promises you made to your partner and to God, even if your partner has not.

Prayer: Heavenly Father, please help us to remain loyal to our partners, particularly when they may wander from you or become unfaithful to us. Keep us prayerful and thankful before you.

One Woman Saves a Clan

Read: 1 Samuel 25:1–42

The Lord will certainly make a lasting dynasty for my master,
because he fights the Lord's battles. Let no wrongdoing be found
in you as long as you live. 1 Samuel 25:28.

Abigail was both intelligent and beautiful—a great combination. Living with her "surly and mean" husband Nabal, Abigail had developed strategies to get around Nabal's obstructive ways. She put these to good use when faced with the possibility of her men slaughtered and her home ruined by David's armed and angry men.

Abigail was approachable; a servant came to her about impending danger. She was resourceful, taking charge of the situation rather than letting it develop. She acted bravely; probably fearing a meeting with a vindictive band of men, see verses 21 and 22. Perhaps in womanly guile, she hoped her beauty would give her some reprieve.

Although Nabal's actions had placed them in jeopardy, Abigail took blame upon herself, thereby saving her men folk and her foolish husband. In seeking David's forgiveness, she presented him with the long view beyond the anger of the moment.

Abigail was devoted to God, mentioning the Lord's name seven times in her plea to David. She probably believed that God would eventually vindicate David and give him the throne. She warned him not to jeopardize his future peace of mind by senseless slaughter or any wrongdoing.

As David conceded to her wisdom, he became aware of Abigail's virtues as well as her beauty, and when Nabal died a few days later David asked her to marry him—which she did.

Prayer: O God, we are encouraged by the resourcefulness of Abigail in a highly stressful situation. Help us to act as wisely, and as husbands, to recognize similar abilities in our wives.

WEEK TWENTY-FOUR: WEEKEND

Finding God's Will

I met a Christian young man who worked for a local concrete company. He relayed his desire to find a place of service to God, and his current work was simply a parking spot awaiting a call to "ministry." He failed to realize that his work at that moment *was* his place of ministry.

Once we become Christians, our whole life is a place of service to God, wherever we may be.

A young lady came to our church from Montreal. She was anxious to ensure God's will for her life, but she had a dilemma. She had prayed for God to guide her decision to move, but did not feel that she had received a specific answer. Eventually she moved anyway, fearing that she had missed or ignored God's direction.

I suggested that perhaps God had left the decision to her; he could use her equally in Montreal or any other city she chose.

The more mature in the faith we become, the less likely God is to direct every decision we make, we are no longer children; we should be able to know God's will in most situations, Romans 12:1–2. God can still intervene to give us specific direction if he desires, as with Paul's experience in Acts 16:6–10.

If we commit ourselves to God's direction, from then on God's will for us is wherever we find ourselves—including our particular marriage and family, despite, or perhaps because of its difficulties.

But remember, being in God's will does not necessarily mean hardship. He will more often call us to those things we enjoy because he has gifted us for them—including the joy of marriage.

Prayer: Dear Father, we desire to grow continually in the faith and know your will. Guide us to those people and places that can lead us in that direction.

Loving Your Enemy

Read: 2 Samuel 1:1–18

Then David and all the men with him . . . mourned and wept and fasted
till evening for Saul and his son Jonathan. 2 Samuel 1:11–12.

David's love for Saul and his son Jonathan, led to his
protracted mourning for them at their death. David
had not only refused to raise his hand against Saul,
but held to account the man who claimed to have killed
him.

In actual fact, Saul had committed suicide when
critically wounded rather than falling into the hands of the
Philistines, 1 Samuel 30:2–4, but David was not to know
this until later. David found no pleasure in the death of Saul
and his sons, although it gave him access to the throne of
Israel.

It defies human logic for David to act this way. Most
people would consider it normal to be thankful Saul was
dead and God had fulfilled his promise to David. Some
might even persuade David to rejoice at these events.

Although David was an ordinary person, he had an
extraordinary understanding of God's character, sensing
the way God thinks, and seeking to be like him. He was a
man after God's own heart.

Enduring difficult relationships is not easy; it can make
or break us. Whether it does or not depends on our choice.
But that choice is not so much a necessary determination
to see the relationship through, but rather finding our
resources in God.

Depending on our own strength may fail us; enduring
strength is found in dependence upon God—increasing our
knowledge of him through his Word, and learning we can
trust him in every situation.

Prayer: Dear Lord, grant us not only the patience to endure
fractious situations, but also to remain true to those that
may create them.

WEEK TWENTY-FIVE: TUESDAY

United under Godly Leadership

Read: 2 Samuel 2:1–11; 5:1–5

The elders of Israel had come to King David at Hebron . . . and
they anointed David king over Israel. 2 Samuel 5:4.

T he split between Judah and Israel had its roots long
before David. While there does not appear to be
animosity between the two prior to David's time, they
were frequently referred to separately.

Judah was the one that would provide royalty, Genesis
49:8–10. Even in Joshua's time and during the period of the
Judges the two were listed separately in the battles to
subdue the land, Joshua 11:21 and Judges 10:9.

After the death of Saul the split began to show itself,
Judah claiming David as king in Hebron, and Israel placing
a son of Saul, Ish-Bosheth, on the throne of Israel. Yet the
history of Israel was then—and we believe still is—
overseen by God himself.

God had promised an anointed David would rule Israel
and David succeeded to the kingship of the whole country.
Now both Judah and Israel united behind their new
commander-in-chief, David, 1 Samuel 18:16.

Marriage is God's idea and plan for most of us. The
break-up of a marriage can have two causes: the wrong
choice of partner before marriage, or failure to understand
or follow God's working plan for marriage.

We identified earlier the servanthood basis for marriage
ensuring the primary goal is for each partner's wellbeing,
desires, and growth.

Both the choice of marriage partners and the
subsequent success of marriage depend on knowing God's
will for it, just as David knew God's will for Israel and
Judah.

Prayer: Heavenly Father, we would be like David, knowing your
promise for us and particularly your desire for marriage.
May your Word and the inspiration of your Spirit be our
guide.

Respect

Read: 2 Samuel 6:1–23

When [Michal] saw King David leaping and dancing before the Lord, she despised him in her heart. 2 Samuel 6:16.

Once David was secure on the throne, he wished to honour God by placing the Ark of the Covenant in a place of prominence. This would signify the Lord's kingship and rule over himself and the people. But David's first experience in returning the Ark was a fearful one.

Uzziah tried to save the Ark from damage, but he violated God's directions for managing it, Numbers 4:5–6, 15. Uzziah's death was a dreadful reminder of the gravity of according honour to God.

Michal's behaviour is harder to assess. She was not by his side rejoicing in the return of the Ark. Perhaps the procession was for men only, or she was sceptical of the whole affair. Her outburst at David for his perceived frivolity appeared to signify resentment, perhaps of his succession to her father's throne or the adulation given the Lord, see verse 21.

Her attitude had changed considerably from the early days of marriage when she protected him, and the barrenness that followed today's events suggests God's displeasure.

The passage reminds us of two things. First, that status and comfort can undermine the sense of our need of God. Power easily corrupts and perhaps her prominence as queen affected Michal's attitude. Her manner was condescending and judgmental, which earned David's rebuke.

Second, David accorded Michal respect. He was careful to state the truth, referring only to himself and his conduct with no censure of his wife. We must treat our partners with love and respect in all situations; God is the eventual judge.

Prayer: O Lord, may we always treat our partners with the respect you have accorded us, in spite of our sin.

ANN AND BRYAN NORFORD

WEEK TWENTY-FIVE: THURSDAY

An Enduring Promise

Read: 2 Samuel 7:1–17

"Your house and your kingdom will endure forever before me;
your throne will be established forever." 2 Samuel 7:16.

Today's reading is a reminder of the permanence of the covenant God made with Abraham and his descendents by its renewal to King David a full millennium later. It reiterated the greatness of the nation and a secure dwelling place for Israel.

David wanted to build a "house" for God—the temple that Solomon would eventually build. But God promised David he would build David's "house"—that is his lineage—and his throne would be established for ever through a son born to him.

It was through Solomon the throne was established. Although the monarchy ceased at the exile some five hundred years later, the lineage continued to the time of Jesus, the Son of David, who will eventually return to claim his throne.

In the intervening time between Solomon and the exile, the nation of Israel "divorced" into two separate kingdoms. David's descendents reigned over the southern portion known as Judah, while usurpers reigned over the northern tribes called Israel.

Some of you will have been through the misery of divorce; the opportunity of reconciliation is over, the damage done to any children of the marriage irreversible, no source of healing is apparent, and remorse and guilt remain.

Yet, although there is no marriage in heaven, Matthew 22:30, it is a place where not only our sin, but the effects of our sin will be erased. God will bring to completion all things that we left undone or broken, and we will rejoice in God's solution to our failures.

Prayer: O Father, we rejoice in your completion of all things through Jesus Christ, and anticipate with joy the time when you will restore all things.

150

Risks of Adultery

Read: 2 Samuel 11:2–13

Then [Bathsheba] went back home. The woman conceived and sent word to David, saying, "I am pregnant." 2 Samuel 11:4–5.

By this time, David was secure on the throne of Israel. This gave David disadvantages in dealing with the temptation Bathsheba's bathing provoked. First, while his armies were away he had spare time, and the devil found work for idle eyes. Second, neither he nor Bathsheba could ever keep their actions secret as they both communicated through others.

As king, David's word was final; he could command Bathsheba to come to him, and it would be dangerous to defy the king.

But her bathing in full view of the palace suggests an interest in the relationship; she might have seen David's walks on the palace roof. But even if her behaviour was seductive, it did not absolve David of his responsibility. As king he had the greater influence.

David could have foreseen the consequences, but the heat of passion rarely sees the big picture. The fact that Bathsheba had just purified herself from her period, Leviticus 12:2, indicates she was not pregnant when she slept with David. Uriah, her husband, was away with the army; the pregnancy was David's.

This forced David into further deception to cover up his sin. He brought Uriah back to sleep with Bathsheba, but Uriah's devotion to his duty foiled that plan.

Like all deception, David entrenched himself deeper with each move—even to greater sin.

Prayer: O Father, we know the power of seduction can blind us to its effects. Keep our eyes open to the risks of illicit sexual liaisons through continual intimacy with you.

Adultery: Pleasure or Misery?

What are the reasons for adultery? Frequently it is an escape from the challenges of home life; pleasure without the accompanying worries. It may be a targeted seduction, or simple adventurism.

Sexual fulfillment and release always produces a sense of pleasure. David's moments of pleasure led into a lifetime of distress, for himself and others. The Bible is clear that David's woes were a consequence of his sin.

Friction which results from infidelity is obvious. Betrayal, anger, and loss of trust by the wife of a philanderer are alone sufficient to cause tension. The variety of attitudes by the husband, from outright denial or excuses to utter remorse and self-reproach can only add to the conflict.

Further, the affair might still drag on after discovery and even if it doesn't, the wife's loss can trigger a long period of mourning countered by the impatience of the husband. Often there is no reconciliation and the marriage breaks up, or it continues in an uneasy co-existence with the wife using guilt to hold the husband hostage.

Infidelity creates a near death experience for marriage, so it is remarkable that many marriages survive and become meaningful for both partners again. Most of David's life is a remarkable record of his source of survival; we find that he never lost his confidence in God, and his psalms are a legacy to us of his victories in times of difficulty.

David found contentment, although he had to face the consequences of his sin, in God's grace toward him and the forgiveness he received. David's example can bring both comfort and strength to continue after we sin.

Prayer: O God, we can only marvel at your grace toward us. Your forgiveness and reconciliation removes our sin, gives us hope, and the joy of restoration.

Adultery Escalates

Read: 2 Samuel 11:14–27

"Put Uriah in the front line where the fighting is fiercest. Then
withdraw from him so he will be struck down and die."
2 Samuel 11:15.

If trickery did not work to mask David's adultery, perhaps murder would. This says little for those around David, particularly Joab, entrusted with his protection.

Joab was violent and self serving, killing rivals for the position of commander-in-chief of David's army, and eventually killing David's son, Absalom, against David's wishes, 2 Samuel 18:9–15.

Uriah's death left Bathsheba free to marry David, bringing her pregnancy into the marriage, and possibly saving David's reputation.

David's position as king gave him opportunity to use murder to conceal his adultery, but most adultery is unlikely to lead to such drastic escalation.

When entering an affair we may feel we can manage the risks, but unknown complications are always a threat. Adultery strikes at the heart of marriage; we cannot assume our marriage will endure the threat of divorce.

Uriah was an innocent victim paying the price for David's sin. Others will pay for our infidelity; particularly children, who suffer the results of likely marriage failure.

As I write this, news reports tell of a Toronto man who threw his five year old daughter from a highway overpass so his wife would not get custody of her. Miraculously the child survived.

The results of a failed marriage which we *can* imagine are serious enough, without the unforeseen costs of our folly.

Prayer: O Lord, adultery seems like a harmless fling and easily
seduces us. Help us to keep in focus the eventual
consequences and damage.

WEEK TWENTY-SIX: TUESDAY

Honest Remorse

Read: 2 Samuel 12:1–14

Then Nathan said to David, "You are the man!" 2 Samuel 12:7.

After reading this passage, it is difficult to see why God considered David a man after his own heart, 1 Samuel 13:14. By our judgment, his sin was greater than Saul's and, like Saul, he did all he could to cover it up until it was revealed to him by the prophet Nathan. What was the difference between Saul and David that condemned Saul but commended David to God?

We have seen how Saul covered up his sin, rationalizing it away when discovered. Saul's confession was not one of true penitence, but rather regret at discovery, further marred by excuses and an underlying concern for his reputation, 1 Samuel 15:24–30.

David by contrast admitted his sin, gave no excuses, and showed true repentance; see Psalm 51 for his prayer of contrition. It is this honesty in the face of factual accusation that draws God's response of mercy and forgiveness, Psalm 51:17.

True honesty requires courage. David's honesty legitimized Bathsheba—both she and her next son Solomon were part of the lineage of Jesus. However, the child of their illegitimate union did *not* survive—a further victim of David's adultery.

Too often, dishonesty is easiest in our marriage relationships because we can manipulate the facts, confuse the detail and often force our opinions upon our partners.

This makes cowardice easier, courage unnecessary and, we hope, avoids unpleasant consequences. But it also makes for an uneasy and distrustful co-existence.

Prayer: O God, help us be honest before you and others about our sin, so we can be cleansed and walk with you.

Consequences of Adultery

Read: 2 Samuel 13:1–21

Then Amnon hated her with intense hatred. In fact, he hated her more than he had loved her. 2 Samuel 13:15.

Although the Lord took away David's sin, it did not absolve him from further consequences. David's household would now be the centre of strife, not peace, which he experienced until his death.

To begin, Amnon raped his half sister Tamar, Absalom's full sister. Later in the chapter Absalom killed Amnon in revenge.

The rest of David's life is a litany of the struggles David faced, mostly stirred up by Absalom. Thus forgiveness did not mean that David "got away with it." He lost the son of his adultery; now it created friction in his household.

The prophecies of Nathan, 2 Samuel 12:11–12 were coming true. His son Absalom ravished David's wives and concubines in full view of the people, 2 Samuel 16:20–22. David found himself fleeing from Israel as Absalom increased his following among the people; even David's throne was in jeopardy for a while.

But as destructive as adultery is to our partner and others, the greater damage is our sin against God: Nathan's rebuke to David was that in his sin he *despised* God, 2 Samuel 12:10.

As Christians, we should be concerned about the effect on God. As his representatives, it sullies his reputation, fostering lies about him to those around us: if we are unfaithful to our partners, then perhaps God is not to be trusted either.

Always remember that a sin against another—above all a partner—*is* a sin against God.

Prayer: Dear Heavenly Father, we thank you there is forgiveness for our sin, even that of adultery. Give us strength to remain faithful to you even if we suffer the consequences of our sin.

155

WEEK TWENTY-SIX: THURSDAY

Perceiving Conspiracy

Read: 2 Samuel 15:1–16

The conspiracy gained strength, and Absalom's following kept on increasing. 2 Samuel 15:12.

R elationships with adult children have their challenges, none more so than those experienced by David with his sons. We noted the strife that accompanied David's reign after his adultery with Bathsheba.

David banished Absalom after he killed Amnon. But David longed for him during the five year banishment from the court, 2 Samuel 13:39, and finally reinstated him, 2 Samuel 14:33. But despite his acceptance by David, Absalom continued to oppose his father for the rest of his life.

Absalom was an attractive man with a vigorous head of hair that shed five pounds when cut yearly. Early in his life he married and had three sons and a daughter, 2 Samuel 14:25-26. On his return to court, he solicited support from those coming to Jerusalem with complaints.

He became the charmer that offered better time and compensation for the complainants than David. Over four years Absalom seduced the people of Israel from his father and set himself up as a rival king to his father.

What was David doing during that time? He must have known what was going on, but his love for Absalom probably blinded him to his son's deception. Eventually David fled from Absalom to avoid bloodshed rather than fight to save his throne, but that gave rise to a period of confrontation and war anyway.

It is easy to let our love for our children blind us to their faults. As they grow older, those faults will have greater impact and more grievous results.

Prayer: O Lord, you have loved us, and you know we love our children. Give us awareness of their actions, and wisdom to warn and restrain them when necessary.

The Sin of the Father . . .

Read: 2 Samuel 16:15–23

They pitched a tent for Absalom on the roof, and he lay with his father's concubines in the sight of all Israel. 2 Samuel 16:22.

Absalom had no sense of repentance for the slaying of Amnon, nor respect for David's forgiveness and reinstatement of him. David had foresight enough to plant Hushai into Absalom's court as a spy. Ahithophel, until then a trusted advisor to David, turned himself over to Absalom, hoping to finish on the winning side.

Ahithophel knew that Absalom sleeping publicly with David's concubines would be obnoxious to the Israelites. They would then consider enmity sufficiently entrenched between Absalom and David to reduce the possibility of reconciliation, always possible from David's history.

Absalom fulfilled the prophecy of Nathan against David, 2 Samuel 12:11, sending his father the most rebellious message yet. David, unwilling to fight against Absalom, nonetheless realized he needed to muster his troops for defence. Hushai's subversive advice to Absalom gave David time to recover from the flight, hear Absalom's plans, and prepare for battle, 2 Samuel 17:14–16.

This reading brings up the problem of responsibility for fulfilling prophecy. Is any behaviour that brings about fulfillment of God's will acceptable? David was responsible for his sins of adultery with Bathsheba and the murder of her husband.

But Absalom was also responsible for his actions, just as Judas was responsible for his betrayal of Jesus, Luke 22:22. Our children can hold us accountable for our failures as parents, but they cannot hold us responsible for their actions when they reach the age of understanding.

Prayer: Dear Lord, we may be holding grudges against our parents, and even using them as an excuse for our own sin. Free us as we forgive our parents, and confess of our own sin.

157

WEEK TWENTY-SIX: WEEKEND

Politics and Cinderella

David had to balance politics and love; he was king and husband and both positions had their challenges. The history of politics is a sordid tale of the power hungry manipulating nations for their own benefit and adulation; of dictators forcing ruthless rule over exploited people.

In contrast, the first love Michal had for David and his remarkable relationship with God, 1 Samuel 18:28, is closer to the love story of Cinderella and seems very different from the politics David needed to practise.

Yet politics and our favourite love stories like Cinderella suggest a common thread to both. Behind those stories and books like Utopia lurks the idea of "Once upon a time . . . happily ever after." They reflect a perfect love and living that our hearts yearn for and our best experiences imply.

Even politics arises from the notion that there is an ideal to strive for beyond the ravages of earthly life; a thirsty longing that wrenches our hearts but is never fully satisfied. As maidens dream of perfect love, so men envision the ideal society and strive for it.

Most politicians probably start off with the desire to better their communities, but easily succumb to the subterfuge, manipulation and compromise that ambition seems to require. If we could read the rest of the story of Cinderella and her prince, it seems probable we might find a degeneration of their love into self-serving manipulation.

But neither of these evidences of fallen human nature should blind us to the desire God has placed in our hearts for the perfection that we can only find in him. If God completes the yearning of the human soul, then he can provide the best that marriage offers also.

Prayer: Dear Lord, we thank you for the yearning of our hearts for you. We pray you will keep that longing alive for the rest of our lives.

Misplaced Trust

Read: 2 Samuel 18:31 to 19:7

For the whole army the victory that day was turned into mourning, because on that day the troops heard it said, "The king is grieving for his son." 2 Samuel 19:2.

Davíd was aware that Joab was a violent man, taking whatever actions he needed to advance his own ends. Leaders often continue to employ such men despite their failings because those very faults support the leaders in their duties.

Joab had no scruples; an asset in war, but Joab's violent passion deceived David. David gave unmistakable instructions to preserve Absalom's life, but Joab took personal revenge on Absalom, killing him in cold blood, 2 Samuel 18:5 and 14.

David was devastated. His cries: "O my son Absalom! My son, my son Absalom! If only I had died instead of you—O Absalom, my son, my son!" ring with the pain that anyone losing a loved one can feel.

His misery and grief were so intense, his army, which had won against the insurgents, returned subdued as if ashamed of defeat. Joab; the one responsible for David's distress, now with typical coldness, berated him for his grieving.

We may fault David for his favouritism of Absalom, but we can sympathize with his loss of a son. But the loss of a child to drugs, crime, and general antisocial or destructive behaviour can be greater, as the grief is ongoing and may last for years.

In his distress, David remained faithful to God, and even showed magnanimity to those who berated him during his flight from Absalom, 2 Samuel 19:21–23. However great our loss and grief, it can only be worsened by a flight from God instead of drawing closer to him.

Prayer: Almighty God, turn the hearts of our sons and daughters back to you. Holy Spirit, guide them into all truth, and give us wisdom and sensitivity to their concerns.

159

WEEK TWENTY-SEVEN: TUESDAY

A Mother's Love

Read: 2 Samuel 21:1–10

From the beginning of the harvest till the rain poured down from the heavens on the bodies, she did not let the birds of the air touch them by day or the wild animals by night. 2 Samuel 21:10.

The basis of this story is punishment for Saul's sin in attempting to destroy the Gibeonites after Joshua had promised to spare them, Joshua chapter 9. The subsequent death of seven sons of Saul ended the three year famine.

However, our interest here is with Rizpah, the mother of two of Saul's sons. She defended the bodies of her sons, slain and laid out on a hillside, from bird and animal predators. She stayed from the "first days of the harvest" until "the rain poured down from the heavens on the bodies."

Probably a lengthy period, but the rain signaled the end of the famine and satisfaction of God's judgment. For Rizpah, the task was daunting, unable to sleep day or night, continually fighting wild animals and birds that would seek to devour the flesh of her sons. In her eyes, although her sons died in judgment, their bodies were not part of the bargain.

Scripture typifies God's love for his people by the love of a mother for her children. When Israel complained that God has forsaken them, Isaiah replied God is less likely to forget them than a mother is to forget the child at her breast, Isaiah 49:15.

When we feel that God has ceased to hear us, the story of Rizpah and our love for our own children reminds us that God's faithfulness is greater than ours and he will be faithful to us even in our darkest times.

Prayer: O Lord, we rejoice in the love you have poured out upon us and the reminder of your faithfulness to us always.

WEEK TWENTY-SEVEN: WEDNESDAY

Advice for Parents

Read: 1 Kings 2:1–12

Walk in [God's] ways, and keep his decrees and commands . . .
so that you may prosper in all you do and wherever you go.
1 Kings 2:3.

D avid gave final advice to the son who was to succeed him later. The passage is in two sections: the first regarding the importance of Solomon's devotion to God, the second with unfinished business.

David failed to deal with Joab's crimes during his reign, so Joab had contributed to David's difficulties and killed Absalom. On his deathbed, David realized the folly of not dealing with violence himself and the need of judgment for Joab.

But the greater importance was urging Solomon to remain committed to God. Whatever else needed attention, David's first concern was Solomon's observance of God's requirements to ensure the nation's future.

The promise of future prosperity and kings in David's line depended on the obedience of his descendants. Although Solomon started well, he failed to heed David's advice, and after his death the kingdom split for 500 years.

David's advice to Solomon is also primary advice for us to give our children, youth, or adults. Solomon started well but finished badly. If we have children who started badly, they have the opportunity to finish well.

Franklin Graham rebelled against his father, Billy Graham, for many years until, as he said: "I became sick and tired of being sick and tired." He became a foremost proponent for the faith.

Solomon himself said, "Train a child in the way he should go, and when he is old he will not turn from it," Proverbs 22:6.

Prayer: O Father, we need all the wisdom you can provide to guide our children. Help us to be examples of faithful readers and followers of your Word.

161

Godly Parents' Advice

Read: 1 Kings 3:4–15

"If you walk in my ways and obey my statutes and commands as David your father did, I will give you a long life." 1 Kings 3:14.

Solomon had many advantages in following the faith of his father. He had David's example to follow and the power to ensure his nation would follow it. In addition, God granted him an extraordinary gift of wisdom.

His admission of inadequacy to fulfill his duties gained for him this gift of God's grace. But his greatest asset was the faith of his father. God promised Solomon control of the kingdom throughout his lifetime specifically based on David's faith, 1 Kings 11:11–13.

But Solomon had weaknesses. He had absolute power, subduing the nations around him and ushering in the longest time of peace in Israel's history. It was easy to assume that he had accomplished this himself, thus reducing his reliance upon God.

The corruption of power is the belief in a personal invincibility and flawless decision making; a sort of divine right to rule. World leaders, as opposite as Adolph Hitler and Margaret Thatcher, both succumbed to this delusion.

If Solomon's greatest asset was the faith of his father, his greatest downfall was not following his father's advice. Solomon had moments of great spiritual awareness, 1 Kings 8:25–27, yet finally succumbed to the desire for many foreign women, 1 Kings 11:1–4, who brought pagan ideas into his kingdom.

Solomon tolerated and supported these, watering down his faithfulness to God. If you are a believer, beware of marriage to a non-Christian, for statistics suggest that a relationship between a Christian and an unsaved partner usually favours the latter.

Prayer: Heavenly Father, it's too easy to think we have achieved success in our own strength. Guard us from the temptation to neglect you from a sense of our own mastery.

Our Faithfulness is our Legacy

Read: 1 Kings 11:1–13

As Solomon grew old, his wives turned his heart after other gods, and his heart was not fully devoted to the Lord his God, as the heart of David his father had been. 1 Kings 11:4.

Solomon can be likened to Saul; he had a lot "going for him." His early life showed great devotion to the Lord who gave him great wisdom. Both men were seduced away from their devotion; Saul by pride and plunder, Solomon by his wives.

Yet God continued to bless Solomon "for the sake of David your father." Solomon's downfall was not simply marrying the wrong wives. These foreign wives brought their gods with them, and Solomon, in true liberal tolerance, simply added them to what became a pantheon of gods which included the Lord, the God of Israel.

Acceptance of these gods led Solomon to worship them, and God predicted the tearing of the kingdom from him. But the separation would not take place until Solomon's death. Why the difference? The unwavering faith of David, despite his failures, provided a legacy of security for Solomon, including the promise of a continuous lineage of Solomon's descendants.

God looks on the heart, even in our times of relapse. But our faithfulness or lack of it can have significant impact upon our families—partners, children and later descendants. It's not just a matter of example for our children who know and see us, as important as that is, but our devotion to God can directly affect generations that follow after us.

For God shows his "love to a thousand generations of those who love me and keep my commandments," Exodus 20:6.

Prayer: O Lord, help us to remember that our greatest gift to our children is faithfulness to you.

WEEK TWENTY-SEVEN: WEEKEND

The Real Gift

Things as gifts are too often apologies for gifts. A true gift is a gift of ourselves for which things make a poor substitute. Of course, gifts given as remembrances at special times are meaningful, but the presence of the giver has greater worth.

Two of our daughters live at a distance, and they send us cards on our birthdays with welcome sentiments. But it is the phone call, the desire to speak with us, to be with us for a while, that we appreciate most.

The gift, as a substitute for love, is probably seen at its most destructive in the relationship between parents and children. The absent father, whose work precludes sufficient time with his children but showers them with gifts and money, may well leave his children empty and rebellious.

Too often they become the "spoiled brats" that plague our society to the astonishment of their parents who "gave them everything they wanted." Everything, that is, except a gift of themselves.

For the real gift is time: time to listen or play, time to give advice, rejoice in accomplishment, complete a task together, or simply be together. Our time is a real gift because it is limited. The minutes or hours we spend with and for another is time we will never have again.

Furthermore, how can our children "catch" our faith if we are never with them? They will absorb other people's ideas easily enough.

The years that our children are with us, difficult and interminable though they may seem at times, eventually pass all too quickly. It's the time we failed to be with them that may haunt us the most.

Prayer: Dear Father, help us to manage our time so we may give ourselves to our children, the greatest earthly gift you have given us.

Trusting God in the Darkness

Read: 1 Kings 11:26–40

Jeroboam son of Nebat rebelled against the king. He was one of Solomon's officials.1 Kings 11:26.

God chose Jeroboam to lead the part of the nation of Israel God would take away from Solomon's son. God would be with Jeroboam, give him a lineage similar to David's, although not outlasting it. But that was dependent on Jeroboam's obedience to God's laws and commands.

Subsequent chapters of the First Book of Kings show that Jeroboam was not obedient. That God chose someone prepared to rebel against the anointed king is significant; he would likely rebel against God himself.

Why would God choose a rebellious individual to rule Israel's northern tribes? As an official of Solomon, Jeroboam had knowledge of the requirements for kingship, and also the requirements of godly rule from the earlier years of Solomon's reign. But surely God's foreknowledge of Jeroboam's future should have precluded his selection for king.

That is like saying that Jesus should have avoided choosing Judas Iscariot as a disciple. We know Judas' selection fulfilled the greater will of God for our salvation. God's plans are more far reaching than our limited vision, for Israel's future as well as our personal ones.

Two principles follow from this. In the bleakest of times—as Israel had yet to experience—we are still in God's hands. His plans, obscured for a time, are still in progress and under his control.

But like Jeroboam, calling into marriage is not a carte blanche for our desires. If we fail to follow God's requirements for maintaining our devotion to him and serving our partner, we place our union in jeopardy.

Prayer: O Lord, your ways are beyond our finite knowledge. Help us trust you in the darkest times of life.

165

Marriage is for Service

Read: 1 Kings 12:1–24

"If today you will be a servant to these people and serve them and give them a favorable answer, they will always be your servants."
1 Kings 12:7.

Ahijah's prophecy to Jeroboam motivated him to seek a reason to take over the ten northern tribes. Rehoboam foolishly gave him one. Especially noteworthy was the advice of Rehoboam's elders to make his reign one of service to his people, but he preferred to rule as a tyrant and lost the northern tribes.

This story raises questions. If prophecy fixes the actions, then are the perpetrators of the actions no longer accountable? Don't they simply fulfill a predetermined role? How can foretelling future actions avoid this trap?

Luke had no problem with this dilemma; he quoted Jesus who held Judas accountable for his actions although he fulfilled God's plan, Luke 22:22.

The answer lies in God's foreknowledge. We look back to choices made freely but now fixed in history. Similarly, God looks to a fixed future and uses choices freely made then to accomplish his plans. This, of course, takes into account the influence that prophecy may have on those free choices.

Wrong assumptions about how marriage works are frequently behind divorce. Rehoboam assumed the people were there to serve him and not vice versa, while Jeroboam assumed a right dealt him by prophecy; the separation was inevitable.

Are your expectations of marriage based on what you expect to receive, or to ensure your rights within the marriage? Your marriage is probably in jeopardy already, unless you reckon marriage is a service to which you plan to give more than fifty percent.

Prayer: Please Lord, forgive each of us for expecting the other partner to fulfill us, rather than using the opportunity serve our partner as you have served us.

WEEK TWENTY-EIGHT: WEDNESDAY

Yielding to Duress

Read: 1 Kings 21:1–16

Jezebel his wife said, "Is this how you act as king over Israel? . . .
I'll get you the vineyard of Naboth the Jezreelite." 1 Kings 21:7.

A review of the Bible's women must include Jezebel, whose name is synonymous with seductive behaviour, Revelation 2:20–23.

Jezebel was from Tyre in modern day Lebanon and brought to Israel to marry Ahab, king of Israel, in a treaty to secure his northern borders.

As with Solomon's similar marriages, this direct defiance of God who promised to be Israel's protector, wrought havoc within Israel.

Jezebel was strong-willed, bringing with her four hundred and fifty prophets of Baal and another four hundred prophets of the goddess Ashtoreth. She claimed worship of these gods equal to the Lord, which brought her into conflict with Elijah, 1 Kings 16:30–33, 18:19, and 19:1–2.

She was forceful and fanatical for her gods, killing the Lord's prophets when they opposed her, 1 Kings 18:13–14. Our reading today shows how ruthless she was in gaining her own ends and those of Ahab.

But of particular note in today's reading is the relationship between Ahab and Jezebel. She considered him weak and indecisive, and took charge of Ahab's dealings, so was literally the power behind the throne. Jezebel could be the self-directed model of some feminists.

But although Jezebel dictated much of Ahab's rule, Scripture indicates that he was still responsible for his decisions, 1 Kings 21:25.

God will still hold us responsible for our actions even if we allow duress of a dictatorial partner to coerce us into ungodly actions.

Prayer: Heavenly Father, may we be faithful to you, even under pressure from our partner or in our efforts to please him or her.

WEEK TWENTY-EIGHT: THURSDAY

God's Unexpected Supply

Read: 2 Kings 4:1–7

When all the jars were full, she said to her son, "Bring me another one." But he replied, "There is not a jar left." Then the oil stopped flowing. 2 Kings 4:6.

Readings for the next two days are about Elisha's care for two mothers and their children. Today's story displays the nature of God in looking after his people. This woman was the widow of a former priest whom Elisha knew had "revered the Lord."

Because her husband was dead she was destitute, and the only way of paying her creditors was to sell her two sons into slavery. It could be up to fifty years before her sons were eligible for release in the year of Jubilee, Leviticus 25:47–55. So she pleaded with Elisha for help.

What help could she have expected? Perhaps Elisha could find the money to pay her creditors, or persuade her creditors to forgo her debt. But God often supplies in ways we cannot foresee.

The solution is one that few would have imagined— pouring oil from a bottomless jug into containers to sell and pay her debt.

People in full time Christian ministry often suffer financial loss as a result of their labour. Those who pastor small churches, missionaries with inadequate support or indigenous pastors in poor countries are constantly anxious about food, shelter, clothing, and education for their children.

Yet they can tell of ways in which God has provided; often in simple ways, but sometimes by extraordinary means and from remarkable sources.

This weekend's commentary provides an example of God's provision for our family during a time of inadequate income.

Prayer: O Lord, you know it is difficult for us to trust under extreme circumstances. May your Spirit increase our faith in those times.

Children: A Gift from the Lord

Read: 2 Kings 4:8–17

"About this time next year," Elisha said, "you will hold a son in your arms." 2 Kings 4:16.

Today's story recounts the second woman Elisha was able to help, but also illustrates the way in which God supplied Elisha's needs. The woman and her husband were wealthy, and provided room and board for Elisha when his journeys took him their way.

They were God fearing and desired to use their resources for the Lord's service. Although the priesthood would normally have provided a salary, Elisha's tenure was during a time of apostasy, and salary was probably a luxury.

He wondered aloud to Gehazi his servant what he could do for the woman in gratitude for her generosity. Finding she was childless, he sought God for a child for her, and promised she would bear a son in the spring.

However, the woman's response showed she had doubts about the possibility and worried that Elisha was raising dubious hopes. Little did she know the later tragedy that awaited her.

In Old Testament times large families were a sign of the Lord's blessing on the family, and absence of children suggested God's displeasure. As we now know—and as Scripture often suggests—childlessness was frequently an accident of nature that God reversed out of compassion for the affected women.

While there are many resources to assist in overcoming barrenness, we recognize that God alone is the author of life. So it is critical that we seek God for children, for ourselves and others who fail to have children.

Prayer: Dear Father, we realize the tragedy of barrenness, even in our current culture. You, Lord, are the author of life, and we pray for ourselves and our loved ones for the joy of children from you.

169

WEEK TWENTY-EIGHT: WEEKEND

In Time of Need

Ann and I felt the call of God into full time ministry which eventually culminated in pastoring two churches in Burnaby, British Columbia. We decided to take full time training and I attended Regent College in Vancouver for over two years to achieve a Master of Divinity degree, and Ann provided indispensable support and assistance. But with a small child beginning school and the need for a home, we ran short of money.

God provided for us in two surprising ways. One of the instructors at the college moved out of a house he had rented and suggested we might rent it. The owners were Christians and were willing to rent it to us for a reasonable figure. We had a house for sale in Alberta, and Ann was led to a buyer who bought it privately, sight unseen, just as our funds dried up.

The money we obtained from the sale enabled us to invest in guaranteed investment certificates for two years. The timing of that investment was remarkable. Interest rates in 1980 had climbed to record highs, mortgage rates reaching twenty percent and higher.

We received interest of over sixteen percent, but the day after that investment rates began a free fall to much lower levels. We had received a peak yield from our investment.

With money Ann was able to make by running her own small secretarial business and over six hundred dollars per month return on our investment, we had sufficient funds to see us through our time at Regent College. God provided for our entire period of financial need.

Prayer: Heavenly Father, thank you for providing for us through our lives, and especially in the difficult times. Help us to remember always you are our provider.

Grief for a Child

Read: 2 Kings 4:18–37

"Did I ask you for a son, my lord?" she said. "Didn't I tell you,
'Don't raise my hopes'?" 2 Kings 4:28.

Ason was born to the Shunammite woman as predicted by Elisha, but died later as a result of a brain disease, perhaps a tumour or aneurism. It is one thing to mourn childlessness, but another to grieve the loss of a long awaited child.

The passage reveals her distress, as she refused to talk to Gehazi and wept at the feet of Elisha. She felt that Elisha's intercession for a son was a bitter hoax, bringing her greater misery and she said so.

Elisha responded immediately. Gehazi was instructed to tuck his cloak in his belt—a sign he was to run—and take immediate action for the boy until Elisha's arrival. Elisha pleaded with God on behalf of the woman for a second time; this time for restoration of the boy's life.

Elisha took what action he could, seeking to revive the boy by breathing mouth to mouth, and warming the small body with his own. But life, whether in the womb or on a death bed belongs to God; God restored the child's life.

Many parents have seen their children healed from disease and restored to the family. But it's not always so. Children's graves are the most tragic places in a graveyard.

We recall words engraved on one tombstone: "For a while in our arms, forever in our hearts." Those words would remain in the parents' hearts for life

The loss of a child will remain for a lifetime. The one consoling fact, in the midst of grief for a Christian, is that the child will forever be in the arms of God.

Prayer: O Lord, we grieve at the death of any child. May we continue to be compassionate, not just at death but over time, to those who suffer this loss.

171

WEEK TWENTY-NINE: TUESDAY

Living in Conflict

Read: 2 Kings 14:1–15

Judah was routed by Israel, and every man fled to his home.
2 Kings 14:13.

During the two hundred years following Solomon's death, Judah and Israel lived in uneasy co-existence in the same land, frequently fighting each other and occasionally forming allies against common enemies.

A general decline in the spiritual condition of each side aggravated the situation, despite a few kings that attempted to return the nations to God.

The two nations squabbled constantly. While both nations could with some justification point to Solomon as the original cause of their misery, they had within themselves the ability to change the course of history.

Ahijah the prophet told Jeroboam that his problems were from his own actions, 1 Kings 14:9–10. They stemmed from alternative, idolatrous worship in Samaria instead of allowing God's people to worship at the temple in Jerusalem. As long as Jeroboam continued to act that way, it prolonged the separation.

Like Israel, a fractious marriage is two individuals living in the same space, but living separate in various degrees of tension with one another. Divorce rarely happens all at once, but is the culmination of a series of disagreements over a period of time.

These disagreements probably have at the core a fundamental disagreement on the expectations of marriage and ignorance or denial of God's expectations. Seeking help to review and adjust expectations may provide direction for reconciliation when desired by both partners.

Prayer: Heavenly Father, guide us to sources of help that can lead us in your ways, for your ways are so much higher than ours.

Sin Reduces Choice

Read: 2 Kings 17:1–13 and 24

All this took place because the Israelites had sinned against the Lord their God. 2 Kings 17:7.

The northern nation of Israel was the first to go into captivity, with the inhabitants of the land transported away and the land resettled with exiles from other lands. The capital of Israel at that time was the city of Samaria. Samaria was also an alternate name for the northern kingdom of Israel.

Because resettlement took place in Samaria, the races mingled and the descendents rejected as true Israelites. When Judah later returned to the land, the residents of Samaria became the hated Samaritans.

The sin of Solomon, and Israel under his reign caused the separation of Israel and Judah. It continued because both nations practised the same sins, and separation became final as each nation turned away from the Lord.

In seeking freedom from the rule of God, Israel and Judah found themselves enslaved by the nations around them. Israel's decline was a loss of spiritual roots and continual skirmishing for possession of the land. Eventually the decline led to slavery and the choices for both nations were no longer theirs.

Marriage problems are firstly spiritual. Ignorance or a loss of faithfulness to God undermines the scriptural understanding of marriage.

Once one or both partners have lost the premise that marriage is service, only the demand for personal fulfillment remains, which may be sought outside the marriage compounding the separation. Subsequent fights and settlements may well decrease freedom of choice for both partners.

Prayer: O Lord, we pray for your Holy Spirit to open your Word to us that we might appreciate the beauty of the roles you give to each of us and wholeheartedly adopt them.

WEEK TWENTY-NINE: THURSDAY

Sin's Ultimate Misery

Read: 2 Kings 24:18 to 25:12

It was because of the Lord's anger that all this happened to Jerusalem and Judah, and in the end he thrust them from his presence. 2 Kings 24:20.

In 586 B.C. Jerusalem fell to Nebuchadnezzar, king of Babylon, the most powerful nation on earth. He executed the leaders of Judah and transported most of the people to Babylon. The poorest remained to till the ground and harvest the crops. Nebuchadnezzar burned the city, including the temple, and fifty years elapsed before any Jews returned to Jerusalem. Today, no temple stands on the site, only the Muslim Dome of the Rock.

This was a time of utmost misery for the Jews, the displaced inhabitants of Judah. Jeremiah records much of this in Lamentations, which records the desolation and despair of the time. Everything that expressed meaning and direction of life had gone; no familiar landmarks or faces, no meaningful work, all desire for life crushed; only grief, pain, and hopelessness filled the void.

The desperation experienced by Judah at this time reflects the grief and pain of marital conflict; the powerlessness when separation and divorce are inevitable. Everything meaningful in life appears in doubt, the present intolerable, and the future empty. It evokes inexpressible anguish for any children of the marriage as they try to make sense of the collapse of their only known world.

Are you thinking that separation is the only answer? If intolerable conditions give you no option, only you can make that decision. But there is wisdom in seeking advice, Proverbs 15:22, and any options for reconciliation are by far the best choice.

Prayer: O Lord, help us who are going through this distressing time of deteriorating relationship to see your plan of restoration for a constructive outcome.

174

The Point of No Return

Read: 2 Chronicles 36:15–23

They mocked God's messengers, despised his words, and scoffed at his prophets until the wrath of the Lord was aroused against his people and there was no remedy. 2 Chronicles 36:16.

Today's reading covers the same events as our last reading. This however, gives a summary of the reasons for the exile and also some hope of return.

Three prophets, Jeremiah, Ezekiel and Daniel and their extensive writings were the mainstay of the Jewish people through the difficult years of exile. Recognizing the context of the exile is necessary to understand these prophets.

The final editor of the two books of Chronicles provided Israel and Judah hope in their exile. Possibly added sometime later, verses 20 to 23 indicate that there was an end to the exile and many Jews were able to return to Israel after seventy years.

The writer clearly expresses the reasons for the exile. God had exhausted the possibility of Judah's return to him from their idolatry "and there was no remedy." The decline had led to a point of no return.

There is usually a point of no return in all disputes. In the early stages of a dispute reconciliation is possible, but there comes a point where all talk and action is complete and no further effect on the situation is possible.

Unfortunately, we cannot always determine the point before which reconciliation is possible and after which it is not. Indefinitely maintaining a position, however justified we feel, is the greatest barrier to settlement.

It is too easy in our anger and sense of injustice to refuse to compromise until it is too late. Don't let that happen to you.

Prayer: Holy Spirit, keep us aware of the point of no return in our marital conflicts. Teach us to love and respect what our partner brings to the marriage.

Responding to Rebellion

The greatest challenge during teen years is how to discipline a wayward child. Where is the balance between punishment that provokes antagonism and leniency that encourages the behaviour? The former risks an escalating confrontation that increases the problem, the latter leaves the problem unresolved.

Making matters worse, while some of us seem born to be natural parents, most of us clearly are not. Here are the three basic approaches to discipline that can be found in Scripture.

First, a sense of justice is necessary if resentment is not to be added to the problem. This means the punishment must fit the crime, and the three Rs of justice give some guidance: retribution, restitution and rehabilitation. Often correcting a wrong where possible is the simplest and most effective form of justice.

Second, the practice of mercy upon genuine repentance reflects a merciful God. This may mean forgoing disciplinary action when forgiveness is the correct response to genuine repentance.

The final response to defiance is release—both physically and emotionally. This is the most difficult, for it separates us from the child we love, and places the child beyond our control. But God treated us that way, leaving our return to him in our hands. The story of the prodigal son is Jesus' example of the definitive act of love.

The return of a child by choice will provide an enjoyable and lasting relationship that will span the later years. In the final analysis, the ultimate source of protection for our teenagers is our total commitment to Jesus Christ, and regular commitment of our children into his care.

Prayer: Heavenly Father, you love our children more than we do, and gave your Son's life for them. Help us to discipline fairly out of love and not anger.

None of Us is Innocent

Read: Nehemiah 1:1–11

"If you return to me and obey my commands, then even if your exiled people are at the farthest horizon, I will gather them from there and bring them to the place I have chosen as a dwelling for my Name." Nehemiah 1:9.

Nehemiah had great sorrow at the state of the homeland that he loved—although the end of the exile was now some ninety years previous and he had probably never lived there.

Like many Jews he had stayed in the land to which his fathers were exiled, and found employment in the palace of Artaxerxes in Persia, rising to a place of prominence. Despite the time lapse since the first exiles returned, much of the city remained in ruins.

However justified the resentment of the Jews at their captors, Nehemiah recognized the reason for the exile was estrangement from God. In his prayer he identifies with the sins of his forefathers, even though he had no personal responsibility.

His prayer justified God's actions as consistent with the covenant he made with Israel. But Nehemiah also reminded God of the promise to restore Israel if they return to him, and sought God's grace for his efforts to assist in that recovery.

No marital dispute is the fault of only one partner; all of us carry some responsibility for our marriage difficulties. If we consider ourselves innocent, it begs the question of our own sinfulness which contributes to the shortcomings of earthly experience.

To pray, justifiably, for God to avenge injustice towards us is only half the prayer; to seek God's forgiveness for our sinfulness that makes us complicit in our distress is the other necessary half.

Prayer: O Lord, our sinfulness adds to conflicts. Strengthen our resolve to work through them. Thank you for the cross, Lord Jesus, where healing and growth begin.

ANN AND BRYAN NORFORD

WEEK THIRTY: TUESDAY

Qualities That Attract

Read: Esther 2:1–18

Now the king was attracted to Esther more than to any of the other women. Esther 2:17.

The book of Esther reads like a novel, with turns and twists in the plot sufficient to engage any reader, but doesn't mention God. Yet the perceptive reader will see the devotion of Mordecai and Esther to their faith and God's influence behind the scenes.

An elder cousin, Mordecai, became her guardian, not only in the parenting sense, but gave whatever protection he could in that despotic regime, enquiring about her welfare daily as she prepared to meet the king.

Mordecai raised Esther well. Her beauty was her obvious asset, but her open and innocent charm "won the favour of everyone that saw her."

Esther was willing to accept advice from those in authority or with expertise. She evidently listened well to Mordecai's tutelage, taking his advice to keep her Jewish blood secret, and took Hegai's advice when sent to the king.

Despite seeing other women of equal or greater beauty, the king favoured Esther and she became queen.

If you have several children you probably wish all your children were like that. Most children learn from their parents, but some learn the hard way.

Esther learned that Mordecai had total concern for her welfare and she had implicit trust in him. This in turn led her to trust others the same way and prepared her to learn from others.

While there is danger in indiscriminate trust, parents who set an example of respect for those in legitimate authority pass on to their children the ability to learn from others.

Prayer: Dear Father, increase our trust in you so we can model trusting relationships to our children.

Risk for the Truth

Read: Esther 4:6–17

"I will go to the king, even though it is against the law. And if I perish, I perish." Esther 4:16.

Mordecai seems an eccentric small man with little to commend him to those in high office. Haman, the Jew's arch enemy, was particularly incensed at Mordecai's indifference to him, as the full story records.

When Mordecai learned of Haman's edict against the Jews, Esther 3:8–9, he openly mourned in sackcloth. Esther, despite her luxurious life at court, continued her concern for Mordecai and sent him clothing to wear. Mordecai refused them, sending back to Esther Haman's edict and seeking her position to influence the king.

Mordecai's message to Esther pulled no punches, probably given in the same vein as instructions to Esther during her growing up years that inspired her to trust his advice. Despite the danger to herself, she agreed to petition the king for the Jews, including herself.

The continuing story relates her courage in facing the king, his favour toward her, and the instructions he gave to help the Jews. The Jews still celebrate that victory over their enemies in the yearly feast of Purim.

For us parents, our children will always remain so even into late adulthood. For that reason we often worry for them. As they face difficult circumstances or decisions, we still feel a responsibility for their pain and subsequent actions.

Especially when they put themselves in harm's way for the Gospel, we want to advise them. Even here they are usually just as capable, as we are, to respond to the challenging situations of life; maybe better.

Prayer: O Lord, we applaud Esther's bravery in saving her people and her trust in Mordecai. May we and our children be prepared to make the same stand even at risk to ourselves.

Faith in Adversity

Read: Job 2:1–10

"Shall we accept good from God, and not trouble?" In all this, Job did not sin in what he said. Job 2:10.

J ob is rarely taught and even less understood, but it states many of the problems that believers in an all-powerful God face. We know that Job's trials were a test of faith, beyond anything most of us will face.

In Job's first chapter he has already lost his sons and daughters and all his wealth. In this chapter he also loses his health, reduced to sitting on an ash heap, scraping painful oozing sores with broken china.

These two chapters teach that results do not necessarily validate beliefs. It highlights the fallacy of pragmatism that results confirm truth. If this was true then Job's wife was right in telling Job that his trust in God was pointless—he should "curse God and die."

Job lost everything including his wife, living an apparent miserable, meaningless existence. But Job had wisdom enough to know that there was nowhere else to go but to God.

Bruce Waltke, an Old Testament professor and translator, tells the story of taking his son for vaccination. The little boy, terrified of the needle, cried on his father's shoulder. But rather than running away from his father and the needle, he clung all the tighter to his father as he was carried to it.

This lad illustrated the difference between faith and denial. His trust in his father was greater than the pain he faced. Job believed he could simply trust God with raw faith when all the evidence seemed to point in the opposite direction.

Prayer: Thank you dear Lord, for the example of Job. Grant us the grace and strength to cling to you more tightly in all the adversities of life.

The Plight of Children

Read: Job 24:1–24

"Why does the Almighty not set times for judgment? Why must those who know him look in vain for such days?" Job 24:1.

In this passage, Job raises several questions but in particular, he is troubled at the violent treatment of the defenceless. In the story of the widow's oil, we read of the practice of selling children into slavery in order to pay debts, and Job lists this as one of his complaints.

Even today, the problem of children caught up in the cycle of violence that engulfed Job's world is an ongoing tragedy. In present times, television advertisements by humanitarian organizations regularly highlight the plight of poor children.

Child slavery is rampant in many countries, westerners making child prostitutes of Thailand a tourist stop. Anti-personnel land mines kill and maim hundreds of unsuspecting children. AIDS in Africa orphans millions of children, some of whom become parents to siblings while children themselves.

It is too easy to feel impotent in the face of such vast problems. Yet children suffer as individuals. Don't let the vastness of the problem blind us to the ability to do something for one child at a time.

A child noticed hundreds of starfish left on the beach by the receding tide. As he started throwing them back into the sea, a passer-by commented that he was making little difference to the vast numbers.

The boy threw another starfish into the foam as he replied: "It made a difference to that one."

Prayer: O Lord, we are horrified at the pain and death of children in our world. May we reflect the love you showed to children in ways that ameliorate the suffering of some.

WEEK THIRTY: WEEKEND

Depravity

When I first learned to ride a bicycle, I was let loose on the streets of my neighbourhood and almost immediately came into conflict with another user. My problem was a very simple one: I was riding on the wrong side of the road as the other user testily informed me.

My father had not taught me the first rule of the road—to ride or drive on the left (that was in England of course). A moment's thought reveals to us the chaos produced without this one simple and basic rule.

When it comes to human nature, most people are poorly informed of the one simple rule that governs all human behaviour: our total depravity. This goes against the grain, especially as it suggests that we have nothing good in us.

But it simply means that everything we do is somehow infected with sin; we act with mixed motives and engage in undesirable fantasies. Conversely, our culture assumes the ultimate good in all, a mistaken notion that contributes as much to society's ills as sin itself. Sin is regarded as a correctable defect rather than a terminal disease.

By contrast the Bible teaches that we are all infected by sin and need inward cleansing by our Creator. The first line of defence for our children is a commitment to Jesus Christ, responding to their recognised need of cleansing and forgiveness; first as an initial experience of salvation, and then as an ongoing source of forgiveness and healing.

Unfortunately, these principles are so basic we tend to take them for granted and forget to clearly instruct our children of them—as my father forgot to inform me of the first rule of the road.

Prayer: Dear Lord, help us to continually remember our fallen state before you, and pass on to our children their need of cleansing and forgiveness provided at the cross.

God Laughs at His Enemies

Read: Psalm 2:1–12

The One enthroned in heaven laughs; the Lord scoffs at them.
Then he rebukes them in his anger and terrifies them in his wrath.
Psalm 2:4–5.

This is a messianic psalm, one that forecasts the coming of the Messiah and points to him as a Son. The ludicrous ranting of the nations against God is set against the awesome power of the coming Son of God, King of the earth.

The ease of final victory for God's appointed King makes a mockery of the power of world rulers, however great they may seem during their brief rule. The psalm ends with a warning to all rulers to "kiss the Son"; to give allegiance to him before it is too late.

I recall my childhood days when "I'll tell my dad on you" was the threat of retaliation for some perceived wrong. I assumed that my father had the capability to put down any other child who harmed me. I recall one boy who made no secret of his resentment when my father reprimanded him—especially as he wasn't totally to blame.

This psalm is a reminder that the Father will give Jesus his power; it is an "inheritance," granted as a "possession." In the same way, God's protection of us is his gift to us. We live under his authority.

Not that he protects us for our selfish desires or deceptive actions, but supports us as we dedicate our lives to him. He will address whatever mockery or persecution we may sustain from others before the final judgment seat of the Son.

Prayer: Thank you Father, that in the fearful times of life we know we are secure in your hands. No-one can ever separate us from you, now or for eternity.

ANN AND BRYAN NORFORD

WEEK THIRTY-ONE: TUESDAY

God's Promise to Sustain Us

Read: Psalm 37:25–28

I was young and now I am old, yet I have never seen the righteous forsaken or their children begging bread. Psalm 37:25.

Today's reading flies in the face of what seems to be true. While we see perpetual violence against the defenceless, David sees God's continual provision for the children of the faithful.

Not only that, David contends that this has been true for his whole life—and he lived to "a good old age," 1 Chronicles 29:28. David qualified his remarks by referring to those who "are always generous and lend freely."

David also stated the general belief of the Old Testament that to "dwell in the land forever" was subject to following God's requirements. Successive kings following Solomon led the nation into sin that eventually sent the nation into exile to Assyria and Babylon.

Later, Jesus' contemporaries assumed blame for the crucifixion of Jesus: "Let his blood be on us and on our children," Matthew 27:25. Within forty years the Roman army destroyed Jerusalem and scattered those children throughout the earth.

On a personal basis, if we are to avoid our "children begging bread" in the future, we must ensure our faithfulness maintains the level of prosperity we enjoy. Tomorrow's thoughts illustrate that danger in more detail.

If we do not live with a clear expression of the importance of faith and recognize God as our provider, our children may believe any prosperity is their right or a result of their own efforts.

Prayer: Heavenly Father, help us to remember that you are the provider to your children. It is a gracious gift from you and not a right to which we are entitled.

Prosperity is a Gift

Read: Psalm 78:1–8

We will tell the next generation the praiseworthy deeds of the Lord, his power, and the wonders he has done. Psalm 78:4.

Asaph, one of David's lead musicians, also penned many of the Psalms. In this one he gives a warning that is a counterpoint to David's encouragement of yesterday. Not only was it imperative that parents lived according to God's covenant, but also that they taught their children to do the same.

Asaph saw the need for teaching succeeding generations if they were not to suffer the fate of their forefathers—"a stubborn and rebellious generation whose hearts were not loyal to God."

We have encountered this idea so many times already in relation to children it must seem like a broken record: the necessity of teaching our children the importance of faith and practical living out of that faith.

There can only be one reason for this repetition: these requirements are so often neglected. We must ask ourselves why this is so when the need for them is so vital.

As we seek God during the difficult times of life, it is natural to teach children to seek God and remain faithful to him. But as faithfulness leads to greater prosperity, children who never face adversity may lose the connection between the two.

Some of the current generation of younger people have a sense that the prosperity we share now is a given part of life, and so believe a godly lifestyle has little to do with maintaining affluence.

Eventually this will lead to a loss of prosperity, and the need to seek God begins the cycle again. We must be vigilant so that succeeding generations do not enter this treadmill.

Prayer: Dear Father, help us teach and so live, that our children see that all we have comes from you, especially the prosperity we may now enjoy.

185

WEEK THIRTY-ONE: THURSDAY

A Healthy Home Environment

Read: Psalm 80:8–11

It sent out its boughs to the Sea, its shoots as far as the River.
Psalm 80:11.

We rarely attain the ideal marriage we desire. Many relationships are quite the reverse and a recipe for disaster for the marriage partners and for their children. But children from dysfunctional homes can become highly effective adults.

Ann developed a strong survival instinct from her poor home life. Annie, her grandmother, took Ann to church where she found the love of God a compelling antidote to her childhood experiences. Ann and I were baptized together at fourteen and fifteen and have been committed Christians ever since.

Ann's experience reminds us that we are never destined to be conditioned by our environment. No-one has perfect parents, and in learning to cope with parents' faults, children learn to cope with an imperfect adult world.

An important motivation for children to seek God's ways for life is to ensure they do not repeat the parents' mistakes. The chaotic setting Ann experienced drew her to seek God's alternative.

Our reading tells us that God brought Israel from the slavery of Egypt, and planted her in a fruitful land where she might flourish, and Israel's faith would provide a protective environment for the land's inhabitants.

It reminds us that our lives placed in God's hands allow him the opportunity to bring healing to us. But of greater significance, it gives us the resources to provide a healthy environment for our family, whatever our previous experience may have been.

Prayer: Thank you Lord that you gave us faith communities as nurturing places for a safe and stable home for our family. May we never neglect this precious resource.

God Cares For Grandchildren

Read: Psalm 103:8–18

From everlasting to everlasting the Lord's love is with those who
fear him, and his righteousness with their children's children.
Psalm 103:17.

If you are parents having difficulties raising children,
then this Psalm should encourage you. While we can
often see the problems and solutions in other families,
our own can seem intractable. Exasperation and despair
follow.

We tend to forget we are dealing with children who are
individuals and make their own decisions; decisions often
made on a superficial understanding of life without the
insight we may have gained.

There are two ideas in this passage that may give us
some help. First, God himself is our example. We know how
stubborn and rebellious Israel was, confirmed by our own
waywardness at times.

He uses our love for our own children to reflect his love
for us, not treating us "as our sins deserve"; he has
compassion "as a father has compassion on his children."

Second, contrary to our brief tenure on earth, his love
for us is eternal, reaching to the generations that follow
us—to our "children's children." As God knows how to deal
with us, so he is our helper in dealing with our children, for
he loves them as he loves us.

We are not alone. While our hearts are right with him,
our children will also be under his care. We may fail on
occasion as our children do, but he remains faithful to us.
That is why we he invites us to "cast all your anxiety on him
because he cares for you." 1 Peter 5:7.

Prayer: O Lord, we cling to that promise that you are with our
children and grandchildren, even the generations that
follow. Keep us faithful to you for their benefit.

187

WEEK THIRTY-ONE: WEEKEND

An Adoption

Ann and I adopted a boy when our first two girls were in their teens. We both felt we had something to give with space in our hearts for another child. The boy's history was one of a broken family, given up to the children's services at the age of six. We first met him in a Salvation Army children's home—his permanent childhood home.

After a year of visits we adopted him into our family at ten years of age. His disturbing background had taught him to survive by using the system and manipulating those he came in contact with. We did not respond well. We had lots of faith and love, but no background in dealing with these challenges

Although he was with us for about three years, his increasing antisocial behaviour and bouts of trouble with the law eventually landed him in juvenile detention. We kept contact with him for a while longer during his stints in detention and later jail terms, but lost contact in later years.

It left us with questions. Did we make a mistake in taking him in? If it was God's leading at the time, why did it turn out so badly? We trusted there was some redeeming value in his time with us, and he continued to be the subject of our prayers that God's Spirit would draw him into his kingdom.

Remarkably, over thirty years later we found out he was living with the sister of a close friend. He was holding a responsible job, and had recovered from a serious bout of cancer.

They have yet to indicate they wish to meet us, and until then, they both remain in our prayers, certain that God has them in his care.

Prayer: We thank you, O Lord, for your provision for our son, and pray for your continued call on his life and the girl he has chosen. May we meet them soon.

Children are a blessing

Read: Psalm 127:1–5

Sons are a heritage from the Lord, children a reward from him.
Psalm 127:3.

Children's behaviour may often remind us that they are infected with a sin nature like ourselves. But that makes them no less valuable than any other human being.

In fact, far from being a curse, our reading states that children are a blessing from God—apparently the more of them, the greater the blessing. Barrenness was often considered a punishment from God in the Old Testament.

Today's attitudes toward children are different. Children are an imposition, interfering with our right to enjoyment. Daycares proliferate as "childparks" allowing parents to pursue their own agendas or singles to work after separation from partners. Some children are still unwanted, abused, and neglected even after decades of abortion rights.

Child pornography has grown exponentially as the internet has brought the world's proclivity for it into our homes. Parental rights become restricted as governments seek to protect children from their parents.

Globally, the picture is the same. Children are deemed an aggravation of the population explosion, richer countries attempting to impose birth restrictions and encourage abortions in poorer countries.

It's easy for us to fall into similar traps. Do we consider large families anti-social or population control unavoidable?

Jesus had nothing but support and protection for children and considered them worthy of his blessing as they are his blessing to us, Mark 10:13–16.

Prayer: Dear Lord, may we ever be aware that children are your creation from conception until death and fight for their right to exist, and continue to love those you have given us.

WEEK THIRTY-TWO: TUESDAY

Family Love for Life

Read: Psalm 128:1–6

May the Lord bless you from Zion . . . and may you live to see your children's children. Psalm 128:5–6.

Ann and I celebrate our birthdays in the spring. It's also the time for mothers' and fathers' days. We receive messages from our children extolling the qualities of mother- and father-hood they see in us.

While we appreciate their thoughts, we are aware we have not really lived up to the standards they express. Senior years are a time for regretting some of the things done or undone during our parenting years.

But we are thankful that they overlook our shortcomings at this time of our lives—although they often expressed them forcefully in their youth.

Ann and I were baptized together in our early teens. The desire and commitment made to God then was real and determined but often less so in practice, particularly during the difficult times of life.

We believe God saw our hearts and graciously forgave our failures, so we experienced his protection and guidance through our lives. We concur with this Psalm, rejoicing in our children and our "children's children."

But it is still with amazement that we see two things: the way God has blessed and continues to bless our children and grandchildren; and the joy that Ann and I find in our companionship together in these latter years. The extent of God's grace to our family, and the unexpected level of joy it has brought is a source of wonder to us.

Ann grabbed my hand the other day—not unusual—but this time added that if I passed on, she did not want to regret missing any opportunity to express her love. A sentiment we should convey at all times of life.

Prayer: Heavenly Father: we are so grateful for your love and grace to us and our family throughout our lifetime. As we recognize our dependence upon you, may you continue to be the source of our praise.

190

Finding Peace in Confusion

Read: Psalm 131:1–3

I have stilled and quieted my soul; like a weaned child with its mother, like a weaned child is my soul within me. Psalm 131:2.

This is probably a good Psalm for the Monday morning rush. Those, and similar mornings, remind us it's during the turbulent times of life we sense that there should be answers beyond ourselves to the dilemmas we face.

This Psalm reflects David's decision to set aside his quest for answers: "not to concern myself with great matters or things too wonderful for me." He makes a decision to calm himself and to seek contentment in his current status. Not an easy thing to do, yet there is no peace without some assurance that there is meaning in the instability of life.

Too often we seek simple answers to complex questions, particularly those that may have no immediate answer. The writer to the Hebrews suggests that his readers needed milksop teaching, not solid food, due to their lack of maturity, Hebrews 5:11–14.

Just as we know our infant children need solid food; so we need to advance in our understanding of the faith and wisdom found in God's Word if we are to find a measure of contentment in life.

Paul himself knew how to find contentment—in plenty or in want—for God could complete his work in Paul under all conditions, Philippians 4:12–13.

Both Paul and David found that maturity didn't necessarily bring immediate answers that gave hope, but it generated trust in God that granted peace when no answers were forthcoming. As David simply said: "Israel, put your hope in the Lord both now and evermore."

Prayer: Dear Lord, grant us the peace to simply trust you when we don't have the answers to life's dilemmas.

WEEK THIRTY-TWO: THURSDAY

Anger Against Injustice

Read: Psalm 137:1–9

By the rivers of Babylon we sat and wept when we remembered Zion. Psalm 137:1.

Today's reading expresses the sorrow, humiliation and anger the Jews went through in captivity. Those who had dragged them from the homeland were now their tormentors, mocking their display of love for the land they had left.

The misery of both captivity and homesickness haunted them, and they could not bear to sing the songs that reminded them of their beloved city. They remembered not only the joys of the now ruined city, but also the taunts of others who had rejoiced in its downfall and scorned them in their distress.

They expressed anger as they sought God for justice for the brutality imposed upon them, seeking vengeance on their attackers. In honesty, they did not repress their feelings and desire for vengeance.

But their cry was to God, knowing that he would avenge them in his own time and in his own way, Deuteronomy 32:35. And because they called on God for justice, they denied themselves the possibility of exacting it.

Divorce raises highly charged emotions, especially anger—at the injustice perpetrated against us and those dependent on us. Despite our own part in the break-up, the injustices against us are real, and the anger natural.

Expression of that anger in some harmless way is justified, but to express it violently simply spreads the venom to others; to suppress it turns it inwards and harms us. Our psalmist found a third way—confess it to God who understands our hurt and anger, and who is big enough to both absorb and avenge it.

Prayer: O Lord, help us confess our anger to you, forgive our oppressors, and trust you to avenge us.

Nowhere to Hide from God

Read: Psalm 139:1–18

Where can I go from your Spirit? Where can I flee from your presence? Psalm 139:7.

The impossibility of escaping from God is the overriding theme in this Psalm. Whether we are for or against him, neither distance nor darkness places us beyond his reach. This may be a fearful thought for those who rebel against him, but is the most comforting to those of us who honour and revere him.

More astonishing is his knowledge of our inmost thoughts, which we would be ashamed to divulge to anyone, yet he loves us still.

Our creation started from the womb, he "knit me together in my mother's womb." Even there "you created my inmost being." Who we would become and plans for our life—if we were willing to abide by them—were already formed in the unformed body.

Even in the "secret place," and "in the depths of the earth"—here a euphemism for the womb—we could not escape him. In God's eyes, human life begins at conception.

The sacredness of life has always been a cornerstone of Christian faith. Whether it is within the womb or on a deathbed, we must weigh our desire to end it for any reason against the fact that life is his creation.

This does not mean that everyone who takes a life is to be condemned, but approached with grace. Many of us know the agony that precedes abortion or euthanasia. But we can never condone the flippant ending of life for convenience or gain. That life is God's and we will give an account for how we dealt with it.

Prayer: O God, we are overcome by your power and knowledge of all things. We are glad we cannot escape from you. Please remain with us at all times and in all places.

193

WEEK THIRTY-TWO: WEEKEND

A Couple That Made It

Darcy first entered our small congregation dressed in his motorcycle leathers. We invited him for lunch and he tried to impress us with his spirituality, mainly of a new age variety.

He continued to attend, mainly—as he told us later—to find babysitters for a young son whose poor behaviour frequently disrupted our services.

Darcy was connected to the drug fraternity, but over a few weeks, became a Christian, leaving his drug connections and starting life over.

Josie came into our congregation supported by a cane. She was a certified quadriplegic after a car accident in her teens. Predicted never to walk again, her slight build belied her fierce determination and she regained the use of her limbs.

She subsequently attended university—in a wheelchair—obtained a degree in social work and became gainfully employed. Darcy and Josie were attracted to each other, but Darcy's sudden disappearance to an open jail tested this relationship—his past life had suddenly caught up with him.

Eventually I married them and the university accepted Darcy as a mature student to study law. Despite his background the Law Society also accepted him.

Today, he is a successful lawyer, and Josie has given birth to two boys, despite her handicap. They are an example of God's work in rehabilitation—Josie from her accident, and Darcy from his old life.

As they put their trust in God, he provided what both of them may never have gained as a result of the accident and choices in early life.

Prayer: Lord, you are a transforming God. It is our deepest desire that you continue your work in our lives by changing and conforming us to your image.

Dangers of Illicit Sex

Read: Proverbs 5:1–23

Drink water from your own cistern, running water from your own
well. Proverbs 5:15.

Sexual permissiveness pervades our western culture
today, but it has been the practice of all generations
to a greater or lesser degree. In his day, Solomon
complained about it, and its attendant dangers. Proverbs
chapters 6 and 7 continue the same theme.

This passage does not dwell on immoral or
promiscuous behaviour; rather it lists its many
disadvantages and gives a variety of reasons for men to
avoid illicit sexual relations.

Solomon does not deny that an affair might bring
temporary pleasure, Proverbs 6:25; 7:18, but the actions of
the adulterous woman are purely mercenary or selfish, and
end in misery. Any affair, however pleasurable for a time,
usually ends in wretchedness for all.

There are other dangers. Sexually transmitted diseases
were likely as prevalent then as now and many would die of
the diseases. The ravages of disease are implied in verse 11,
and death in verses 5 and 23.

Not only are there physical dangers, but verse 14 also
lists loss of status. Despite loose morality in current
western culture, society expects ethical standards from high
profile people. President Clinton came close to
impeachment for his sexual behaviour and Jimmy
Swaggart, the television evangelist, lost credibility
consorting with a prostitute.

However, adultery is not wrong because of its risks; it is
wrong because there is a commandment against it, Exodus
20:14, and Deuteronomy 5:18. Ignoring it distorts the image
of God—the ultimate faithful One—within us.

Prayer: Dear Lord, keep us from the folly and eventual misery of
illicit sex. Draw us close to you and to each other during
times of temptation.

The Foolish Woman

Read: Proverbs 11:22; 14:1; 21:9

The wise woman builds her house, but with her own hands the foolish one tears hers down. Proverbs 14:1.

The word "house" in the above text is better translated "household." It refers to a wife building the home she provides for her family, not the structure in which they live. These Proverbs warn against women who are destructive.

The woman of loose morals breaks another's home, but today's readings are of a wife whose actions tear down her own home. No woman deliberately sets out to destroy her home, but some conduct does just that.

A wife can damage her family several ways. First, the quarrelsome wife stirs up strife. It can be the nagging wife whose constant harping on faults makes a "corner of the roof" a welcome retreat.

Nagging—generally referring to women, but can also refer to men—is counterproductive as it alienates the target. Wives may use this in a desperate effort to convert their husbands. Jesus made his point clear, but left people to their own decisions.

Second, the wife with poor judgment "turns aside" from discernment. This usually refers to moral issues; she is the "wayward wife" lacking judgment, Proverbs 6:23-24. It also refers to one who is spiritually obtuse for it is "the fool [who] says in his heart, 'There is no God,'" Psalm 14:1.

Foolishness makes beauty purely ornamental and of no family value. There's nothing wrong with beauty; every man wants a beautiful wife. It is outward attraction and inner virtue together that provide the unique combination towards a secure comfortable home, however poor.

Prayer: Dear Father, I really desire to be a good and faithful wife. Reveal those areas where I can make my home happier and more secure.

The Wise Man

Read: Proverbs 13:22; 14:26; 20:7

He who fears the Lord has a secure fortress, and for his children it will be a refuge. Proverbs 14:26.

These verses reveal the benefits of godly fathers. Inheritance is not only financial, but includes support during a child's lifetime; a home that is a secure refuge.

During childhood setbacks, those from good homes know the comfort of a secure place that the bond between husband and wife provides. Fracturing of that bond breaks the cocoon that produces joyful and strong development in growing children. That is the inheritance that godly parents leave their children.

Few TV shows reflect normal family life. The impression TV writers have of "normal" life are desperate housewives, the partner swapping of the soaps, or hilarious rounds of meaningless sexual encounters.

Even shows depicting professionals—detectives, doctors, and nurses for example—usually cast the actors as swingers, divorced, single parents, or struggling with marital problems.

The media have given us a negative confirmation of today's verses by depicting the results of ungodly sexuality; usually promoted by men, but in which women are increasingly the predators.

Unfortunately, the breakdown of Christian families also denies the truth of these verses. But no family is immune from the difficulties of life, and Proverbs are a general rule.

Families that model godliness, not those that only pay lip service to it, are the most likely to pass their blessings on to the children. Fathers have an initial role in guiding that conclusion.

Prayer: Heavenly Father, you are my role model as husband and father. Teach me your wisdom to guide my family as I read your Word and listen to you.

WEEK THIRTY-THREE: THURSDAY

Discipline of Children

Read: Proverbs 13:24; 22.15

Folly is bound up in the heart of a child, but the rod of discipline will drive it far from him. Proverbs 22:15.

Several readings from Proverbs are isolated verses, and today's readings follow that pattern. Much of Proverbs is collections of sayings that have stood the test of time, but not set in any obvious order. Thus, every verse is a sermon in itself, demanding deeper thought.

The second of today's proverbs suggests that a child is foolish—not very acceptable in current western culture that dotes on its children, and it even appears to oppose Jesus' teaching to become like little children.

We need to recognize imitable child*like* qualities that are easily lost in adulthood: innocence, trust, and simplicity to name a few. But that does not mean that we should become child*ish*. The self-centred nature of the newborn to ensure its survival is not a trait to foster as the child grows.

We need to teach the quality of self sacrifice to oppose the strong instinct for self preservation. Jesus taught that we should love our neighbours as ourselves; a direct allusion to our propensity to ensure our own needs first.

Solomon reckoned we need to oppose childish and foolish ideas through discipline. In fact, the first proverb indicates that lack of discipline displays lack of love for the child.

Thus the motivation for opposing childish actions is not from of anger or for personal convenience; it's for the eventual well being of the child and ultimate acceptance into an interrelated community.

Prayer: Heavenly Father, you know we love our children dearly. Help us discipline fairly, not out of anger or selfishness.

We Are Created Perfect

Read: Proverbs 20:11; 29:15

Even a child is known by his actions, by whether his conduct is pure and right. Proverbs 20:11.

While example is necessary in raising a child, it alone will not impart wisdom. The first of today's verses questions the innocence of a child. The idea that a child is born an empty moral package for the filling is foreign to Scripture.

The temperament given at birth reveals itself in the way a child behaves, with both the negative and positive use of that temperament expressed. While temperaments are diverse, they all have one thing in common: they are God given characteristics as much as hair and eye colour.

So why would God create temperaments that produce corrupt qualities? To ask this question reveals a misunderstanding of temperament. All elements of temperament are perfect; it is the use of them that is good or bad.

For instance, an ignorant stubbornness is simply the flip side of steadfastness; superficiality is a symptom of the ability to see the big picture, while attention to detail often precludes depth of vision. Try viewing the characteristics of your family and note the positive value of those qualities you dislike.

The second verse indicates the need for training. Our youngest daughter was the ultimate strong willed child. Early on we realized that it is strength of will that produces results in a world that is hard to change.

Our challenge was to retain that persevering nature while we channeled it into positive directions. Wisdom imparted by example is established by careful discipline. Our calling was not to break the will but to mould it.

Prayer: Dear Father, we come in deep gratitude for the children you have given us. Help us discern and encourage the positive characteristics you have created in each of them.

WEEK THIRTY-THREE: WEEKEND

Children Are a Joy

Ann and I had two families, two girls born early in life when making a living and setting up home was an arduous time. Our youngest girl was born sixteen years later as the older girls left home.

For myself, I had treated the older girls quite seriously, missing much of the enjoyment I should have had with them, and probably made their childhood harder than necessary.

But with the youngest, this was one for fun and enjoyment; leading to the accusation from her sisters and mother that she was spoilt.

Life stretches endlessly before us in our youth, but looking back from old age, it seems to have passed in a moment—"where did the years go?" David understood that, having that sudden inspiration from God on the brevity of life, Psalm 39:4–5.

That life seems to pass more quickly as we age is also a common experience. The end of life is shorter than the beginning and we need to run faster to catch up on those things we neglected earlier in life.

Old age is a time for rejoicing in our children and grandchildren. Ann and I take a considerable interest in the growth and education of our grandchildren, watching them grow into mature adults and choose marriage partners.

We frequently hang out with them and our children with the greatest joy. In return, we regularly receive complimentary cards and notes from them—more than we deserve.

For those unwilling to have children, they will miss one of the greatest blessings life has to offer. But God has other joys for those unable to have children.

Prayer: O Lord, keep us from by-passing those opportunities to enjoy our children during those young years.

The Virtuous Woman

Read: Proverbs 31:10–31

Charm is deceptive, and beauty is fleeting; but a woman who fears the Lord is to be praised. Proverbs 31:30.

When we receive unsolicited advice regarding our relationships, how can we know what is good or bad? Let me suggest two approaches.

First, is the advice really for our own good? Frequently it's from people who don't have a real interest in our welfare, or else have an agenda of their own. When it comes to a lifetime partner, listen to those who *really* care about us.

Second, does our lover stand up to the scrutiny of Scripture? Love for a woman of the qualities described in this passage is a good foundation for marriage.

Ann and I met when we were young teenagers, and considered ourselves meant for each other. After four years of courtship, we were married when Ann was 18 and I was 19, with the blessing of our families.

Ann came from an unsavoury neighbourhood, and a severely dysfunctional home. I still had several years left to complete my architectural degree, and we had no place to live. We received messages about how foolish we were, destined for break-up due to our youthful marriage.

Despite my adoration for Ann, I saw in her the qualities listed in today's reading. I had no doubts about her ability to provide the partnership that marriage required, and we both had an unwavering commitment to our faith in Jesus Christ. Needless to say, our families' reservations were unfounded, and those who predicted disaster for our marriage are still waiting for it.

Prayer: Lord, we thank you for the Scripture extolling the woman of virtue. Please guide our children to pursue a partner of like integrity, whether male or female.

WEEK THIRTY-FOUR: TUESDAY

A Time for Everything

Read: Ecclesiastes 3:1–8

There is a time for everything, and a season for every activity
under heaven. Ecclesiastes 3:1.

Today's reading is disturbing because it outlines both good and bad activities that will always infringe on our time. It is almost as if we are being counseled to make room for those things that are distasteful, rather than avoiding them and concentrating on the agreeable.

Yet evil, as well as the world's demands, invades our relationships. There is a time for war as well as peace: a time to confront one another rather than act in toleration or appeasement. Even more surprising is the assertion that there is also a time to hate. Who could we possibly be exhorted to hate?

Perhaps the answer is in defining hate as the Bible defines love: not a feeling but an action and often a warning of danger. We can act "hatefully," not in the common idea of a vindictive response, but in creative, positive, even fierce opposition, to falsehood, stupidity, and cruelty.

Anger always has a reason, but seldom a good one. Yet anger is sometimes justified: when one is deceived, betrayed, or undervalued. Similarly, we might describe courts as hating and angry when convicting a felon, but they practice justice, not revenge.

God expresses anger frequently, but it is always just, even at one point hating Esau, Malachi 1:2–5. Is there an issue you need to confront your partner about? Maybe this is a time, not for love, but—in its redefined sense—a time for "hate."

Prayer: Heavenly Father, help us always be transparent with our partners. May our critique of others be with gentleness and respect, and willingness to admit our faults in justified complaints against us.

Setbacks: Part of the Process

Read: Ecclesiastes 3:9–14

He has also set eternity in the hearts of men; yet they cannot
fathom what God has done from beginning to end.
Ecclesiastes 3:11.

There's nothing like a day of accomplishment when
everything goes according to plan and is complete.
But we also have frustrating days of redo, repair, or
failure, achieving nothing of significance.

Upon reflection, we realize that there must be times for
preparation, planning, and evaluation; times for correcting
previous work or adapting to changing circumstances; even
times for rethinking and renewing the way we live.

In the big picture both the time of advance and
apparent retreat are all part of the same process. To
advance tomorrow as we did yesterday, we may need to
retrench today. Today's reading gives some rationale to this
process. In it we recognize a bigger picture than we can
see, even when questions are unanswered: "the burden
God has laid on men."

This is particularly true of the setbacks of life, which
baffle us. At those times Ecclesiastes exhorts us to find
satisfaction in the daily routine, recognizing that every day
has meaning in God's bigger picture beyond our grasp.

Relationship in marriage is much the same. The conflict
and abrasion between partners discourages us. Stopping
and dealing with interpersonal relations seems an
unnecessary disruption in other important areas of life.

But in the larger picture, it is part of the process, as
necessary as the times of joy and companionship
together—and in the end deepens the relationship.

It's often necessary to leave the big picture to God and
trust him with what we can't figure out.

Prayer: Almighty God, we are so glad you know the end from the
beginning. Help us to trust you in the perplexing times of
life.

WEEK THIRTY-FOUR: THURSDAY

Four-Way Marriage

Read: Ecclesiastes 4:9–12

A cord of three strands is not quickly broken. Ecclesiastes 4:12.

It's a common misconception that marriage is a union between two people. In fact there are four parties to a marriage. Weddings are public for they announce to the community the couple's union and their responsibility to each other and to the children that may arrive.

That's why marriages are registered and witnesses sign the register. The community has a place at the wedding as a witness to the union.

God is the other witness to the union, religious or not. He is a silent witness at all wedding ceremonies for marriage was his idea. His register also records the union and he is a witness to any action of a partner who threatens the relationship, Matthew 19:4–6.

God is more interested in the outcome of the relationship than any earthly authority, for he is the protector of any orphan or widow left from a break-up. Husbands and wives will give account to God for the treatment of their partners and children.

God is also interested in sustaining the marriage. A partnership has synergy—the work of two together is greater than the sum of each working alone; each can provide help, comfort, and protection to the other. But the last verse reminds us it is the third strand in the cord that maintains relationship that "is not quickly broken."

After the wedding the state has little interest unless there is a problem. God desires to be with us in our marriage, rejoicing in the good times, and supporting us through the bad—if we will let him.

Prayer: Dear Lord, it's a fearful thing to know you are a witness to every action in our marriage. Motivate us to act towards each other and our children with loving care in response to this truth.

Sex: God's Creation

Read: Song of Solomon 4:8 to 5:1

I have come into my garden, my sister, my bride.
Song of Solomon 5:1.

There have been those through the centuries that have tried to ban sex on the basis that it was inherently sinful, even forbidding marriage, 1 Timothy 4:3-4, but all that God has created is good—and that includes sex.

The Song of Solomon is King Solomon's love song to his bride. Despite difficulties in identifying characters in the dialogue, it is clear that the subject matter is the celebration of sexuality, sometimes dressed in symbolic language, at other times explicit.

This short book reveals sexuality as a gift of great beauty and wonder, for each partner to lavish upon the other. It describes in delicate song the intenseness of longing, the inexpressible beauty of the loved one, the exquisite sense of the other's presence.

Today's reading finishes up with joy at consummation of the relationship, expressed as final entry into the garden of his beloved, while the background chorus urges them to "drink your fill of love."

Does this sound like your marriage? Perhaps not, yet there is an echo in most of us that yearns for that level of companionship. It is a reminder that under the stress and reversals of wedded life, that experience of vitality is ready to awake.

Don't be discouraged to the point of despair in a difficult marriage. There is renewal for the most jaded of marriages; the deepest joy is still found in the most vital relationship that God has provided for us.

Prayer: Father, thank you for this incredible gift you designed for us, and the close companionship that accompanies it. Increase our awareness that it reflects the companionship you desire with us.

WEEK THIRTY-FOUR: WEEKEND

Love and Marriage

An old song says: "Love and marriage go together like a horse and carriage." Unfortunately, too many think that idea went out with the horse and buggy era. Sex is now perceived as a recreational activity, generally divorced from the idea of marriage or children.

Even a cursory knowledge of Scripture will reveal its message of sexual satisfaction only within marriage, confirmed by marriage and family as the bedrock of civilization across the world.

At the risk of being legalistic, the restriction of sex to within marriage must be the basis not only of a stable society, but also of a secure and happy family life for husband, wife, and children.

However, this ideal requires us to practise certain fundamental features, the foremost of which is fidelity. Infidelity causes consequences beyond emotional trauma, particularly the prevalence of venereal disease, and its possible transmission to the family.

It is no coincidence that AIDS has blossomed with the sexual revolution and is sustained by indiscriminate sexual union.

But infidelity, while inexcusable, often has its reasons. Sexual availability is the reason for and the promise of marriage, 1 Corinthians 7:5. To withhold it or used as a weapon is a primary departure from the covenant and may promote infidelity.

Other critical requirements for a happy marriage hinge on Christian servanthood and submission to the other as discussed earlier. Simply put, as Ann is fond of saying: "Be good to each other." Lack of these practices can be just as harmful to marriage as infidelity.

Prayer: Thank you, Heavenly Father, for the partners we married. Keep our relationship with you strong, so we may be able to withstand the temptations that too easily beset us and hinder our relationship with each other.

The Dangers of Delay

Read: Song of Solomon 5:2–6

I opened for my lover, but my lover had left; he was gone.
Song of Solomon 5:6.

The last reading may have given a rapturous look at the joys of the marriage union, but a study of the book also describes some of the challenges found in marriage. Today, there is the particular warning of boredom or apathy setting into the relationship.

The bride hears her beloved at the door calling to enter, but she has settled for the night: "I have taken off my robe—must I put it on again? I have washed my feet—must I soil them again?"

His call was inconvenient, not necessarily inappropriate, or demanding. Her situation was not one of inability but of disinterest. Yet the desire for him was not lost, and as he tried the door, the old fervour reappeared.

But when she reconsidered her initial denial and dressed, he had left. The longings of yesterday had dissipated into indifference on her part and impatience on his. But the story goes on to record her change of heart, her search for him and their final love for each other.

The critical factor in any personal disruption is time. Perhaps this is why Paul exhorts us not to "let the sun go down while you are still angry," Ephesians 4:26. The longer we put off reconciling, the more entrenched each position becomes and reconciling becomes harder.

Every time that occurs, it becomes easier not to reconcile at all. Love cannot bear the pain of separation; it is *this* pain we need to embrace and provoke us to make up before the day is done.

Prayer: Dear Lord, it is too easy for busyness to interfere with our intimacy. Help us take the time keep our love for you and each other fresh, especially in times of conflict.

Disciplines of Marriage

Read: Song of Solomon 8:6–12

Love is as strong as death, its jealousy unyielding as the grave.
Song of Solomon 8:6.

A rarely raised difference between humans and animals is that animals grow, mature, and propagate, by following their instincts. However, humans debase themselves when instincts are not controlled and disciplined.

Love is strong, but it eventually requires the choice of discipline over instinct; a distinctive and ennobling mark of humanity based on their freedom of choice.

Verse 6 raises the issue of commitment. Not only does this involve a pledge of allegiance for life, "a seal over your heart," but also a "jealousy unyielding as the grave;" a God given emotion that will try to protect the relationship.

Solomon compares faithfulness in marriage to a vineyard. He had a natural vineyard let to tenants, but the fruit of his lover's vineyard—her sexuality—is for him alone.

Both lifetime commitment and sexual faithfulness are the key disciplines that guard the continuing joy inherent in the relationship.

Solomon discusses the virginity of a younger sister. Will she be a wall that shuts out intruders and maintains her virginity, or a door that will let all come in? Today's culture suggests sexual experimentation will provide better adjustment for marriage.

But the reverse is true. Sexual discipline *before* marriage is the same discipline required *in* marriage. To play loosely with sex prior to marriage is to enter into marriage with the same ease of sexual adventurism and a correspondingly greater risk of infidelity and break-up.

Prayer: O Lord, we know that our first priority is to be faithful to you, which is the basis of ensuring our faithfulness to each other.

God Identifies with Us

Read: Isaiah 9:1–7

The people walking in darkness have seen a great light.
Isaiah 9:2.

We recall each Christmas the amazing fact that God himself, creator of all things, became a created being for a while. We would have expected him to come in some sort of majesty and power, yet he chose to come as a child. That has several implications.

First, he gave meaning and dignity to every life. By becoming a baby he identified with the poorest and weakest of humanity. Thus the life of any child, the poor, disabled, oppressed or disadvantaged person—all with more power than a baby—all become significant to him. We cannot imagine the depth of sacrifice necessary for the Lord of all to become a child.

Second, he determined to experience firsthand the trauma of life—including that of childhood and the erratic events of family life. He had brothers who mocked him, John 7:3–5. He was rejected, tortured, and killed by the nation he considered his family. Jesus experienced the same emotions that you experience in your own family.

We have few options in our family experience. But Jesus chose to become the child of a poor family. In doing so, he placed himself in the most vulnerable place of human experience, identifying with the weakest human state and becoming a victim of our fallen world.

As a result, this One, now exalted to the pinnacle of power, understands and provides strength and support to those who trust him in the uncertainty of earthly existence.

Prayer: Dear Lord, you have experienced all that we have to go through, including family problems. You know what we are experiencing right now, and we can experience your comfort and compassion for us in our time of distress.

WEEK THIRTY-FIVE: THURSDAY

God Identifies with Children

Read: Isaiah 11:1–9

The earth will be full of the knowledge of the Lord as the waters cover the sea. Isaiah 11:9.

Today's reading takes us forward to the coming of Christ to earth a second time. Then he will come as judge of all the earth, not as a vulnerable human being. He will retain all the human characteristics of compassion and justice, and his judgment will be fair.

In part, his mission will be to bring deliverance to children from the dangers that threaten them: he will release them from the fears of life; certainly from wild beasts, but by implication from other dangers also.

It is from this perspective that we view the suffering of our own children. While we cannot always reduce or dispel the pain of a child's suffering, it is of temporal duration. The Bible sees this life as a breath, our "days are like a fleeting shadow," Psalm 144:4.

Children killed, molested, those with incurable or terminal diseases, and the vicarious pain the parents experience for their children draw our heartstrings the tightest. But to forget the coming of the One who will bring final healing and justice to the earth is to live without hope.

No child suffers without Christ participating in their pain. He suffered the barbs of childhood and later the pain of rejection and shame of the cross. He knows and records the suffering of children now and reserves judgment for those who inflict it, Matthew 18:6.

He doesn't judge by hearsay or perception, verse 3, but by the Spirit of knowledge based on truth. No-one will gainsay his judgments "for the earth will be filled with the knowledge of the Lord as the waters cover the sea."

Prayer: Lord, thank you for the instinctive love you have placed in our hearts for our children, even though it causes us pain at times. Help us to remember you love them as your children also.

210

Strength at Any Age

Read: Jeremiah 1:4–10

"Before I formed you in the womb I knew you; before you were born I set you apart. Jeremiah 1:5.

We generally consider two periods of life are the most vulnerable and also the least productive. Childhood's lack of strength and experience are a disadvantage when competing in the world. That was Jeremiah's excuse as he responded to the call of God to prophesy.

Moses took a similar approach when called by God to lead Israel out of Egypt, Exodus 3:11. Moses and Jeremiah both appeared humble, but it was a false humility motivated by fear and an excuse not to cooperate with God's call.

On the other hand, a sense of inadequacy is essential if we are to recognize our dependence upon God and his ability to use us. As Ann and I approach old age, it is tempting to revert to the excuse of childhood that we now lack the strength needed to continue in God's call.

And although we have a lifetime of experience, a simple library of facts is useless without the wisdom to use them. And the source of wisdom is in God; we are dependent on him.

Like us, Jeremiah failed to grasp that strength and ability—even for his persecution that followed—is not a product of age. He should have consulted Isaiah, who reminds us that: "Even youths grow tired and weary, and young men stumble and fall."

Trust in God provides strength for any task he gives us, and that is available at any age, Isaiah 40:30–31. No wonder Jesus taught us not to despise childhood.

Prayer: O Lord, thank you for the reminder that you will provide the strength needed for the tasks to which you call us.

Maintaining Fidelity

Women predators are in the minority, but even Scripture records some. The Bible frequently pictured the nation of Israel as one in her unfaithfulness to God; Proverbs speaks of the seductive adulteress, Proverbs 5:3–6, and we can recall Potiphar's wife, Genesis 39:6–12.

But men are generally the initiators to which women respond. Prostitution is mostly a response to the demands of men, not the desire of women. Men generally propose, and women—where they have this freedom—choose to accept or reject the proposal.

Thus men have the initial responsibility for maintaining a moral standard. When they fail, women's ability to say "no" becomes the final line of defence of a culture's morality. When the liberation of women to personal freedom motivates illicit sexual encounters the culture begins its descent into moral anarchy.

Even though Eve committed the first sin, Adam's participation made him complicit. In an ironic reversal of fortunes, while men are responsible for entry into illicit sexuality, women become complicit when they consent to it.

This discussion of male and female infidelity holds true for the marriage partnership that God has provided. Each is a guardian of the other in faith and fidelity.

Jealousy is a tool given to us by God to rein in unfaithful partners, and a natural and required response when the promise of faithfulness is broken. God is a jealous God, requiring our continued commitment to him.

It is our crucial service to him; each to protect loyalty to the other, and the devotion of each other to him.

Prayer: Dear Lord, we recognize we are both liable to be unfaithful, and pray for your protection from those who would try to subvert and separate us.

Escalating Rebellion

Read: Jeremiah 31:18–20

Is not Ephraim my dear son, the child in whom I delight?
Jeremiah 31:20.

Following the reign of Solomon, Israel was split into two kingdoms, the southern called Judah and the northern known as Israel but here called Ephraim, the main tribe.

At the time of Jeremiah's call, the people of the northern nation of Israel were already in captivity in Assyria. It is clear from this passage that Israel had realized that sinfulness resulted in slavery in exile and they determined to repent of their sin.

This passage likens God's relationship to his people to the relationship between parent and child and uses that comparison to show God's love for Israel. The question arises: how can God claim love for his people when subjected to such privation?

The answer is a long one; not in space but in time. For four hundred years since David, God repeatedly rebuked and chastised his people for their continuing sin; sometimes resulting in a short behaviour change but rarely in meaningful ongoing repentance. It is a story of escalating penalties culminating in their exile.

I recall the Cuban missile crisis when Khrushchev of the Soviet Union was planting nuclear missiles in Cuba, which President Kennedy of the United States opposed. Kennedy's response was to raise the stakes for Khrushchev incrementally until Khrushchev eventually backed down and removed the missiles.

Similarly, censure of our children should match, not only the severity of the action that occasioned it, but also evidence of any escalating level of rebellion.

Prayer: O Lord, the extent of discipline for our children is often difficult to assess. Give us your insight into attitudes as well as actions that require our intervention.

WEEK THIRTY-SIX: TUESDAY

The Final Covenant

Read: Jeremiah 31:31–37

"Only if the heavens above can be measured and the foundations of the earth below be searched out will I reject all the descendants of Israel because of all they have done." Jeremiah 31:37.

This passage promises God will eventually establish a New Covenant (New Testament) with Israel. The Old Covenant (Old Testament) had its limitations— primarily because Israel was unable to abide by its terms, and so repeatedly lost the benefits of the covenant.

The New Covenant would be written on their hearts, not on tablets of stone. It specifically speaks of a time when "they will all know me"; a time when the knowledge of God would be universal, Isaiah 11:9.

Much of this is still future, but the New Covenant was introduced by the coming of Jesus Christ and is already available, although awaiting its full consummation at the return of Christ to earth.

God's commitment to this covenant toward Israel is guaranteed as long as his creation continues, stated unequivocally in verses 36 and 37. In the meantime, this age provides for Gentiles to enter the New Covenant.

I am sure that making a similar level of commitment of love to our partners would be intimidating for most of us, even if our desire is the same. But Israel's Lord is as faithful to us in our personal lives as he is toward Israel as a nation.

We can bring that same God into our lives as we commit to trust him, not only for our salvation, but also for his investment in our marriages; to strengthen our ability to be faithful to our partners.

Prayer: Heavenly Father, thank you for the everlasting and secure covenant you have made with us. Help us imitate you in keeping the covenant we made with our partners.

God Keeps His Covenant

Read: Jeremiah 32:1–15

This is what the Lord Almighty, the God of Israel, says: "Houses, fields and vineyards will again be bought in this land."
Jeremiah 32:15.

Ann had two great-uncles who were brothers. They bought a row of cottages just before the outbreak of World War Two for a song; they might not be standing at the end of the war, or valueless because of possible Nazi occupation.

But the cottages were still standing as the war ended at a time when property values were at their highest. After some expense in upgrading the cottages they sold for enough money to retire on.

Jeremiah faced a similar dilemma: he was told to buy land when the army that was besieging Jerusalem already occupied it. It was worthless. Jeremiah's uncle owned the land and wanted Jeremiah to buy it, perhaps thinking that the prophet was a little dense and would jump at the chance to buy it cheap.

Jeremiah did buy it, not as a financial investment, but to provide a practical illustration of God's promise that the exile was not permanent and God would bring Judah back to the land.

Despite Israel's deserved exile, God remained their covenant Lord, committed to watch over them and eventually restore them to the land and to himself.

Whatever the outcome of any marital conflict we may face, whether it results in break-up or reconciliation, our status with God will never change.

It is the same God that we worship and who keeps his covenant with us. A failed marriage is not a barrier to God's love and forgiveness and an eternity with him.

Prayer: Lord, you know the guilt that comes with a failed relationship. I pray for your forgiveness and thank you for the promise of reconciliation with you.

God Chooses His Bride

Read: Ezekiel 16:1–14

I gave you my solemn oath and entered into a covenant with you, declares the Sovereign Lord, and you became mine. Ezekiel 16:8.

The words adultery and idolatry sound similar and there is a significant bond between the two in Scripture. Regularly in the Old Testament, as with this chapter, idolatry symbolizes a form of adultery against God. In the New Testament, the relationship between Jesus Christ and his Church is seen as a marriage union, Matthew 22:1–2, Ephesians 5:22–27, Revelation 19:7–8.

This passage illustrates the mercy of God in rescuing the infant nation from its forbears, and implies the establishment of Abraham, rescued from his pagan ancestors, as the origin of Israel.

Later, when this despised one, as Israel is depicted, became marriageable, God became her husband and protector, lavishing his love upon her. This portrays the nation of Israel, born as a slave to Egypt, ill treated, persecuted until the exodus, and eventually under the reign of Solomon, a sovereign nation controlling her own destiny and at peace with her neighbours.

For our purposes, the picture of the love of God for his bride mirrors the love of a husband for his wife.

Women reading this may justifiably bristle at the depiction of the infant Israel as representing them; it hardly illustrates today's independent woman. Never-the-less, many of the world's women suffer exploitation from men rather than flourish under men's protection.

The care and concern lavished by God on his selected bride demonstrates my part as a husband to ensure that my wife's freedom and gifting advance the family and the community beyond.

Prayer: Thank you Lord, for reminding us that you have betrothed us to yourself ensuring our eternal security.

The Bride Turns to Prostitution

Read: Ezekiel 16:15–29

You trusted in your beauty and used your fame to become a prostitute. Ezekiel 16:15.

When I was a teen, some-one explained to me that every privilege carries a responsibility. The privileges afforded to Israel by God gave her the responsibility to respond wisely.

Today's reading pictures Israel as an unfaithful bride; she fell under the seductive power of affluence, which alone is insufficient to fill the longings in our hearts. It leads to boredom and a search for entertainment to fill the void. God led Israel to a place of prosperity and she was bored with him.

The charge of prostitution was not totally symbolic. The sexual activity of the Canaanite gods supposedly provided fertility to the earth, but they had to be encouraged and shown how. Ritual prostitution provided the example at shrines in public squares and streets.

Charges of prostitution with the Egyptians, Assyrians and Babylonians, were symbolic of military alliances sought for protection. Both the religious and military "prostitution" was a rejection of God's promise to provide fertile crops and protection from Israel's enemies.

Wouldn't it have been better for God to ignore the discarded baby if she eventually turned out so immoral? Not necessarily. Israel had freedom of choice; she could have chosen a better path.

Both husband and wife have a similar responsibility: for him to discharge his duties to his wife and for her to respond to the advantages she receives. Israel's idolatry was a symbol of adultery against God and rejection of his promise. In the same way, seeking fulfillment outside of marriage also denies God's faithfulness to us.

Prayer: O Lord, help us always remember that unfaithfulness to each other belies your faithfulness to your people.

217

WEEK THIRTY-SIX: WEEKEND

Marriage Made in Heaven

We make the most critical choices in life when we are young and the least prepared for them. Surely, the best time to choose a marriage partner would be in old age when life experience and wisdom would ensure the best choice—although even that could be suspect.

But God did not create us this way, so how can we ensure our children and grandchildren make the right choices? We do not have the ability to arrange marriages as some cultures do. However, parents and grandparents can still be influential and provide guidance for later generations to develop sustainable marriages.

As our grandchildren were born, we felt constrained to pray for them. This was probably because they mostly lived major distances away and so we had less hands-on influence with them. Our prayers were that they would come into fellowship with God through accepting Jesus Christ as Saviour.

But we also prayed for the ones they would marry, that those our grandchildren chose to marry would be God's provision. So we began to pray for those children also, although we did not know who they were.

To date, we've had the privilege of seeing two grandchildren marry, and of welcoming into the family a fine grandson-in-law, and a beautiful granddaughter-in-law.

It was a special joy for us to tell our granddaughter-in-law that we had been praying for her since her husband was born, and then to hear her say that *her* grandfather had be praying for *our* grandson for the same length of time.

Prayer: Dear Father, we continue to pray for our grandchildren that you will guide them through the difficult times they may encounter to maintain a secure home for their children.

Decline of the Prostitute

Read: Ezekiel 16:30–42

"I will put a stop to your prostitution, and you will no longer pay your lovers. Then my wrath against you will subside and my jealous anger will turn away from you." Ezekiel 16:41–42.

Following the last passage, this reading shows Israel's behaviour went from increasing adultery to loss of dignity. The punishment described for Israel is only partly symbolic. The action of stripping her bare and naked is certainly suggestive of the pillage of the land by the Assyrians and Babylonians shortly after Ezekiel's writing.

Frequently, the result of immoral or addictive behaviour is not a punishment inflicted from outside. The decline and final defeat of Israel was an inevitable result of her seeking solutions for legitimate needs by illegitimate means.

The same is true of life generally; frequently after failure to obtain enduring satisfaction we engage more deeply in the practice that has failed us. Until we find our fulfillment in God and the provision he has made for us, we will always be disappointed, however deeply we engage in independent pursuits.

For both men and women, there can be a lasting satisfaction in marriage where each is pre-eminently concerned for the other's welfare. Seeking to guard this relationship—however hard at times—can bring us unparalleled contentment.

Despite the record of broken marriages, the vast numbers of couples portraying the truth of this passage attest to the wisdom of Scripture, and the merit of following God's plan for the sexes.

Prayer: O Lord, the results of prostitution are too horrific to contemplate. Open our eyes to see the value of obedience to your ways which are so much higher than ours.

219

WEEK THIRTY-SEVEN: TUESDAY

The Sacrifice of Reconciliation
Read: Hosea 1:1–11; 3:1–3

"Go, show your love to your wife again, though she is loved by
another and is an adulteress. Love her as the Lord loves the
Israelites. Hosea 3:1.

From a Christian viewpoint the story of Hosea and
Gomer is unexpected. God called Hosea to marry a
prostitute. We don't know whether Gomer was a
prostitute before Hosea married her or afterwards.

Either way, the story is an extraordinary one of
reconciliation under the most adverse circumstances. After
she had borne Hosea children, Gomer went into a life of
prostitution, which led to her slavery and she became
available in a slave market. On condition of her restored
faithfulness to him, Gomer purchased her back as his wife.

The reading indicates this was an acted parable,
frequent in prophetic writing. The behaviour of Hosea and
Gomer reflected the relationship between God and his
people Israel.

Previous readings recall a similar story of Israel's
unfaithfulness and God's determination to restore her to
himself. Both these stories reminded Israel of God's
enduring love that would never cease, Hosea 11:9.

Our lives are also acted parables. Our lives tell others
about God. Our faithfulness reflects his; our unfaithfulness
suggests we can't trust him. Faithfulness, especially
reconciliation, reflects his love for us.

But reconciliation is not simple acceptance. God's offer
of forgiveness is available upon our repentance. But what
especially characterizes the love of God is the patience to
await that change.

The opportunity to repair a relationship requires
patience, dedication, and love for the other and above all a
reliance on God who demonstrated these characteristics.

Prayer: Lord, we recall the sacrifice you made to reconcile us to
yourself. May each of us be prepared to make the
sacrifices necessary to remain faithful to each other.

God's Love for His People

Read: Hosea 11:1–11

'How can I give you up, Ephraim? How can I hand you over, Israel?" Hosea 11:8.

Yesterday's poignant story of Hosea and his wife Gomer, illustrated the relationship between God and Israel. Today, that comparison is gone and the language is straightforward.

In past readings we noted the severity of Israel's exile and the suffering it created. Today, we see God's love for his people despite their continuing waywardness. He speaks of their "childhood" and his care and compassion for them after rescuing them from slavery in Egypt.

A few years ago, a 23 year old son of a millionaire was abducted at gunpoint in Vancouver. The parents appeared on television pleading for the son's safe return; their distress was agonizing to watch.

It illustrates the heartbreak of God at his people's suffering, his yearning for their return to him and his promise of eventual restoration. He cannot treat them like Admah and Zeboiim, cities of the plain destroyed with Sodom and Gomorrah, Deuteronomy 29:23.

The phrase: "Out of Egypt I have called my son," refers to Israel, but the phrase is later used in relation to Jesus' return from Egypt after his parents fled there to avoid Herod's threats, Matthew 2:15. God showed the same protection for the infant Jesus as he did for the emerging nation of Israel from Egypt.

As we watch our own children growing up and notice their vulnerability, we can be confident that God has that same love for the children that's our privilege to bear. Even in the most difficult of times, we can rest in the assurance that God has them in his hands.

Prayer: Thank you, Lord, for your unfailing love to us and to our children. Even in the most distressing times, we know they are safe in your hands.

WEEK THIRTY-SEVEN: THURSDAY

Handling our Resources

Read: Haggai 1:1–14

"You earn wages, only to put them in a purse with holes in it."
Haggai 1:6.

Probably the greatest source of friction in marriage is the use of money. Even for frugal couples, income is often insufficient to cover necessary expenses and argument reigns over how to apportion it.

The advice of a good consultant may alleviate the problem, and a wise man once said that each of us is entitled to keep something of what we earn—always put a percentage aside.

While this passage can suggest Christians should provide a percentage of their income to support their local church, there is a more general application. Our spirituality may directly affect our ability to assure the provisions of life.

Haggai made a direct connection between Israel's neglect of God's honour and their lack of prosperity. It may well be the prosperity enjoyed by the western world results from the Christian roots of that civilization—however erratic, meagre, and poorly understood.

Thus, as God becomes increasingly irrelevant to western culture, its prosperity will decline. The huge indebtedness of western governments and their citizens is just the beginning.

Culture starts with the individual. How do we honour God in our everyday life? How do we divide up our time and resources? Answering these questions may be the key to our personal prosperity and the freedom from economic friction in our marriages.

A happy home is a healthy home, and distress over money is one risk we can eliminate from the dangers to marriage.

Prayer: Dear Father, we need wise, godly advice in the management of the resources you have given us.

Marriage Failure

Read: Malachi 2:10–16

Guard yourself in your spirit, and do not break faith. Malachi 2:16.

Adultery in the Old Testament required the death penalty as did murder, for sexual immorality has the same power to destroy marriage. Like death, it splits in two those who have become "one flesh."

In our reading, divorcing Jewish women to make way for foreign wives was violence against them. To consider divorce as a form of violence against women, provoked God's formidable statement, "I hate divorce," and puts into perspective the seriousness of divorce.

If so, why did the law and Jesus provide for divorce? Deuteronomy 24:1–4, Matthew 5:32; 19:9. Fortunately, Jesus recognized that in our fallen state there would be occasions when marriage would fail, or living conditions would become intolerable.

Scripture presumes marriage failure is a sexual violation of the marriage and divorce could provide release from insufferable conditions. The break-up of some marriages is unavoidable, but it is not the unforgivable sin.

Most of us have engaged in behaviour that posed danger to our marriages. If by God's grace our marriage has remained intact, we are no less guilty than those whose marriages have failed; we are all in the same boat, equally needing God's forgiveness for abuse in our marriages.

Our reading encourages us to "guard yourself in your spirit, and do not break faith." This clearly relates to breaking faith with our partners, but if a Christian is unfaithful to a wife or husband, the example is a lie about God himself, for he is never unfaithful.

Prayer: Heavenly Father, we implore you to be the guardian of our marriage and our children. We want our marriage to be a witness of your faithfulness to those who put their faith in you.

For Us or For Him?

The Bible says little regarding marriage directly. As Christians consider marriage to be the cornerstone of society, this seems to be a strange omission. Today, a thriving industry is devoted to marriage and family guidance—even this book could be included—much of it inspired by Christian belief.

But while little is written specifically on the marriage relationship in Scripture, there is a great deal on interpersonal relationships based on the relationship between God and his people.

Of even greater significance, Scripture considers our service to one another as service to God himself, Matthew 25:40. Additionally, our personal relationships are a witness to the faithfulness of God in his relationship to us, his people, Ephesians 5:25 and Philippians 2:5.

However, these ideas are strictly Christian. For someone with a secular outlook on life, the marriage relationship depends purely on what each partner needs or desires. On this level, human love can do great things, but marriage cannot provide resources that come from God alone.

As our culture has moved away from its historical Christian roots—even worse, as Christians have adopted much of the culture's philosophy—marriage has become less secure. This is evident in the number of broken marriages, single parents, and displaced children.

Marriages are a barometer of our cultural commitment to God. If we are serious about our Christian faith and its impact on life, we will lean less on interpersonal resources and look to our relationship with God to guide us in our commitment to one another.

Prayer: We thank you, Lord, for the marriage you have given us, despite its imperfections. Discourage us from expecting from our partner what only you can give.

224

An Unmarried Pregnancy

Read: Matthew 1:18–25

Mary was pledged to be married to Joseph, but before they came together, she was found to be with child through the Holy Spirit. Matthew 1:18.

Mary's pregnancy may have filled her with awe and wonder but was a source of great distress for Joseph. Engagement in that culture was equivalent to marriage but without sexual union.

Pregnancy out of wedlock was a source of great shame and stigma. So Joseph was not happy about the pregnancy, and initially he did not believe her story. After all, her revelation was hardly a common occurrence.

For Mary, the situation was just as distressing; knowing her innocence yet knowing few would accept her. But misunderstood by Joseph would have been harder to take, even if expected.

But Joseph was a compassionate and devout man. Even though he could not accept her story at the outset, he wanted to provide the least grief and "divorce her quietly." But God intervened, and Joseph learned the truth through his dream. Despite the scorn and stigma, he responded to the angel's instructions and stood by Mary.

A daughter who becomes pregnant has many questions. How will she cope with a child and no income? Will the father accept responsibility? How will her parents respond? What will family and friends think? Is an abortion the answer?

It is a life changing experience, but whether for better or worse largely depends on the parents. If their love for her is greater than the fear for their reputation, they can steer their daughter through her turbulent waters, and eventually find great joy in the grandchild God has given.

Prayer: O Lord, we trust you with our children and grandchildren and ask you for compassion and wisdom in the difficult circumstances our children face.

WEEK THIRTY-EIGHT: TUESDAY

The World Attacks Children

Read: Matthew 2:13–18

[Herod] gave orders to kill all the boys in Bethlehem and its vicinity who were two years old and under. Matthew 2:16.

The concern over a pregnant daughter is natural, but it often overshadows the welfare of the unborn child. Herod saw the child Jesus as a threat to his throne, so he did all he could to destroy the newborn child. Again it was God's intervention that saved the child's life.

The worldwide tragedy today is that the unborn and young are under immense threat from a variety of sources. In this story Herod, in his attempt to destroy the Giver of life, is the archetype of all those who place young life in jeopardy.

The threat to life is ubiquitous, from the parents, boyfriends, and husbands of pregnant girls, to systematic abortion by decree in nations like China, and western pressure for abortions in developing nations.

Infanticide is widely practised in India and China where daughters are a liability. In the west, the inconvenience of children is the major threat to the unborn, abortions numbering millions every year.

The trauma of an unwanted and inconvenient pregnancy is no excuse for taking the unborn child's life. Whatever the reason for the pregnancy, God is still the giver of life.

Even if the young couple's sin is the cause of the pregnancy, the child's life should not be sacrificed for the sin of its parents.

That is true even if there are unintended consequences the unborn child may have to endure due to its inconvenient entry into a mother's womb.

Prayer: Heavenly Father, we thank you for the children you have given us. Give us the moral courage to support young lives and reduce their suffering or death.

Practising Hypocrisy

Read: Matthew 5:17–20

"Whoever practices and teaches these commands will be called great in the kingdom of heaven." Matthew 5:19.

Today's reading opposes the view that the Old Testament is no longer relevant for Christians. Jesus taught the whole law remains in effect, and the punishments associated with the law also continue in effect.

Throughout his earthly ministry Jesus never disallowed judgments under Moses' law, but did question the right of accusers to impose it, John 8:7. Further, Jesus summarized the law as loving God and loving one's neighbour—"All the law and the Prophets hang on these two commandments," Matthew 22:34–36.

Jesus' exhortation to maintain a better standard of righteousness than the scribes and Pharisees seems especially difficult. They lived exemplary lives, and displayed them for all to see, yet Jesus had his greatest condemnation for them.

In today's terms, they had a clean face on the Sabbath, but in their hearts they were driven by less honourable motives—in particular, to maintain status, Matthew 6:2, 5, and 16. So Jesus characterized them as hypocrites, clean on the outside, but dirty within, Matthew 23:25–28.

Simply put, the Pharisees were playing games with their devotion to God. Unfortunately, we tend to do the same, often using poor attitudes or negative actions to manipulate our partners. A husband's anger and violence are not unusual in "Christian" families, yet that husband may project a calm and pious veneer to the world.

If we are serious in our faith, we will avoid God's wrath by admitting our games and ending coercion of those closest to us.

Prayer: O Lord, we admit we act in frustration, anger, or resentment in trying to have things our way. Forgive us, as we seek the forgiveness of our partner.

227

WEEK THIRTY-EIGHT: THURSDAY

Attitudes: Not Just Actions

Read: Matthew 5:21–28

"I tell you that anyone who looks at a woman lustfully has already committed adultery with her in his heart." Matthew 5:28.

After his instruction to attain a greater righteousness than the Pharisees, Jesus did not leave us without help. He gave examples of the Pharisees' righteousness. They believed that simply complying with lists of laws was sufficient, and other actions or attitudes were irrelevant.

This led to contradictory results which Jesus himself pointed out. Pharisees would dedicate money to God which should have assisted their parents, Mark 7:10–13, and ensured accurate tithing without considering virtues necessary to serve God's people, Matthew. 23:23–24.

Jesus extended the idea of sin beyond actions to attitudes revealing a desire to sin. While the law clearly defined murder as killing an innocent party, Jesus considered anger equal to murder; similarly a lustful look at a woman as adultery.

The sin was already committed in the heart, whether or not acted upon. For someone defrauded, Jesus required a change of heart leading to repayment to the victim before being sued.

These requirements may seem unattainable, but they serve to underline the sinfulness of our hearts and the need of God's grace. As we have received his grace, we should also give it, for our partners battle the same sinful hearts that we do.

But of greater significance, we must be prepared to deal with anger, lust and other negative attitudes that precede sinful acts. In so doing, we take a pre-emptive strike against potential sinful situations and avoid those occasions that jeopardize our marriage relationships.

Prayer: Dear Lord, we need your strength to keep our thoughts and attitudes under control, as well as our actions. Help us seek your daily cleansing and purity of thought.

Avoiding Temptation

Read: Matthew 5:29–37

Simply let your 'Yes' be 'Yes,' and your 'No,' 'No'; anything beyond
this comes from the evil one. Matthew 5:37.

A lady, addicted to drugs but who had a soft heart towards God, attended our church. She was aware of these verses, and continually threatened to cut her hands off. She was sufficiently unstable at times that we feared she might actually do it.

We pointed out there are few one-handed Christians around, that most understand the passage as hyperbole— exaggeration to make a point. She would follow our reasoning for a while, and then simply state she was going to cut her hands off. Fortunately, she never did.

The great third century theologian Origen took this passage more literally, castrating himself to eliminate sexual temptation. The point of the passage is strictly to avoid situations or practices that seduce us into sexual sin.

Wandering eyes are a major cause of divorce, as desire for someone else breeds dissatisfaction with a current partner. Jesus recognized sexual uncleanness as grounds for divorce, as it broke the marriage vows.

Jesus summarizes these instructions with advice not to make an oath before God. After all, an oath is only necessary if normal commitments are not trustworthy, with the added danger of invoking God's wrath on us if we break it.

His concern is that we keep the promises we make, for in doing so we reflect the image of God who keeps his promises. Following the passages on avoiding sexual temptation and divorce, maintaining our promises to our partners is of primary importance in maintaining those relationships.

Prayer: Lord, you have been teaching us that attitude is as important as action. Help us control our thought patterns and avoid potentially seductive situations which can lead to infidelity.

WEEK THIRTY-EIGHT: WEEKEND

Peace

The earth sorely needs those who can bring peace to a planet that has known conflict since its beginning. We know that final peace will elude the world until the coming of the Prince of Peace, but how do we find inner peace amid the current conflicts of life?

First, the world will always have war as long as individuals cannot find peace with their neighbours. While watching the many peace marches world wide—and agreeing with their desire—I often wonder if those marching are at peace with those they live with.

To berate the leaders of the world for failure to achieve peace while at personal loggerheads with legitimate authorities, adjacent neighbours or family members is the height of hypocrisy.

Second, those who cannot live with people around them are generally not at peace with themselves. Conflict with others is usually a result of conflict within oneself; internal anger, dissatisfaction, turmoil or resentment are frequently displaced and directed at others. But how can we find that often elusive peace for ourselves?

Last, the Bible teaches that the source of peace is outside of ourselves; we can have peace within when we have peace with God.

Although the coming of the Prince of Peace will finally bring peace on earth, Jesus has already offered us peace with God by his sacrifice on the cross for our sin. We can trust God with the inequities of life that cause conflict—even our own guilt.

The knowledge that our status is settled for ever gives us an inner peace that we can share with others.

Prayer: Thank you, Lord Jesus, for making the sacrifice that reconciles us to a holy God. Thank you for peace with God in Christ, our earthly and eternal security.

Responding to Injustice

Read: Matthew 5:38–48

Love your enemies and pray for those who persecute you, that you may be sons of your Father in heaven. Matthew 5:44–45.

How does a Christian cope with a relationship that has deteriorated to that of uneasy co-existence? Any communication is more like defending against an enemy rather than communing with a friend.

When the Bible says we are to love our enemies—"If someone strikes you on the right cheek, turn to him the other also"—how does this work out in practice? Does today's reading suggest that we should submit to any injustice?

Jesus' teaching is best understood by how he responded to his enemies. While on trial, Jesus set the record straight. He asked for legitimate witnesses and requested just treatment, John 18:20–23.

He made clear statements confirming the truth about himself, based his final exoneration outside of earthly courts, Matthew 26:64, John 18:36–37. He set Pilate straight on the limits of Pilate's authority, John 19:11, and faced his martyrdom with resolution, not resignation.

He was silent "as a sheep before her shearers," exhibiting no anger, resentment or revenge, but rather showing compassion towards his persecutors by praying that they would be forgiven, Luke 23:34.

Love for a partner in a broken relationship especially means praying for them as Jesus prayed for his tormentors. It is not possible to pray for someone without loving him or her and if we pray in love, we will pray for them as we would pray for ourselves.

If prayer is an expression of love, it also increases our love and consequently our ability to weather the storm.

Prayer: O Lord, draw me closer to you so I absorb more of your nature, and respond with the grace and truth Jesus showed in opposing personal attacks.

WEEK THIRTY-NINE: TUESDAY

Children Make Choices

Read: Matthew 7:13–23

"Enter through the narrow gate. For wide is the gate and broad is the road that leads to destruction." Matthew 7:13.

This passage is a picture of those who have rejected Jesus Christ by following self-destructive paths, or falsely represented him for their own advancement.

But it becomes a tragedy when we conceive of God releasing his own created children to perdition. Parents should be encouraged to know that even God, as a perfect parent, did not raise perfect children.

How often have you beaten yourself up as a parent for the behaviour of your children? We do this when we recognize ourselves as imperfect parents, losing patience or making errors of judgment.

Most parents regret something in the handling of the childhood years, and while we—as opposed to God—may foster some legitimate guilt, our children often make their own decisions, irrespective of our desire for them to make better ones.

But even our mistakes are not completely lost. A child with perfect parents would never learn at an early age to face difficulties that later life will present.

When our two girls were small, we couldn't afford the heating we would have liked in our home, and Ann walked them in the winter air to avoid lighting a fire too early. The girls were robust and healthy; unlike two neighbour boys of similar age in a centrally heated house who were continually weak and sickly.

If childhood is preparation for adulthood, then they will learn from our mistakes. But also over protectiveness may expose them, unprepared, to hazards in later life.

Prayer: Lord, you know we try the best for our children. We know they will make their own decisions, but we pray you will continually make yourself known to them, so they will always be aware of you.

232

The Source of Authority

Read: Matthew 8:5–13

Just say the word, and my servant will be healed. For I myself am a man under authority. Matthew 8:8–9.

This passage reveals an important fact about authority. The centurion clearly perceived that his authority was derived, not autonomous. He could only command because he was under authority of the army he served and he wielded that greater authority.

Paul elaborates, explaining that all earthly authority comes from God. To disobey those authorities risks the judgment of God, Romans 13:1–5. But those authorities cannot act as they please; God will judge them according to their record of furthering God's will on earth.

A mother explained to her small daughter that God wanted her to act in a certain way, and then instructed her. The child, defiant, retorted that her mother was not God. Her mother replied: "I am God to you."

The mother had grasped the principle that all authority is derived; we do not wield our own. She was God to her child as long as she fulfilled God's desire for the child.

The centurion realized that Jesus had the Father's full authority behind him just as the centurion represented the authority of the Roman Army. That was the basis of the centurion's faith.

This should give us caution as well as encouragement in the raising of our children: caution that we cannot exploit the authority given to us. To exceed that authority may harm the children and bring us reprisals.

But we can be encouraged that we have God's authority to steer our children in the right path. As we obey his Word and teach our children his ways, we can trust God with the future outcome.

Prayer: Heavenly Father, we thank you for the authority you have given us. Grant us the wisdom to wield it in accordance with your plans and purposes.

WEEK THIRTY-NINE: THURSDAY

A New Relationship

Read: Matthew 9:14–17

"How can the guests of the bridegroom mourn while he is with them?" Matthew 9:15.

Jesus uses wedding imagery in the New Testament, portraying himself as a Bridegroom to his people. But the Husband of the Old Testament is a stark contrast to the Bridegroom of the New. Under the Old Covenant, Israel was in continual danger of losing fellowship with God and reaping the consequences of disobedience.

But under the New Covenant, the Bridegroom has already paid the price of infidelity, and to be with him is a time for rejoicing, not fasting.

The difference is not just a matter of adding the new ideas to the old. The new is incompatible with the old. To patch the old garment with the new material will tear the old, and similarly, the new wine poured into the old wineskins will burst them.

Jesus' coming exploded the old relationship to make way for the new. But the basis of the relationship was unchanged. In both, God loved his people and provided for them according to his character which *doesn't* change.

Jesus took our failure upon himself and in so doing gave us freedom to fail. Similarly, we are able to cover our partner's failures without expecting atonement. This, of course, is for minor irritants, not major injustices which need dealing with directly.

To rearrange the dishwasher my partner loaded haphazardly for a more efficient wash is a form of sacrifice, as opposed to complaining and expecting some form of penance.

We can repeat this a dozen times daily, letting that spirit of grace and forgiveness give us joy in living with each other.

Prayer: Dear Lord, you have done so much for us, how can we not do a hundred little things for our partners?

Facing Persecution

Read: Matthew 10:16–25

I am sending you out like sheep among wolves. Therefore be as shrewd as snakes and as innocent as doves. Matthew 10:16.

The persecution of Christians has been an ongoing atrocity since the time of Christ. As he was maligned and crucified, so his followers have been mistreated simply for believing in him.

This persecution is not only from outside. The Church has also had its own program of martyring "heretics" who held different views on secondary issues of the faith.

The greater tragedy is the splitting of families over the issues of faith as predicted in this passage; worse the willingness of parents to put their children to death and vice versa.

A local church in our hometown had a pastor whose daughter befriended a non-Christian man. The pastor decided her "sin" must isolate her from her family and the congregation. The girl eventually married her choice and the separation from her father was complete.

By all accounts she had a good marriage, but the church split over the issue and folded. God in Christ had extended his saving grace and forgiveness to the father who in turn refused that same grace to his daughter.

Christian parents and children often argue on issues of faith. Like the example above, it is not always the children that are entirely to blame. A child's rebellion against the guidelines of faith demands careful insight of the parents toward themselves as well as their child.

Certainly extend discipline required during the early years. But let the grace of acceptance be our ongoing attitude to them as they enter adult life, just as God accepted us before we trusted him.

Prayer: Lord, you know how much we wish for our children to follow you. Help us maintain a loving relationship with them, and show our love always as you have loved us.

235

WEEK THIRTY-NINE: WEEKEND

Faith or Works?

Some of this week's devotionals must have raised the questions about acceptance by God as a result of obedience—especially the value of that obedience under persecution.

The foremost tenet of the Christian faith since its inception has been that faith in God is the means of salvation and reconciliation with him. Yet Israel was continually encouraged to obedience of the Ten Commandments which formed the basis of all Old Testament laws. But a couple of things illustrate faith as the governing factor in relationship with God.

The Israelites' salvation was not in keeping the law which no-one could keep and only condemned them, Romans 7:9, but in believing that God accepted their sacrifices as atonement for breaking the law.

It was faith in that promise that saved them. You may recall that it was Abraham's faith that God counted as righteousness, Genesis 15:6.

Second, actions betray belief. While what we do cannot save us, our actions are evidence of what we really believe—that is, evidence of the faith that saves us.

Jesus said "If you love me, keep my commands," John 14:15. Jesus considered our actions confirm our love for him. Our children may say they love us, but we judge the claim by their actions toward us.

James takes up a parallel idea when he says: "Show me your faith without deeds, and I will show you my faith by what I do," James. 2:18. Our claim to believe in God's promise to us cannot be sustained if we act in a way that is contrary to that belief.

Prayer: Thank you Lord Jesus, for doing what we could not do for ourselves—keep the law. But also for taking our punishment upon yourself so we can be free of condemnation and enjoy relationship with you.

Rest in Jesus

Read: Matthew 11:20–30

No one knows the Son except the Father, and no one knows the
Father except the Son and those to whom the Son chooses to
reveal him. Matthew 11:27.

Parents have reason to be confused regarding the
rearing of children. A billboard recently had a picture
of a baby with the caption, "It doesn't come with
instructions." Add to that the plethora of advice by
"experts" and the bewilderment deepens.

The Bible does not open its wisdom to the "the wise
and learned," but reveals it to "little children." The Son
chooses to reveal knowledge about the life-giving God; it is
not some lofty secret imparted by a cadre of specialists.

Jesus raises the issue, common in Scripture, of
understanding spiritual things. The message Jesus brought
is by revelation, not the result of investigation alone—he
has "revealed them to little children."

This doesn't mean only children can understand, but
rather the humility and acceptance practised by young
children is the key to understanding, for his message is
spiritually discerned, 1 Corinthians 2:12–14. Acceptance of
Jesus Christ at face value gives spiritual insight and
understanding.

Those willing to accept him in this way Jesus calls to
himself, not just to live in fellowship with him, but also to
find rest in him.

It may seem strange that rest is being "yoked" to him,
but being "yoked" means partnership; he takes the heavier
part of the work, for "my burden is light."

Through the centuries God's people have found that
retreating into him is a place of quietness and rest, a place
to unburden and renew strength in him. If you are living in
difficult circumstances, this is your inheritance.

Prayer: Thank you, Lord, we do not have to bear life's burdens
alone, but you have promised to walk with us through the
dark times, and take the heavier load.

237

ANN AND BRYAN NORFORD

Truth by Revelation

Read: Matthew 13:11–17

"The knowledge of the secrets of the kingdom of heaven has been given to you, but not to them." Matthew 13:11.

This passage picks up the theme from yesterday's reading that understanding of spiritual things is through revelation.

People do not hear the Gospel for a number of reasons. It is too simple, an infantile and insufficient response to a complex world. Its simplicity offends the intellect which is better served arguing against the Gospel in complex terms.

For others, the Gospel interferes with their desires in life, and they devise arguments against it to bolster unbelief.

Of course, underlying these evasions—for all of us—is sin. Our sinful nature distorts the real truth about life. Sinfulness and flawed understanding feed off each other creating a downward spiral leading us further from the truth.

Those who are seduced from the truth this way are "ever seeing but not perceiving," because their "heart has become calloused." All of which leaves us with the provocative question: how can anyone find God?

As we saw previously, Jesus taught that understanding of spiritual things was a gift of revelation from God; the Holy Spirit came to convict men and women of their sinfulness and need of him, John 16:7–11.

Knowing that conversion is the work of God and not our responsibility can bring a great sense of relief. We are in partnership with God and it is the Holy Spirit who convicts of the truth.

If you are in a difficult relationship, God can reveal the truth to your partner, and prayer is your greatest resource.

Prayer: Heavenly Father, there is so much I don't understand. Holy Spirit, continually reveal your truth to our flawed understanding, and to our children, according to your promise.

Faith is Persistent

Read: Matthew 15:21–28

"Woman, you have great faith! Your request is granted."
Matthew 15:28.

This may seem like a "run of the mill" story about another healing by Jesus. However, each story has been included for a reason, usually to illustrate something of significance. So what is the significance of this story?

There are a number of items that stand out. Jesus initially refused to answer the woman, and when he did he refused her request because she was not Jewish. Was this plain old racial discrimination—especially when he suggested her people were dogs?

This woman was persistent and innovative. Perhaps Jesus knew this, responding in a way that drew her out, even enjoying the brief repartee they engaged in. His initial feigned indifference could not hide his compassion and he healed her daughter.

That this woman was an unlikely candidate for Jesus' care is the main point of the story. She was outside of the people he came to—"the lost sheep of Israel." Even his disciples didn't think she was worthy of attention, so we draw two lessons from this story.

First, Jesus was illustrating that Gentiles were not outside his care, in fact as the Gospel unfolds in Scripture, it is evident that the blessing of Abraham was to *all* peoples, Acts 3:25. Those of us outside the Jewish race are recipients of that promise.

Second, Jesus' compassion reaches beyond ourselves to those *we* might consider unworthy. Families are his concern, many of whom struggle outside the faith.

Are we willing to engage hurting fathers, mothers, and children outside of our faith as Jesus was?

Prayer: O Lord, thank you for the reminder you came for all people. Grant me the same compassion for anyone in need, irrespective of ethnic or spiritual status.

239

Humility the Greater Virtue

Read: Matthew 18:1–7

"Whoever humbles himself like this child is the greatest in the kingdom of heaven." Matthew 18:4.

We have already noted that real wisdom, beyond earthly wisdom is available to all who ask for it. Today's reading views the quality of humility as another asset in the resources of the spiritual person.

Jesus compares the humility of children who naturally defer to their immediate adults with those who are greatest in the kingdom of heaven. With few exceptions, children are generally content to live a carefree life unbothered with ambition for fame or fortune.

It seems in this context that humility is not to play the "doormat"—as is so often suggested—but the ability to fulfill God's requirements in our life without expecting accolades we think should be forthcoming. Jesus is explicit that the desire for public recognition is opposed to spiritual maturity.

In fact those who desire earthly recognition receive their reward in this life; it is those who work for him behind the scenes that will receive God's reward, Matthew 6:1–6, 16–18. That is not to say that we should shun public recognition—we all need encouragement at times—but it should not be our motivating factor.

We spend a lot of time teaching our children and ensuring right teaching, but spend too little time in learning from them.

It is their qualities of innocence, humility and trust that endear them to us; the qualities that we need in relation to our heavenly Father. It is those who exhibit these qualities that are the greatest in the kingdom of heaven.

Prayer: Lord, thank you for the children you have given us and for the example they can be for us. Give us teachable spirits.

The "One Flesh" Family

Read: Matthew 19:1–12

"The two will become one flesh, so they are no longer two, but one. Therefore what God has joined together, let man not separate." Matthew 19:5–6.

While a family may be various groupings, the Bible defines marriage between a man and a woman. Marriage is established as a procreative setting, Genesis 1:28, and as such, other unions are excluded.

But the sexes were also created for companionship, for it was "not good for man to be alone," Genesis 2:18, so Eve was brought to Adam as his companion, Genesis 2:20–24. Jesus quotes liberally from the Genesis passages, endorsing its message and restating the "one flesh" principle.

The relationship between man and wife is so strong, it is sufficient to break the bond with parents—to "leave" one and "cleave" to the other. Jesus reminds his listeners that they "become one flesh," just as Adam and Eve came from the same piece of clay.

This not only highlights the strength of the marriage bond, but also the pain associated with marriage break-up.

Jesus also recognized singleness as a viable option. In addition, Paul saw a spiritual advantage for those whose energies are not split between family and God's service, 1 Corinthians 7:32–35. In this way he supported singleness without denigrating the family.

However, if God has placed us in a family, our service to him is to serve them. It is illogical to consider that family is secondary to our service to God. Don't fall into the trap of letting either our family or outside ministry dominate the other.

Prayer: Thank you Lord, for the companionship you have given us in our partners. Keep us mindful our service to them is our service to you.

241

WEEK FORTY: WEEKEND

He Was Ready

A friend of ours, Brad, died recently, leaving a wife and two children. He had lived a precarious life due to sickness, and living until his fifties was a miracle. He had been near death several times earlier in life, but had survived long enough to witness the answer to his prayer: that he might live long enough to see his children become adults.

Brad, spurred by his sickness, continually invested himself in his family, ensuring his home was secure and a place of peace and comfort for its members. His wife, a registered nurse, supported him in his infirmity and through numerous medical operations.

Together they accomplished what neither could do alone: they established a place of refuge during the distressing times of life, recognizing God's grace and affirmation in their lives and marriage.

The story of Brad's last days is an illustration of his entire life. He had come to a place where critical heart surgery was necessary but loss of his life might occur.

He retrieved all his belongings and trophies from his work and finalized all the outstanding matters on his desk at home. He wrote to his church expressing his gratitude for its support during his sickness, and wrote to his family thanking them for their love and reaffirming his love for them.

He stated his confidence in God for both life and death, for himself and his family. He bought new furniture and appliances for the home, so that the succeeding years would be trouble free.

Finally, he emptied his personal bank account, giving his wife the check on the day of the operation that took his life. He was ready.

Prayer: O Lord, may we have the same courage to serve the partner that you have given us.

Children: A Temporary Gift

Read: Matthew 19:13–14

"Let the little children come to me, and do not hinder them, for the kingdom of heaven belongs to such as these." Matthew 19:14.

What we have read earlier helps us understand Jesus' rebuke to his disciples when they considered he was too busy to respond to children. Here, he repeats the basic concept that the nature of children is the quality that gains easier entrance to the kingdom of heaven.

But he not only used them as examples, he also cared for them; before he continued with his work he blessed them. The pictures of children surrounding him, sitting on his knee, seated or standing around him in fascination ring true, as does his enjoyment of the children.

His recognition of their qualities also made him angry at their mistreatment. To see the suffering of children widely disseminated in the media gives a real sense of the judgment awaiting the perpetrators.

But it is parents that abuse children who bear the greatest judgment. Our children are not really "ours," but lent to us for a time for our enjoyment. Placed in our care during a vulnerable period, we will account for their welfare.

While this may seem daunting, it is comforting to know that the mistakes we make will not be held against us. Children adapt; rarely holding our errors against us and forgiving as we admit our mistakes to them.

If our desire for our children is good and we get it right most of the time, they will probably be just fine. And when we acknowledge and confess our mistakes they are cancelled by our Saviour's blood.

Prayer: Dear Lord, thank you for our children, and thank you for the forgiveness they extend to us; a mirror of your care for us.

WEEK FORTY-ONE: TUESDAY

Service: Not Status

Read: Matthew 20:17–28

"The Son of Man did not come to be served, but to serve, and to give his life as a ransom for many." Matthew 20:28.

It is not unreasonable for parents to want the best for their children, but it is often sought at the expense of others. The mother of James and John sought special status for her two sons, above the other disciples. Her sons were also complicit in the request and the other disciples were indignantly aware of it.

The danger of conflict in this case was only part of the problem. Jesus' first response was that they didn't know what they were asking. So why did they not expect the answer they received?

Jesus had already told the disciples he would shortly be condemned and crucified, and later explained his death was one of service to mankind. This was the "cup" he was to "drink": one of suffering for the sake of others, and the disciples themselves would share with him.

James and John did not understand that only if their service with him accorded them the lowest status would they share his place of honour.

Perhaps today, this type of favouritism is the abusive hockey parent's tirade and violence when their child gets less than the parents want. They mirror Jesus' words: "that the rulers of the Gentiles lord it over [others]," by pushing their child in front.

But as Jesus said, "many who are first will be last, and many who are last will be first," Matthew 19:30. This does not legitimize humiliation or deny fairness but it reminds us and our children that the aim of Christian life is service, not status.

Prayer: Dear Jesus, you provided the ultimate example of the selfless servant. Keep us close to that pattern in our dealings with each other and those in need.

Childhood Perceptiveness

Read: Matthew 21:14–16

Replied Jesus, "Have you never read, 'From the lips of children and infants you have ordained praise'?" Matthew 21:16.

Children are often more perceptive than adults, probably because they are not contaminated with the skepticism that life and living brings us. This appears to have been the case in this passage: children saw Jesus healing and simply made four by putting two and two together. To them, he was the heralded Son of David.

The chief priests and teachers who had far more resources and reason to recognize Jesus' real identity failed to do so. In fact, they vehemently denied the children's claims for Jesus.

Jesus not only recognized the perceptiveness of the children around him, his response showed that it was God's plan to use children in the revelation of himself. They would be the ones who would recognize and proclaim the true identity of Jesus to the world.

Possibly these children were the ones who had stirred up the populace to welcome Jesus into Jerusalem earlier in the day as he rode into the city on that first Palm Sunday, Matthew 21:8–11.

It has been said, "Give me a child up to the age of six, and I will have him for life." This acknowledges that what children learn is likely to stay with them for life.

Our youngest daughter made her lifetime commitment to God at the age of three. She needed to rethink her understanding as she approached adulthood, and this is a time to question, possibly even reject their childhood conception of faith.

But the reality of childhood experience remains strong and many recognize the truth of their faith as they see it anew through adult eyes.

Prayer: Dear Lord, give us the perception of childhood, but the wisdom of your Holy Spirit as we attempt living daily according to your nature.

WEEK FORTY-ONE: THURSDAY

Unreliability

Read: Matthew 21:28–32

"I tell you the truth, the tax collectors and the prostitutes are entering the kingdom of God ahead of you." Matthew 21:31.

This story has a parallel with the two sons in the parable of the prodigal son. Two sons had opposite responses to their father's wishes. The defiant one eventually changed his mind and obeyed his father; the other agreed to his father's wishes but then failed to obey.

Jesus explained the basic lesson of this parable by pointing out that the religious leaders of his day failed to fulfill God's desires, but sinners repented and found acceptance into his kingdom.

However, the different responses of the two sons provide insights into the behaviour of all people; but the second son's response is certainly the most frustrating.

Children frequently give a positive response to a parent's command, but through laziness or distractions end up not complying. Outright defiance is simple animal behaviour, but deception is a greater fault for it is a sin of reason—God's gift peculiar to humankind deliberately used to mislead.

A child that lies tacitly admits wrong behaviour and guilt, and is using reason to avoid discipline. By willfully failing to carry out an agreed task, a child is testing a parent's resolve for the child to complete the task.

Without compulsion to obey, a pattern of deception—saying one thing and doing another—may be set, earning the Pharisee's reputation abhorred by Jesus. Setting a time limit, even letting the child do so, provides a measurable method of ensuring compliance and will discourage similar behaviour in the future.

Prayer: Heavenly Father, we need all the help we can get to discipline our children, May we set the example by following through on all our agreements.

Assurance for the Future

Read: Matthew 22:23–33

"'I am the God of Abraham, the God of Isaac, and the God of Jacob.' He is not the God of the dead but of the living."
Matthew 22:32.

The Sadducees were wrong on two counts: not believing in life beyond death, and in sarcastically postulating marriage beyond death.

Jesus responded to their argument against resurrection by showing that the patriarchs, Abraham, Isaac, and Jacob must be alive, for God "is not the God of the dead but of the living." That God's people will survive death has been the solid hope of Christians through the ages, assuring them that those who have gone before will be there to meet us; especially that our Saviour will be there to greet us in person.

But Jesus also corrected their imaginative view of heaven, by stating that there would be no marriage in heaven—men and women "would be like the angels in heaven."

It may come as a shock or disappointment that there is no marriage in heaven. For those with happy marriages on earth, it is a natural hope that the relationship will continue. But even our marriage vows indicate that marriage and the fidelity it demands ends at death.

In addition to partners, there are a host of loved ones that have gone before who we hope to see. That there will be a reunion is clear in Scripture, which is why we do not "grieve like the rest of men, who have no hope," 1 Thessalonians 4:13.

The reunions will be real, but the relationships will be different because we will be different, and the final union will be with Jesus Christ, whose bride we will be.

Prayer: Dear Lord, we are so thankful for the truth of eternal life and the reunions we shall experience. Most of all, we shall see you face to face, betrothed to you for eternity.

WEEK FORTY-ONE: WEEKEND

Idealism or Realism

I dealism is a feature of youth; realism a growing understanding gained later in life. Idealism sees "what should be done," while realism perceives "what can be done." These viewpoints are often the basis for dispute between the generations, the older and "wiser" having the experience to know the setbacks for any project.

On this basis, logic says that the older ideas should prevail. But realism often degenerates into "what can't be done." However, all the reasons why something can't be done often require only one way in which it can.

Childhood and youth see everything through young, fresh eyes, including methods and ideas not anticipated or available to their elders. They have the advantage of not being restricted by systems and processes adopted by the older and traditional generation, and are more able to "think outside the box."

The 1851 Festival of Britain in London a held a competition to determine the design of the main building. Many architects presented designs, but the winner was a huge steel and glass building (the Crystal Palace) designed by a gardener familiar with greenhouses.

He wasn't inhibited by the standard building techniques of his day, and his design was the forerunner of many later steel and glass buildings.

I am always amazed at the occasional news reports of children who have pioneered a fund collection or humanitarian project, often with remarkable results.

Rather than recount why a child's idea cannot be done, enable them to think through their own ideas on how problems can be overcome. We may be amazed at what their idealism can accomplish.

Prayer: O Lord, give us the perception to recognize the idealistic ideas of our children and help them develop ways of accomplishing those desires.

Love from the Heart

Read: Matthew 22:34–40

"All the Law and the Prophets hang on these two commandments."
Matthew 22:40.

You may recall that Jeremiah forecast a time when God would write the Law on hearts, not on stone, Jeremiah 31:33. It is the Spirit of God, placing us into the salvation offered in Jesus Christ that transforms the Law into a life giving reality, 2 Corinthians 3:6; love fulfills the Law, Romans 13:10.

In today's reading, Jesus teaches that to love God with heart, soul, mind, and strength and to love our neighbour as ourselves are the supreme commandments, which summarize all the Law and the Prophets.

The Ten Commandments, Exodus 20:1–17, are about love; the first four about our relationship to God, and the remaining six how we live with our neighbour.

These commandments tell us how we relate to God and our neighbour. For instance, if we love our neighbours we will not kill them, commit adultery against them, or steal from them.

This means we have flexibility in fulfilling the Law. Jesus completed the Law for us—both by keeping it and dying for our failure to do so. We no longer obey the Law out of fear, but in the grace of God's forgiveness, freeing us to love from the heart and not by the letter.

Our marriage partners are our neighbours. As we live in the freedom of God's grace and forgiveness, we can love them from the heart covering them with *our* grace and forgiveness. The blood of Christ covers their mistakes and faults in trying to love just as ours are.

Prayer: Dear Lord, thank you for freeing us to love from our hearts and not according to the letter of the Law. Grant us the power and wisdom of your Spirit in fulfilling your commands in this way.

249

The Pain of Rejection

Read: Matthew 23:33 to 24:2

"O Jerusalem, Jerusalem, you who kill the prophets and stone those sent to you, how often I have longed to gather your children together, as a hen gathers her chicks under her wings, but you were not willing." Matthew 23:37.

We may think knowing the future would be an enormous advantage for life. But for Jesus, being God incarnate, that knowledge was a distinct disadvantage.

John spelt it out in the opening words of his Gospel that "though the world was made by him, the world did not recognize him. He came unto his own, but his own did not receive him," John 1:10–11. Jesus knew in advance that the city he loved and cared for would reject him and be destroyed.

But it was not just the rejection that distressed him; it was also the desolation that would come to Jerusalem: sacked by the Roman army and the city's inhabitants scattered to the four winds some forty years later.

He describes in chapter 24 the destruction of the temple that would accompany that attack. Today, only the temple platform remains of the original temple—apart from the Muslim Dome of the Rock built later—and the Wailing Wall that supports its foundations.

The parent-child relationship that Scripture often uses to illustrate God's relationship to his people occurs again here. If Jesus can mourn over the condition of a defiant Israel, he can identify with parents of rebellious children.

Your children may have cut themselves off from you, seeking a precarious life of their own and you mourn the loss of intimacy with your child. But you are also painfully aware of the outcome of a child's poorly chosen lifestyle. Jesus, who has travelled this pathway before, travels this rugged journey with you.

Prayer: O Lord, hear our cry for our straying children. Have mercy on and us, and draw us all together again in you.

WEEK FORTY-TWO: WEDNESDAY

Being Ready

Read: Matthew 24:42–51

"The master of that servant will come on a day when he does not expect him and at an hour he is not aware of." Matthew 24:50.

Two related parables in today's reading ensure that the house is secure from outside threat, and also protected from failure within.

These stories refer to our readiness for the return of Jesus Christ to earth, but we need to be ready for him to take us at any time. Thus, we must be reconciled to him and our affairs in order, Some are keenly aware of dying because of lingering sickness or other threatening tragedy, but for many it is a distant, dormant prospect.

The first parable illustrates the necessity of providing a secure place for our family. Security for a house means locking doors and windows and setting the alarm system.

Security in marriage requires trust in the faithfulness of our partner. And that living and working arrangements are set to reduce the outside threat of infidelity and clear alarms sound when a risk is apparent.

Even so, securing a home is pointless if there is a threat from within. Is my home-life and attitude a threat to my family?

We have a great deal of influence over our household, particularly the happiness of our partner. Love makes the lover vulnerable; it places us at the mercy of those we love, and gives us power over those who love us.

Will we use it to bring joy to our partner and children, or for our own self-interest, producing a resentful and rebellious home? If we love our family as we love ourselves we will try to provide them with a sense of security in an insecure world.

Prayer: O Father, there are so many threats to our families. But our security is in you. Thank you for showing us how to love our partners and children completely.

WEEK FORTY-TWO: THURSDAY

Ability Sets Expectation

Read: Matthew 25:14–30

"To one he gave five talents of money, to another two talents, and
to another one talent, each according to his ability."
Matthew 25:15.

This parable suggests it is insufficient to guard the home and so fulfill our responsibility to it. The steward with one talent guarded it well, produced it intact, but it still fell short of the master's expectations.

Caring for our families is of vital importance, but may not be an expression of love. Duty or compliance with a court order can provide these. Love goes beyond what is required; it seeks to invest in the growth of each individual's potential through direction, encouragement, and purpose for life.

Primarily, this means ensuring they understand that the foundation for life is a personal relationship with God—understanding the need for and accepting the freedom of forgiveness in Christ.

That is essential, but following through on that commitment provides fulfillment in living. Does your partner have unfulfilled potential that could enhance not only his or her life, but also the life of others—children, family and friends?

Others may make tremendous gains for God's kingdom, but fulfilling God's will for us as individuals is accomplishment—however limited it may seem. None of the stewards in our story had the same responsibility; the master only expected results in proportion to the talents given. Banking the money for interest would have been sufficient from the steward with one talent

If we are married, our primary responsibility before God, beyond the well being of our family, is that we encourage the fulfillment of God's investment in them.

Prayer: O Lord, we need to translate our love for our family members into actions that complete their God given potential. Open our eyes to those possibilities.

252

The Tragedy of Rejecting Jesus
Read: Matthew 27:19–25

All the people answered, "Let his blood be on us and on our children!" Matthew 27:25.

The last verse of our reading today must be the most heartrending cry of world history. Despite Pilate's insistence of Jesus' innocence, and his request for an indictable charge, the crowd, incited by the Jewish leaders, simply cried for Jesus' blood.

On Pilate's warning that the crowd would be responsible for Jesus' death, they willingly took the blame, and in an arrogant and heartless undertaking, called judgment down on their children also.

A generation in Scripture is forty years, and it is no accident that the destruction of Jerusalem and the exile of the Jews from Israel for the next 1900 years took place in 70 A.D., forty years after Jesus' crucifixion.

Some might argue that they spoke in ignorance; not really knowing the One they wanted crucified and goaded on by their leaders. But ignorance, then as now, is no excuse; any unfounded accusation and sentence, especially of this cruelty, is subject to justice for the victim.

There is a parallel here; today's generation has largely denied the claims of Christ, passing their skepticism to their children with tragic consequences. Whereas today's parents may not be calling directly for Jesus' death, rejection of any claim he may have upon their lives is the same as that which instigated his crucifixion.

We may consider we have gentler ways of casting him aside, but encouraging our children to reject him is to call judgment down on them also.

Prayer: Thank you Lord, for revealing yourself to us. We ask you to reveal yourself to our children and guard us from any words that discourage them from faith in you.

WEEK FORTY-TWO: WEEKEND

Justice

A ny good justice system, like any good table, is built on four legs. First, retribution: a debt to be paid, a punishment or penalty. Second, restitution: damage to be repaired. Third, rehabilitation: behaviour to be changed or correction to be applied, and finally deterrence: a warning to others.

All these attributes of justice are promoted in Scripture, but our present society only recognises the last two, pays lip service to the second, and abhors the first. Punishment is characterised as vindictive and vengeful and generally considered inappropriate.

Yet all sports identify penalty as a necessary part of the game, even though the culture refuses to apply it to life. Offences against the rules of society produce a debt to society that requires repayment. The Bible sees sin—that which produces real guilt—as a debt against God, a wrong for which a penalty must atone.

This idea is fundamental to biblical thinking and essential to the Christian faith. Our guilt incurred a debt to God which has been dealt with at the cross—the meeting-place of justice and mercy.

The fact that our penalty has been paid at the cross does not absolve us of our debts to society; those we incur here still have to be repaid. Nor does loving our neighbour mean letting a thief who invades our home go free. Our responsibility is to see that he receives the justice he deserves and the help he needs, and to ensure protection for our neighbour.

We may forgive the thief and absorb the loss ourselves at times, so practising both justice and mercy, practical ways we can teach our children the justice and mercy of God extended to us.

Prayer: We thank you Father, that Jesus Christ has met all the requirements of justice at the cross, by which we have received your mercy.

WEEK FORTY-THREE: MONDAY

Genuine Compassion

Read: Mark 5:22–43

"My little daughter is dying. Please come and put your hands on her so that she will be healed and live." Mark 5:23.

Jesus genuinely cared for children and that care extended to families, to the parents of children and the pain they endured when their children suffered.

Jairus was a synagogue leader; he may even have been the type of Jewish leader that Jesus often reproached. Yet Christ's compassion went beyond concern for poor theology. Jesus practiced what the Pharisees failed to do: he had compassion for people.

The unusual part of this story is the distraction Jesus had on his way to see Jairus' daughter. Surely he should have made the dying child a first priority, and dealt with the sick woman later, because the child died while he was engaged in healing the woman.

While we know that he eventually raised this girl to life, children still die despite our prayers to God for healing. The greatest mistake we can make is to consider that he does not care.

Also unusual, Jesus had little time for those who came to mourn. The mourners were probably paid to wail and cry on behalf of the bereaved and had little personal sympathy themselves.

Many who attend funerals have little in common with the one who has passed on, and their brief words of sympathy fade during the lonely days that follow.

In contrast, Jesus drove out the mourners and spent time with the parents in their distress, raising the child and ensuring her welfare. He remains with us in our times of grief when the presence of others wanes.

Prayer: Thank you Lord that you are always there when we are alone with our sorrow. Increase our trust in your promise you will never leave or forsake us.

255

WEEK FORTY-THREE: TUESDAY

Pedophilia

Read: Mark 9:42 and 10:13–16

"If anyone causes one of these little ones who believe in me to sin, it would be better for him to be thrown into the sea with a large millstone tied around his neck." Mark 9:42.

The proliferation of internet pornography around the globe means that these products are easily available in countries where the practices depicted are illegal. News reports constantly document cases of men with computers full of pictures of children in sexual poses.

These children appear trained in adult preferences, or may be sexual slaves in some countries. While this violation of children is offensive, its practitioners still actively pursue it as a legitimate sexual orientation.

As arguments in favour of liberalizing homosexuality have carried the day; similar arguments for freedom of sexual expression by pedophilia may be hard for future liberal-minded governments and courts to deny.

Even assuming this does not occur, the free dissemination of pedophiliac material can only break down the moral defences in individuals, providing a false sense of legitimacy, and widen its practice. This puts all children at increasing risk.

Pornography is insidious, posing as harmless entertainment, but is addictive and destructive. Pedophilia especially rejects scriptural injunctions in today's reading to protect children from harm.

Pedophiles may argue that their practice does not harm children because it is a loving relationship. But this is clearly at odds with the results of pedophilia in residential schools in Canada.

Seek help, if necessary to eliminate these destructive influences from your home.

Prayer: Heavenly Father, we know in this highly sexualized culture, pornographic materials are rampant. Help us keep our home clean of these damaging influences.

Loving Our Neighbour

Read: Mark 12:18–34

"The second [commandment] is this: 'Love your neighbour as yourself.' There is no commandment greater than these."
Mark 12:31.

I believe in love at first sight—I have to; I fell for my wife Ann at our first meeting. From then on I lived in a twilight world without her, and a dizzy disorienting daze when with her. The whole universe took its hue from her absence or presence, and concentration on anything else became laborious and half-hearted.

It is probably necessary that these times usually evolve into something more practical or life would become almost impossible.

But when the Bible speaks of love, love is revealed as a form of service, feeding and caring for our wives as we do for ourselves, Ephesians 5:28–29, not the sense of physical attraction. Our reading today raises this idea of loving oneself as a means of gauging our love for a neighbour.

This is frequently cited as a command to love ourselves before we can love others. Loving oneself is then interpreted as having good self-esteem, liking and valuing ourselves, perhaps verging on narcissism, but necessary in order to love others the same way.

This interpretation is understandable in a society that constantly psychoanalyses itself. But loving ourselves is simply caring for ourselves; ensuring we have sufficient food, clothing and shelter.

Jesus' priority was for the physical well-being of our neighbour—don't talk to him of self-esteem if he is hungry or cold. When the Bible tells us to love our neighbour—which *includes* our wives—this is what it means.

Prayer: Heavenly Father, may our love be genuine service, not simply a response evoked by feelings.

WEEK FORTY-THREE: THURSDAY

Every Child is from God

Read: Luke 2:8–20

"I bring you good news of great joy that will be for all the people. Today in the town of David a Saviour has been born to you; he is Christ the Lord." Luke 2:10–11.

Mary found it true. The trauma of an inconvenient pregnancy eventually gives way to rejoicing over the child's birth and years of pleasure watching the child develop.

Today's reading is the ultimate example of this; the heavenly angels themselves rejoicing over the birth of the Saviour. The birth of your child may not herald the same fortune for humankind, but the birth of every child is a potential joy to the parents and benefit to the world.

God brings no-one into this world to live without purpose, exist without reason, or function without meaning. None of us are here by chance, but each of us is a unique creation of God.

He loves, cares about us, and wants us to know him as he knows us. God is able to use every life to benefit the world and to make his great plan known to its generation.

But how that child responds to God's call, to follow him or waste the life given by God, is their choice to make, not ours to assume or terminate for personal reasons.

However, some may believe it would have been better not to have been born. Both Job, 3:1–26, and Jeremiah, 20:14–18, felt that way during times of personal distress, yet their lives had a resounding value in promoting the knowledge of God in perilous times.

During the ordeal of determining the problems that an unwanted pregnancy entails, never lose sight of the joy that awaits the arrival of the baby and the potential that child may have for the Gospel and the world.

Prayer: O Lord, we thank you for each child you have brought into our family, children, and grandchildren. Help us love them emotionally and practically so they discover a unique purpose in our world and the joy they are to us.

Seeking God for Our child

Read: Luke 2:21–24, 39–40

The child grew and became strong; he was filled with wisdom, and the grace of God was upon him. Luke 2:40.

Joseph and Mary fulfilled the requirements of the Old Testament law by having Jesus circumcised and, being their firstborn, redeemed with the required sacrifice. The consecration of the firstborn was a sign that God spared the firstborn of Israel when the destroying angel killed the firstborn of the Egyptians, Exodus 13:1.

Thus, Mary and Joseph demonstrated their devotion to God, and ensured Jesus was included within the covenant God made with the Israelites, Genesis 17:9-14. It was an act of faith in the promises of God.

Most Christians have their children either baptized, common in liturgical churches, or dedicated to God, mostly in the non-conformist traditions. Either way, the parents signify desire to bring their children into the family of God for his oversight and direction.

Child baptism or "sprinkling" parallels the Jewish rite of circumcision; to bring the child into the New Covenant which the child later endorses at "confirmation." Children "dedicated" at birth confirm their parents' desire for them later in baptism by immersion.

If we believe that God answers prayer, performing these procedures is a public confession that we seek God's direction in the lives of our children.

Joseph and Mary fulfilled the Law's requirements, and Jesus grew in wisdom and the grace of God. Jesus, knowing his destiny, would surely grow in this way. However, *his* parents' role at birth for him underlines the importance of placing *our* children in God's care, as their destiny is far less certain.

Prayer: Dear Lord, we desire our children to follow you. Thank you for baptism, a way you have shown us to publicly express our desire to follow you.

WEEK FORTY-THREE: WEEKEND

Some NOs in Raising Children

No! Not a string of don'ts to avoid, but rather resources not available to us. Certain expectations are outside our control, and if we don't recognize that we set ourselves up for disillusionment and frustration.

First, there are no formulas for raising children. Certainly there are guidelines, but no two children are the same and require different handling. What our oldest child would take as a warning, our second would accept as a challenge; even experience was a limited asset.

Our third—the ultimate strong-willed child—was different again. That strong will would be invaluable when well-directed in later life, and needed molding and not breaking.

Second, we have no final control over our children. In the earliest years we have some control, but in the end we can only influence our children. We are not creators, making others into our own image; our children are people with their own God given personality and decision making ability.

Increasing independence only lessens our power over them, and good parenting will prepare them to channel their independence into constructive and creative ways.

Last, there is no guarantee that our children will turn out the way we desire. We are all aware of children from good families that turn out imperfectly, and vice versa.

Our biggest mistake may be in planning to bring up good children. As we have seen, this is outside our ability. We can plan to be good parents, praying for God's wisdom and direction for us in these uncharted waters, for his call upon their lives at an early age, and guidance in their major choices of life.

Prayer: Heavenly Father, we know we have limited control over our children. Grant us the grace to live lives that capture their imagination and desire to reproduce a godly heritage.

Respect Within Families

Read: Luke 2:41–52

"Son, why have you treated us like this? Your father and I have
been anxiously searching for you." Luke 2:48.

The only information about Jesus' growing up years is
this one passage. I doubt Jesus went through the
rebellious teens, but today's reading does suggest his
parents had their times of frustration, caused mainly by
their lack of understanding of his role on earth.

It is easy to consider Jesus thoughtless for his lack of
sensitivity to his parents' worry, and Mary spoke plainly in
expressing it. He was missing for three days. One wonders
how he ate and slept during that time, although debating
the teachers of his day probably comes as no surprise.

What is also surprising is the fact that his parents left
Jerusalem without him, assuming he was in the company of
their friends. The culture of the day and the intermingling
of travelling companions may partly explain why.

I always found it hard to accept their leaving without
him, until the day Ann and I left church without our four
year old daughter; we were halfway home before we
realized she was missing. Back at church we found her
happily among friends, unaware we had left.

Our experience reminded us that we all make mistakes
with our children, often inadvertently or under stress. The
experience of Mary and Joseph underlines the fact that our
mistakes may also be a lack of understanding of our
children's grasp of events and feelings during their
childhood and teen years.

Although discipline is necessary in forming a child's
character, it is not a substitute for empathy with their
evolving situation and needs.

Prayer: O Lord, we always want our children to be aware of our
needs and feelings. Help us to be more aware of theirs.

WEEK FORTY-FOUR: TUESDAY

Faith Plus Practice

Read: Luke 6:46–49

"Why do you call me, 'Lord, Lord,' and do not do what I say?"
Luke 6:46.

This parable is often misused, suggesting that faith in Christ is the foundation for a secure life. But hearing, even believing, the message that Christ brought does not constitute a sufficient foundation. The man that built on the rock is he who "puts [Christ's words] into practice."

Practice should be an outcome of faith; practical experience reinforces faith. Strength for troubled times is gained from practical experience in the easier times. Set a firm foundation for life at its beginning; it may be too late when difficulty arises.

This is especially true of marriage. It is doubtful if the needs of an enduring marriage and family are in the forefront of a couple's thoughts when engaged. It is the "heady time" it should be.

But it should also be a time of commitment for both to place faith in Christ and pledge to put his Word into practice in their life together—a foundation upon which they can build their marriage, family and even old age together.

Moreover, Jesus gave warning of the consequences of not acting upon his instruction. The house built on sand may last for a long while. It continues to stand because no storm has yet occurred, not because the sandy foundation is sufficient support.

Many marriages based on the wrong values may seem secure and endure for a time, but may not stand the attack of adversity. Adversity brings reflection and even recognition of God's claims upon us, but it means starting from scratch: building a new foundation to sustain our marriage.

Prayer: Dear Lord, prompt us to read your Word daily, but also to put your instructions into practice every day to ensure a stable and lasting marriage.

Jesus Enters Our Grief

Read: Luke 7:11-17

When the Lord saw her, his heart went out to her and he said,
"Don't cry." Luke 7:13.

Today's story, together with raising of Jairus' daughter we read previously, proved Jesus' power over death, Scripture clearly stating that the son was dead.

It also records Jesus' concern for the mother: "His heart went out to her and he said, 'Don't cry.'" Again, in his anger over death and the misery it brings, he raises a child, somewhat older than Jairus' daughter, in order to end the grief of the mother.

In a church we pastored, a young couple had several children and expected another. Early in the pregnancy the child was diagnosed with only a brain stem, and the couple advised to have an abortion. Their faith made this option unacceptable, although it may have reduced the heartache they knew would come.

The child, a daughter, was born and they nursed her for the few hours that she lived. At the funeral, the young father carried the tiny coffin down the church aisle, weeping as he came.

God loved this helpless child and took her to be with him, letting her stay with her parents for that brief time, although she would remain in their hearts for life.

But our reading today emphasizes the compassion that Jesus had for this lad's mother, illustrating for us the compassion God has for all bereaved parents. How could it be otherwise?

God knows firsthand what it is to see his own Son die—worse, to die a cruel and ignominious death at the hands of evil men.

Prayer: Dear Lord, it is of great comfort to know that you are involved in our times of grief and adversity. Thank you for caring for us as you loved your Son.

WEEK FORTY-FOUR: THURSDAY

"Hating" Our Families

Read: Luke 14:25–33

"If anyone comes to me and does not hate his father and mother, his wife and children, his brothers and sisters—yes, even his own life—he cannot be my disciple." Luke 14:26.

In today's passage, the standards Jesus requires from those who would follow him appear to challenge the need for cohesive and loving families. God is intimately concerned with families, and to require hatred of them as a stipulation for discipleship is against his nature.

Attempts to reconcile the conflict elicit two responses. Either the conditions are unattainable for the average person and refer to exceptional calls of God, or they are an exaggeration to make the point that we all need to have clear priorities.

There is truth to both viewpoints. In places where it is dangerous to propagate the Christian faith, a parent may court death or imprisonment and leave the family neglected as a result of God's call.

Children especially may follow God's call to foreign, even hazardous lands, and lose regular contact with family. The requirement may not be *hatred* of family but certainly a *priority* to follow Christ in these ways which risk great heartache for them.

Although love for our families is evidence of our love for God, it cannot supplant it. In setting family priorities, we need to ensure God's desire for our lives comes before our own; particularly when differences in belief within a family may promote different goals for life.

Not only is this fulfilling the command to "hate" our families, but Jesus promised that God will provide alternate "families" to replace the ones we may lose for the Kingdom, both now and for eternity, Luke 18:29–30.

Prayer: O Lord, when obedience to your call brings misunderstanding in our families, keep us faithful to you. Give us ongoing love for those family members who may reject us.

Straying Children

Read: Luke 15:11–24

"This son of mine was dead and is alive again; he was lost and is found." Luke 15:24.

This parable of the prodigal son is probably one of the best known. While the story illustrates the love of God for his erring children, the comparison made with an earthly father also illustrates the strength of love a father has for his child.

It also shows the sense of belonging the son retained despite his foolish and divisive behaviour. For all stray children, they rarely lose the parental connection; a desire for reconciliation lurking in the subconscious of every child.

Most instructive in this story is the father's willingness to let the son go. He freely gave the son his share of the inheritance, probably knowing its dissolute use.

In a child's early life we have ability to control and influence. But the hard time comes when the child reaches an age of independence capable of making his or her own choices. How do we react then?

Can we respect their choices even when we disagree? Even more, are we prepared to receive and support them upon their desire to return from a destructive lifestyle?

There is wisdom in giving freedom to a child who opposes parental advice, but being open to receive that child again later when a child returns to the parents.

After all that is the way God has dealt with us; maintaining both his requirements of us and his love for us. He will leave us to our own devices as long as we want to live independently, but he is amazingly willing to receive us upon our repentance.

Prayer: Lord, we thank you for the love of parents or guardians who reflected your love for us. Grant that we may show the same patience and forbearance toward our children.

265

WEEK FORTY-FOUR: WEEKEND

Growing a Teenager

The growth of children into the teens is a voyage into uncharted waters for child and parent, but the best protection for teen years is training from the earliest years. If a child has not learned respect for parents, it is unlikely he or she will heed instructions as a teen.

Respect is established in two ways. It has to be earned. A child must develop a confidence in consistent and equitable treatment of failures and successes: both sanctions when guidelines are flouted and encouragement when they are met or exceeded, always with genuine respect towards the child.

But respect is also taught by instilling obedience to authority during childhood. A child who can disobey or manipulate his or her parents with little impunity will carry that attitude into the teens and adulthood with potentially disastrous consequences.

This does not mean that as an adult he or she should obey all authority regardless, but rather that authority will be obeyed, but if necessary disputed with thoughtful respect.

Obedience is not generated because you love the child, he or she will obey if the child loves you, John 14:15. Discipline will not undermine a child's love for his or her parent, although abuse will distance a child from a parent. A child feels safe and is happier with secure boundaries.

Children who continually get their own way may develop contempt in place of love for parents and set their own boundaries.

Do you need to be a perfect parent? Take heart. Children have an amazing capacity for adaptability and forgiveness if we are honest with them. We need to get it right most, not all the time, to maintain a bond that lasts.

Prayer: Dear Lord, we admit our ignorance in bringing up teens. Show us wisdom from your Word at our times of uncertainty.

Dealing with Jealousy

Read: Luke 15:25–32

"'My son,' the father said, 'you are always with me, and everything I have is yours.'" Luke 15:31.

The story of the prodigal son is really the story of two sons, but also of a prodigal father. Prodigal is the opposite of frugal, meaning extravagance which may be wasteful or generous; the father was prodigal with his love for the wayward son in the generous sense.

In contrast, the older son had very little of that extravagant love. His attitude to his younger brother is probably the more natural human response: why should a waster receive so much welcome and the devoted son apparently ignored?

This problem of sibling rivalry fed on false perceptions. The older considered celebration of his brother's return unfair, and it fostered jealousy. Really, he had little to be jealous about. His inheritance was all his father owned, the younger having had his share. His father recognized his loyalty; he had his father's favour.

The younger son was entitled to nothing save what the father graciously provided him. They both shared equally in their father's love. What more could the older brother desire?

Sibling rivalry is a constant in all families; from the youngest age children squabble. Because children are different, they often need to be treated differently, which can be misconstrued by a child as *better* treatment.

Head off jealousy by explaining to children they are being treated fairly, although differently. This father took pains to mollify his elder son's anger, explaining that because the younger son had frittered away his inheritance, the older brother was far better off.

Prayer: Dear Father, thank you for the gift of your Holy Spirit who leads us, and your Word which instructs us. Give us listening ears in dealing with rivalry among our children.

WEEK FORTY-FIVE: TUESDAY

Recognizing God's Image

Read: Luke 20:20–26

"Give to Caesar what is Caesar's, and to God what is God's."
Luke 20:25.

The stamped image of Caesar on Roman coins is similar to the image of God created in humankind. Scripture gives little indication how that image of God shows itself in us, but today's passage gives some guidance to its meaning.

As we found in earlier readings, Adam and Eve's joint responsibility over the earth was also a reflection of the image of God. We do not own what we have. Those things are lent to us for the duration of our lives; we are only stewards of all that we possess, responsible to God for our use and treatment of them.

This applies supremely to people for whom we have responsibility, especially our families, and we will give account for the way we have served or used them.

Jesus, on hearing his opponents confirm Caesar's image stamped on the coins of the day, identified the coins as belonging to Caesar. In the same way, the image of God within men and women signifies his ownership of each human being; they are his with his stamp upon them.

As with Adam and Eve in Eden, we have responsibility to care for those God has given us. If we fail to care for our families, we risk losing our relationship with God by not recognizing and so rejecting God's image in them.

In turn, this will reduce our ability to care for them, leading into a downward spiral. This worrisome scenario should encourage us to be vigilant in our treatment of those closest to us.

Prayer: O Lord, sometimes it's difficult to see your image in our children and each other. Grant us your discernment to accurately respond to those situations.

Rejection by Our Own

Read: John 1:9–13

He was in the world, and though the world was made through him,
the world did not recognize him. He came to that which was his
own, but his own did not receive him. John 1:10–11.

His own people the Jews, and his creation, rejected
Jesus. This rejection parallels much parental
rejection by youth in today's western culture. When
children evaluate parents in the light of their maturing
understanding, it is a shock for them to find that parents
are flawed individuals and not the final authority on
everything of childhood.

For the most part, children retain attachment to their
parents, often with a few bumps along the way as they pass
through puberty.

But a significant minority rejects parents, despite the
parents' best efforts. Many of you reading this will have
been through such an experience; a heart-wrenching
rollercoaster ride of hope and despair for which entreaties
and prayers seem unanswered. Every ring of the phone
brings a jolt of apprehension; living in a state of daily
tension exhausts you.

Jesus still walks the same road himself; his deity does
not soften the despair he feels over those who reject his
call. Parents will find the greatest comfort in seeking God to
walk with them on the road he knows so well, sensing the
presence of God daily.

Prayer is the key, for it is natural to pray under stress
and to silently call on him in moments of crisis, but pray
also for reconciliation with your child. Our reading reminds
us that many accepted Christ and became his children, and
his joy at their response can also be yours when a child
returns.

Prayer: O Lord, you know that feeling of estrangement and loss
so well. Be our daily comfort in the ongoing crisis we may
be facing.

No Barriers to Christ

Read: John 4:9–30

"If you knew the gift of God and who it is that asks you for a drink, you would have asked him and he would have given you living water." John 4:10.

This woman had several counts against her. First, she was a woman. Women did not have the status that Jesus gave to them—the disciples were surprised that he was even talking with her. She was also a Samaritan, a member of the impure race that the Jews despised—she was surprised he made a request of her.

Finally, she had a disreputable background, married five times and now living common law—and Jesus knew about it. Yet all these factors did not stop Jesus seeking to draw her into his kingdom.

She could not help being a Samaritan or a woman, but her life style was largely a result of her choices. Yet his attitude toward her was one of care and respect and her response was joy that overflowed to others.

In her excitement she brought others to meet Jesus, who invited him to stay with them. Many believed on Jesus because of the woman's testimony; still other Samaritans believed on Jesus as they listened to his words.

Race, sex, and colour are no bar to receiving Christ; his approach to the despised Samaritans made this clear. But our lifestyle, which we may have chosen, is also no barrier.

You may have been involved in life experiences that you regret, but now you are accepted in Christ, to receive his forgiveness, and make a fresh start for living—everything is new in Christ, 2 Corinthians 5:17. Your desire for a stable relationship can come alive as you commit yourself to his care for you.

Prayer: Dear Lord and Saviour, thank you for your grace which is more than sufficient to cover all my sin.

Healing: a Step Toward Faith

Read: John 4:43–54

The royal official said, "Sir, come down before my child dies." Jesus replied, "You may go. Your son will live." John 4:49–50.

John is very sparse with his report of miracles, recording only six or seven in his Gospel. He called them signs, recording those that had special significance in revealing the true identity of Jesus Christ.

Jesus often dealt with people of status as this man was, a royal official, although in this case he began by rebuking the man, but finally healing the man's son from a distance.

Jesus refused to perform miracles just to prove his identity. He was no travelling showman, Matthew 16:1–4. But despite John's claim that miracles were signs of Jesus' deity, he also performed them out of compassion for the bereaved.

But he wanted this official to understand that the basis of belief was not the miracle he was about to do for the official's son: "Unless you people see signs and wonders . . . you will never believe." Despite this rebuke, the man continued to entreat Jesus, who lovingly responded to his request. As a result of the healing, "he and his household believed."

Because we generally consider we have life under control when all is going well, it is usually adversity that wakes us up to our need for God. It is far better to seek God's direction for our lives at all times than wait for family dilemmas to drive us to seek him and believe on him.

Prayer: Lord, we thank you for the miracles you have performed in our lives, but above all, we praise you for making your Word real to us by the Holy Spirit. Help our unbelief.

WEEK FORTY FIVE: WEEKEND

Provoked Parents

At times it seems that the blessing children are supposed to be is replaced by the trials they incite to cultivate our patience. No circumstances of life can stir our emotions more than our children.

But the range of emotions we feel change as our children move into the teen years. Our earlier frustrations with them turn to fear for them and earlier anger toward them turns to mistrust and suspicion.

Our ability to assert ourselves gives way to inadequacy as the control we once had lessens. While we had the ability to be emotionally detached in directing our small children, teens evoke a greater emotional response.

We have high expectations for our children. Yet in the early teen years they are still not adults but often act as though they were, with that typical characteristic of confident folly.

For ourselves, our limitations begin to show, as we discover we don't have all the answers and find ourselves with an empty authority. We may discover our lack of communication skills—particularly active listening, and find that we have previously not really heard *and* understood.

Finally, the teen years will find the weak spots in our marriages. Marriage conflict is a primary source of insecurity for teens and they are old enough to try to find that security elsewhere.

A dozen years of child raising should have taught parents to operate together, giving no opportunity for a child to divide and conquer. During this time of greater stress they would learn Scripture's picture of the Trinity is our guide—to offend one is to offend all.

Prayer: O Lord, teach us parenting skills while our children are still young, and guide us by your Spirit as they progress to the maturing years.

Supporting Children

Read: John 9:1–23

"Is this your son?" they asked. "Is this the one you say was born blind? How is it that now he can see?" John 9:19.

This passage raises the question: how far should parents go to support children? These parents had grave difficulties with a son blind from birth.

Apart from the obvious problem of providing for a son that would normally have helped to support them, they probably had to bear the taunts of those who assumed that the blind son was punishment for some sin. The healing of their son by Jesus only added to their woes.

The son was feisty enough to stand up for himself; he didn't really need his parents, but the Pharisees' need to establish the son's identity drew them in. The son had personal experience with Jesus and so decided that he no longer needed the approval of the Pharisees.

But his parents were still dependent on the synagogue for acceptance, so their answers were non-committal to avoid disgrace in the community. Thus the son had to defend himself and was eventually thrown out of the synagogue.

There is often a fine line between recognizing a child's unacceptable public behaviour and maintaining support for him as a person.

Some scold their children in public, leaving the child shamed. Others deny the child's responsibility, tacitly condoning the behaviour. Still others may disown the child like these parents, leaving the son to defend himself.

But something like: "Son, let's go home and work this out together," may provide support and dignity for the child, but still leave the appropriateness of the behaviour to be dealt with.

Prayer: Heavenly Father, we want to be supportive of our children even when they misbehave. Help us tread that fine line between condoning and condemning their actions.

Jesus: Our Resurrection

Read: John 11:17–37

"I am the resurrection and the life. He who believes in me will live, even though he dies; and whoever lives and believes in me will never die. Do you believe this?" John 11:25.

The home of Mary, Martha and Lazarus was a place of rest and recuperation for Jesus, a family that would be the object of his compassion. Yet both Martha and Mary accused Jesus of the same thing: "Lord, if you had been here, my brother would not have died."

Some voiced the thought: "Could not he who opened the eyes of the blind man also kept this man from dying?" If Jesus had healed Lazarus before death rather than restoring him to life after, he would have saved his sisters much misery.

This raises the age old question of why God does things the way he does when we cannot see the reason. Here, at least, we have an explanation: this event was to glorify him, John 11:4.

Jesus' response to Martha clarified it further; he proclaimed himself "the resurrection and the life," and raised Lazarus as proof. God's primary purpose is that his "will be done on earth as it is in heaven," Matthew 6:10. We may experience situations like Martha and Mary, but unlike them have no explanation.

The most poignant examples of distress are those within families, for they are the closest to us. The answer that God has his reasons for our distress may add to our stoicism, but it is cold comfort.

We are more comforted knowing Jesus is the resurrection and can breathe life into dead situations. But resurrection to our final destiny will clarify and restore all things, for what we see and understand now is temporary; it is the unseen that is eternal, 2 Corinthians 4:16–18.

Prayer: Dear God, while we understand your purposes we do not always comprehend your ways. Help us to trust you when we have no answer to our situation.

WEEK FORTY-SIX: WEDNESDAY

Love: An Action Word

Read: John 14:15–24

"If anyone loves me, he will obey my teaching. My Father will love
him, and we will come to him and make our home with him."
John 14:23-24.

We noted previously that the Bible rarely refers to physical love, even when talking about marriage. This seems like a strange omission, when the Bible is a book about God's love for us.

We consider this strange because of a misconception of love, considering it primarily a "feeling" word. So what happens when the feelings subside?

There are several Greek words used to describe love: eros refers to sexual attraction or desire, Philos deals with the love between friends and family, hence Philadelphia, the city of brotherly love. Both these concepts deal with feelings derived from a natural affinity.

However, agape, more often found in the New Testament, reveals love as an act of the will, replacing desire with decision. So our relationship to God is not conditioned by feelings, but by our commitment. The feelings may vary, but our commitment can remain irrespective of how we feel.

Further, a change of feelings can be generated by the will; by a decision to *act* in a way that displays love. Feelings or attitudes are helpful, but not necessary to generate actions.

In contrast, actions can generate feelings; hence the importance of understanding verse 15 where obedience and love act as a spiral, each reinforcing the other.

God's love for us was not just communicating his feelings, but his action in sending Jesus to die for us. Actions that demonstrate love will help to keep the feeling alive in our relationships.

Prayer: Thank you, Lord, for expressing your love so clearly at
the cross. Help us to act thoughtfully as well as on
impulse.

WEEK FORTY-SIX: THURSDAY

Sorrow will be Turned to Joy

Read: John 16:16–22

"Now is your time of grief, but I will see you again and you will rejoice, and no one will take away your joy." John 16:22.

Carrying and having a child is a long period of relative discomfort, followed by several hours of painful labour. For women, there appears little redeeming value in the whole process, except the hope of birth.

Men can only relate vicariously, unaware of the real burdens women carry. Bringing husbands into the delivery room enables them to share some of it. One woman put it this way: "My husband was happy enough to be present at conception; he can be there at the delivery as well."

Whether a woman completely forgets the trauma of childbirth once the little one is in her arms is debatable. But the Bible doesn't mitigate labour pains; in fact, it uses them as an illustration of severe suffering, see Isaiah 13:8, 21:3 and Micah 4:9–10.

But it conveys the general idea of joy a child brings, eventually outweighing past pain. Thus, the Bible refers to the pain of childbirth as a symbol of the difficulties that will eventually give way to the joy of final union with Christ, see also Matthew 24:8.

We know we will always be subject to adversity. But Christians live in hope; not the earthly wish that things *may* improve, but the *certainty* of the promises of God.

Whether it is the loss of a loved one to death, or the failing attractions of the world, we do not "grieve like the rest who have no hope,"1 Thessalonians 4:13. We know that our suffering is temporary, but joy will last forever, Romans 8:18 and 2 Corinthians 4:17.

Prayer: O Lord, during the dark times of life, help us keep alive that enduring hope your sacrifice has given us.

WEEK FORTY-SIX: FRIDAY

The Promise of the Holy Spirit

Read: Acts 2:14–21

"'In the last days,' God says, 'I will pour out my Spirit on all people.'" Acts 2:17.

Further to the promise of the next life discussed yesterday, today's reading records God's intervention into earthly life; there is hope for coming generations who accept and honour Christ.

The first coming of Jesus to earth and his return to heaven led to the day of Pentecost and the indwelling Holy Spirit promised to all believers. In the intervening time until his return to earth, we are promised the inspiration of God's Spirit in visions and dreams.

This is a promise given to all Christians that God will work in lives to accomplish his will on earth, irrespective of age or sex, referring to "all people . . . sons . . . daughters . . . young men . . . old men . . . men and women."

Dreams and visions may not just be visible spiritual manifestations, but clarity of what the future holds and clear understanding of the outcomes of various plans or actions.

Recognizing our own sin involves us in Jesus' crucifixion, and seeking the forgiveness he promises ensures a rich heritage for our children. Those who sought his crucifixion brought Christ's blood on their own children. In contrast, we bring upon our children the promise of the Spirit and his involvement in their lives.

Their dreams and visions will contribute to God's plan to bring hope to a fallen world; even change the course of world history as "everyone who calls on the name of the Lord will be saved." Isn't this what we desire for our children?

Prayer: Dear Lord, not only do we thank you for the children you have given us, but also for the Holy Spirit who will guide them through life after we have passed on.

WEEK FORTY-SIX: WEEKEND
Pornography

Of the many forms of aberrant sexual behaviour, pornography is a major driving force in the decay of western society. At one time it was generally unacceptable by the mainstream, hidden in magazines from public view.

Today the internet inserts pornography into the mainstream media, instantly accessible with the click of a mouse to indulge in complete privacy. No longer limited by the printed page from the corner store, the full range of global deviancy is instantly available.

As pornography becomes available to youth, young males may begin to view females as sexual objects for gratification. This may even lead to sexual exploitation of juveniles, spoiling them for sustainable marriage.

Over time this activity has dire consequences for families and, as a result, eventually for society as a whole. But pornography also has its effect on marriages. It can redefine a wife as a sexual object rather than recognize sex as an aid to deeper personal intimacy.

Further, the use of pornography to initiate sex can be addictive, becoming increasingly necessary—and possibly increasingly deviant—to promote sexual activity.

Use of pornography may reinforce a sexual deviancy a married partner already has. The variety of sexual practices on the internet provides a smorgasbord of ideas that highlight and legitimize aberrant sexual preferences which in turn undermine the marriage relationship.

The internet not only provides these fantasies, it also provides opportunity for practice by connecting to likeminded individuals. For a user, pornography's varied attraction will constantly threaten marriage.

Prayer: Dear Lord, thank you for your Word which gives strict guidelines on illicit sexual practices. Help us heed them, and seek help to overcome unacceptable behaviour when necessary.

Descent to Depravity

Read: Romans 1:18–32

Although they know God's righteous decree that those who do such things deserve death, they not only continue to do these very things but also approve of those who practice them. Romans 1:32.

This passage is perhaps the most quoted for demonstrating the steps of descent into evil. We are all aware of the normalization of much current sexual practice and the compassionate response we are constrained to make as sinners ourselves.

This passage also claims homosexuality is a result of refusing to acknowledge God and the evidence for him, and a lack of thankfulness to him for life and its provisions.

The reading traces the increasing confusion between good and evil and the eventual approval of evil. Fuzzy thinking about evil leads to the eastern idea that "all is one," nothing is inherently evil. The notion that circumstances determine an action good or evil removes the objective distinction between good and evil.

Today's passage records homosexuality as unbiblical and not confined to our age, Isaiah 5:20. It leads to confusion about good and evil, which the Bible calls depravity.

A clear understanding of good and evil is going to help any relationship, particularly the close one of marriage. A positive approach to today's reading shows that acknowledgment of God and thankfulness to him will clarify our thinking on sexual and other issues.

The Bible clarifies this. Many references in the New Testament cite good and evil, often spoken by Jesus. Thus, daily reading and study of the Bible is critical to maintaining a healthy marriage.

Prayer: Heavenly Father, it's easy to conform to the biblical illiteracy of our day. Grant us your Holy Spirit to constrain us to seek your truth daily.

WEEK FORTY-SEVEN: TUESDAY
Eliminating Hypocrisy
Read: Romans 2:17–24

You, then, who teach others, do you not teach yourself?
Romans 2:21.

W e exhibit a distorted image of God—perhaps more discernible in some than others. Close relationships magnify that distortion, tempting us to judge and act accordingly toward our partner.

This should rather evoke pity, even humility as we are in the same condition. It was because God loved us and responded to us in mercy instead of judgment that caused him to make the ultimate sacrifice to reconcile us back to himself.

If we are to display a true image of God to others, it must be a reflection of God's concern for them. This may be old news to you, but do you practice this with your partner?

Today's reading was written to the Jews who considered themselves superior to the Gentiles because of their relationship to God. It can just as easily apply to us who place ourselves in judgment over our partners.

God does not recognize or accept this kind of superiority; he sees us both on level ground at the foot of the cross and in need of his continuing forgiveness and grace.

If we are to be a supporting member of our marriage team, we can only approach another's failure with the recognition of our own. Motivation based on superiority or judgment will maintain inequality in our marriage and ensure a dysfunctional relationship.

It may also foster similar behaviour in our children and in their marriages as they learn from us and mimic our attitudes.

Prayer: Dear Lord, it is easier to see the faults in others than in ourselves. Give me a glimpse of my own faults, that I may respond to others with empathy and compassion, and not judgment.

Overcoming Irritants

Read: Romans 5:1–11

God demonstrates his own love for us in this: while we were still sinners, Christ died for us. Romans 5:8.

As we grow to know our partners, the glow comes off the relationship, and we begin to see our partner's faults. It is often the little things that can destroy a marriage. One lady, when asked what irritated her about her husband, replied that it was his habit of peeling a grapefruit like an orange.

Even in the midst of her love song, the beloved in the Song of Solomon recognized that it was "the little foxes that ruin the vineyards," Song of Solomon, 2:15.

Today's reading provides a clear picture that we should build our relationship on grace as much as love. We must foster the ability to forgive and accept imperfections in marriage.

But in dealing with irritants in a marriage, it is critical to decide what is really important. The irritants may magnify underlying major problems that require dealing with first, either between partners or with outside help.

Most of us have a limit to patience and tolerance, and some marriages cannot be saved when destructive behaviour like drugs, alcohol, or infidelity continues. Failure to hold our partners accountable may make us resentful; we will fail our partners and leave the marriage vulnerable.

God loved us, demonstrating "his own love for us in this: while we were still sinners, Christ died for us." While we were still rebellious against God, he loved us enough to go to extraordinary lengths to reconcile us. This is may be a tough act to follow, but it's the basis of any lasting relationship.

Prayer: Father, it's true that marriage is hard work at times, needing more grace for our partners than we can muster. Grant us greater insight into our need of your love and grace for us, that we might love more completely.

281

ANN AND BRYAN NORFORD

WEEK FORTY-SEVEN: THURSDAY

We Are God's Children

Read: Romans 8:12–17

Now if we are children, then we are heirs—heirs of God and co-heirs with Christ, if indeed we share in his sufferings in order that we may also share in his glory. Romans 8:17.

The Bible frequently talks about our relationship to God as that of child to parent. The New Testament defines this in two ways; being born into God's kingdom, or children by adoption; the first reflects our choice, the second, his choice.

The Bible makes no distinction between the two—both have the same privileges and inheritance. Today's reading uses the idea of adoption, receiving "the Spirit of sonship" and calling God Father. We are called into God's family by his choice, with the full benefits of a child.

Knowing that he has the same interest and heartache over us as we do over our children is one of the benefits of becoming a child of God. Our pain, waywardness, or foolishness affects him just as we are affected by similar behaviour in our children. His guidance of us is similar to what we need to raise our children, and he can teach us much on bringing up our family.

How does God work with us to encourage, mature, and discipline our children? The answers are in Scripture that "is God-breathed and is useful for teaching, rebuking, correcting and training in righteousness, so that all God's people may be thoroughly equipped for every good work," 2 Timothy 3:16–17.

This book will increase your knowledge of God's Word and encourage you to seek him and his ways regularly. That practice will provide resources for ensuring your children's happiness and fulfilling your God given role.

Prayer: Dear Lord, thank you for the example you have shown us by calling us to be your children. Grant your Holy Spirit's insight into understanding your Word and training our children.

282

God is the Judge

Read: Romans 14:1–12

Why do you judge your brother? Or why do you look down on your brother? For we will all stand before God's judgment seat.
Romans 14:10.

In a church we pastored there was a young couple who had remarkable ability with children. They had three of their own, and adopted two more, one with Fetal Alcohol Syndrome.

Rick was a gung-ho Christian, demonstrating his commitment to God in outspoken ways. Mary was more subdued, fulfilling her responsibilities in practical ways. Much of the commendation for the children's growth was hers.

However, Rick complained of her lack of spirituality, meaning of course, that it did not measure up to his. Eventually he left her, taking the children with him and joining up with an unmarried mother with four children of her own. Mary, feeling betrayed, promptly divorced him.

When I asked Rick for his reasons for this move, he indicated that he and his new partner "were one," meaning one spiritually, enabling them both to serve the Lord. This rationale apparently trumped the obvious injustice against his former wife Mary. The act of desertion was itself wrong, as it reflected a mistaken judgment Rick was not qualified to make.

It is all too easy for us to judge another's spirituality, which means we assume ours to be superior. It fails to take into account the differences in temperament and that we cannot see into another's heart where God judges.

But above all we have no right to judge those whom God has accepted—they stand or fall before him who is their only Master. We become hypocrites and earn the well-deserved right to be called Pharisees.

Prayer: O Lord, keep me from judging my partner just because he or she expresses the faith differently to the way I do.

WEEK FORTY-SEVEN: WEEKEND

Celebrate the Difference

Common remarks heard about a marriage is the difference between the partners—"how could two people so different get along?"

Marriage partners should have common interests as a bond between them, but when it comes to temperament and abilities, we tend to admire in others those things absent in ourselves, and fall in love with those that are opposite to us, coveting their differences.

A reclusive, self-contained young man, attracted to a vivacious young woman, is astonished that she should fall for him. She is drawn to his steadiness and self assurance.

Sexual attraction is essential for a good marriage but quickly fades without the attraction of personality as glue in the relationship. But differences in temperament that initially attract can become the source of irritation as the relationship matures, because each does things differently.

Then the husband may try to make his wife over into his own image, perhaps even with her compliance in her anxiety to please. In doing so, the difference that attracted him fades and he sets himself up to venture outside of marriage for that lost attraction. In another couple, the wife might try it.

The disordered way in which the dishwasher is loaded, compared with his efficient arrangement, is not the time for irritation and rebuke. Rather it is a time to rejoice that the vitality he most admires is still in the house, both physically and temperamentally.

The French would say, "Vive la difference," referring to the sexes. We should incorporate that idea into differences in personality that first drew us together.

Prayer: O Lord, help me realize that my partner's differences are a gift from you and allow those characteristics to grow and flourish and maintain the attraction that drew me.

Seek the "Foolishness" of God

Read: 1 Corinthians 1:18–31

The foolishness of God is wiser than man's wisdom, and the
weakness of God is stronger than man's strength.
1 Corinthians 1:25.

Why should we consider the wisdom of the Bible superior? Aren't there other resources that can bring the same benefits? Many claim there are, but none has provided a better or lasting alternative.

Our permissive culture has been destructive rather than beneficial to human relationships. Today's passage warns us of the arrogance of assuming our own wisdom above that which comes from God. Actually, developing our own ideas on what constitutes wisdom can lead us away from God.

We cannot, in the end, develop sound wisdom for life if it is not founded on truth. The Bible maintains that God exists and he responds to those who seek him, Hebrews 11:6.

Thus, to consider God non-existent or irrelevant to life is to build on an insecure foundation, and all that stands on it will be flawed and eventually unsustainable. So our reading maintains that "God chose the foolish things of the world to shame the wise," because lack of wisdom of the "foolish" drove them to God's wisdom.

Perhaps you have sensed this feeling of inadequacy. Despite the variety of voices offering guidance you don't know where to turn for lasting direction.

If you feel this places you among the weak and foolish, then be encouraged, because that gives place for our Creator's wisdom to enter and bring joy and meaning to your life and relationships. As our Creator is the wisdom within the Bible, so he can also be the guide and sustainer in all the relationships of your life.

Prayer: Dear Heavenly Father, we are beginning to find that it is in the extremities of life that we can find you. Thank you for being the wisdom that clarifies our direction for life.

285

WEEK FORTY-EIGHT: TUESDAY

We Can All Be Changed

Read: 1 Corinthians 6:8–13

That is what some of you were. But you were washed, you were sanctified, you were justified in the name of the Lord Jesus Christ and by the Spirit of our God. 1 Corinthians 6:11.

This passage places homosexuality together with a list of unacceptable practices. This passage is not so much rebuke as a reminder that these practices can be changed. The propensity to sin is in all of us and it is not hard to find unacceptable tendencies within ourselves such as adultery, pornography, or other devious sexual practices.

Gay claims that homosexuality is genetic is still debated, and Paul lists homosexuality under the category of sexual preferences that can be resisted or reversed.

Jennifer married a fine Christian man and had several children. One day, her husband notified her that he was gay and divorce followed. He had lived straight, as heterosexual marriage and several children attested.

Even if the claim of homosexuality was real, it was simple adultery and equal to leaving for another woman. Both homosexual and heterosexual dalliance outside of marriage breaks the marriage vow through adulterous sexual choices.

However, it is critical for us to realize that the tendency to homosexuality is not a sin. Temptation is not a sin—Jesus was tempted without sin, Hebrews 4:15.

We all have temptations to deal with and as such we are all in the same category. Unacceptable orientation of any sort only reminds us that we are all "oriented" towards sin, whether sexual or not. It is indulgence in our tempting desires that converts them into sin.

Prayer: O Lord, help us to stay aware of our own sinfulness and so empathize with those maintaining illicit relationships, while pointing them to the cross.

Sex Within Marriage

Read: 1 Corinthians 7:1–9

Do not deprive each other except by mutual consent and for a
time, so that you may devote yourselves to prayer.
1 Corinthians 7:5.

This passage deals primarily with sex: the need for it,
the provision for it and consent to it. Paul claimed
that remaining unmarried like him was a gift, but for
others marriage was also a gift. In this he identifies sex as
good, and its outlet in marriage.

This means that sexual co-operation is a condition of
marriage, and his instructions are that each should fulfil
their marital duty; to deprive the other of sexual intimacy is
fraud, a refusal to abide by the marriage vows.

However, this does not mean that a couple cannot
exclude sexual contact for an agreed period for prayer—a
type of sexual fasting to concentrate on spiritual matters.
But the period cannot be indeterminate or too long, or it
may result in "lack of control" and cut short the agreed
devotional time.

But even this suggestion of mutual abstinence is given
"as a concession, not as a command." Clearly, Paul
believed that mutual satisfaction in the marriage
relationship is critical to maintaining fidelity and
permanence of the union.

I'm sure that this is a message that the guys want to
hear. Yet, as someone said, there are no frigid women, only
inattentive men. Men are turned on by sight, but women
respond to more intimate companionship.

Warmth towards a husband is fostered by a wife's
sense of being looked after, protected, and cosseted;
knowing she and her ideas are valued; that her needs and
desires—besides sex—are important to her husband.

Prayer: Dear Lord, help me as a husband to know and respond
to my wife's needs, as I desire that she fulfills mine.

WEEK FORTY-EIGHT: THURSDAY

Mixed Marriages

Read: 1 Corinthians 7:10–15

If any brother has a wife who is not a believer and she is willing to
live with him, he must not divorce her. And if a woman has a
husband who is not a believer and he is willing to live with her, she
must not divorce him. 1 Corinthians 7:12–13.

Today's reading discusses mixed marriage—not one
between people of different colour, but between a
believer and an unbeliever.

Two kinds of mixed marriages exist: one where a
Christian marries an unbeliever and the other where one
partner becomes a believer after marriage.

The former is inadvisable, because mixed marriages
entered into knowingly statistically favour the unbeliever,
the believer losing faith. This may be a result of persuasion
from the unbeliever, or compromise by the believer. Worse,
marriage entered into on the promise or hope of another's
conversion is a form of spiritual blackmail.

But what are the responsibilities of the believer if one
partner becomes a believer after marriage? Paul opposes
the idea that a new Christian should opt out of such a
marriage because it seems more appropriate to his or her
new spiritual state.

Rather, in verses 12–15, Paul lets the unbelieving
spouse set the agenda to continue in the marriage or leave.
There are many mixed marriages where there is genuine
love between the partners, even if the intimacy of faith is
missing.

To destroy these based on faith is irresponsible,
especially where there are children from the marriage. In
fact, Paul shows his concern for children, indicating that
they are under the umbrella of the believer's faith by the
extension of his or her sanctification to the partner—
presumably for the period of the children's dependence.

Prayer: Dear Lord, help me to maintain a good marriage for my
unbelieving partner and a loving family for my children.

Let the Unbeliever Go

Read: 1 Corinthians 7:15–16

If the unbeliever leaves, let him do so. A believing man or woman is not bound in such circumstances; God has called us to live in peace. 1 Corinthians 7:15.

We noted previously the decision regarding the future of a mixed marriage is the non-believer's choice. The Christian is under no compulsion to persuade the partner to stay or leave.

But if the non-believer decides to leave, the believer "is not bound" to try to save the marriage. The desertion of an unbelieving husband is grounds for the dissolution of the marriage. Thus Paul adds desertion to infidelity as the basis for divorce.

Marriage is not an evangelical institution. By saying, "How do you know . . . whether you will save your [partner]?" Paul indicates there is no guarantee that an unbelieving partner who wishes to leave will be saved if constrained to stay unwillingly in the marriage.

However, where a believer takes the initiative to leave a marriage which is intolerable, he or she should remain unmarried, providing for reconciliation, 1 Corinthians 7:10–11, reconciliation being the first option.

Two phrases in the Corinthian passage that often cause confusion are the statements, "not I, but the Lord" and "I, not the Lord," 1 Corinthians 7:10 and 12, that qualify Paul's writing.

Some assume this to mean that what the Lord has said takes precedence over what Paul has written, disqualifying the options that Paul gives. In fact, Paul in the first instance is quoting Jesus, see Matthew 19:9, and in the second is writing as the Holy Spirit leads him.

Thus both are the Word of God to us and are for our guidance and benefit.

Prayer: Lord, thank you for clear guidelines on these marriage conditions. Help us to be faithful to you in the way we conduct ourselves in these situations.

WEEK FORTY-EIGHT: WEEKEND

Remarriage

There has always been debate in Christian circles about divorce and remarriage. Some will deny the possibility of divorce for the believer, because God hates divorce, Malachi 2:16.

Others will agree that God has made allowance for divorce because of the hardness of our hearts, Matthew 19:8, but deny the possibility of remarriage. Still others maintain that the reason for divorce is to allow remarriage; divorce is unnecessary if remarriage is disallowed.

This debate stigmatizes those who have sought divorce for legitimate reasons, and casts additional suspicion on those who remarry.

It is one thing to be passionate about marriage and its permanence as we all should be. But it is cruel to translate that into lack of compassion for those caught in intolerable marriages.

It was our practice during our time of ministry to remarry divorced persons, and a close friend castigated me roundly for doing so. How could I marry those who had been divorced when it was clear that God hated it?

I could not argue that divorce was God's ideal, but it was clear to me that God's provision for it was an act of grace towards us all, for none of us would make the perfect marriage and some of us could not sustain one.

But God's grace provided more than that; it was the source of forgiveness for all sin, and I had accepted that grace for me personally. How could I not pass the same grace of God to those coming to me? If I was to err at all, it had to be on the side of grace and not law.

Prayer: Dear Lord, thank you for the grace you extended to us. Guide us how to show your grace to all caught in marriage dilemmas, while being clear about your ideals.

True Love

Read: 1 Corinthians 13:1–7

If I give all I possess to the poor and surrender my body to the flames, but have not love, I gain nothing. 1 Corinthians 13:3.

This passage deals in depth with our love for each other, and is key advice for marriage. However, in contrast to previous passages we have looked at, it reverses some ideas we discussed.

We recognized that love without actions is dead, but this passage reminds us that not all actions are motivated by love. Lesser, even offensive motives can provoke seemingly good actions. What might these be?

It doesn't take long to look around us, or even inside us, to find some answers. Desire for personal recognition, fanatical dedication to an ideology, creating a sense of indebtedness to oneself, or even plain old manipulation can provoke apparently loving actions.

But these actions are done without care or concern for the person to whom they are directed, and they will not last. Once the desired end is gained or unattainable, or irritation or impatience sets in, the actions cease. On the other hand, real "love never fails."

In extolling the permanence of love, Paul lists qualities of love in verses 4–6 revealing attitudes that cannot exist with the lesser motives listed previously. Love "always protects, always trusts, always hopes, always perseveres," for love is motive enough in itself.

Of course, our earthly relationships are not always altruistic. Most of us need a "pay-off" somewhere along the way, and most of the time real love gains a response.

But if genuine love for the focus of our actions is the primary motivation, it will stand the test of time, displaying the characteristics that Paul lists.

Prayer: Heavenly Father, you are the source of love. Continue to teach us from your Word how to love each other and so reflect your love to others.

WEEK FORTY-NINE: TUESDAY

Love Trumps Knowledge

Read: 1 Corinthians 13:8–13

Now we see but a poor reflection as in a mirror; then we shall see face to face. Now I know in part; then I shall know fully, even as I am fully known. 1 Corinthians 13:12.

While Christians may invest their lives learning about God and how to live, Paul sees it as temporary and limited. What we know now is but a "poor reflection as in a mirror," inadequate for the life beyond this one.

Knowledge is necessary and commended by the Bible, but it can produce a self-righteousness that measures another's spirituality. The man who "knows it all" is simply unaware of what he does *not* know, 1 Corinthians 8:1–2.

Similarly, the gifts of the Spirit, prophecy, tongues and others, are temporary and not an indicator of special approval from God.

Am I proud of greater spiritual prowess than my partner and use it to control or browbeat her, pointing out deficiencies or lack of devotion? Paul shows the difference between my partner and me is insignificant compared with my near complete ignorance of spiritual things.

But what I do know is not insignificant when used in love to encourage and commend my wife. If my gifts of knowledge and spiritual gifts are used with love they will be real and effective.

Of real significance in this passage is the listing of the primary virtues of Christianity; faith, hope and love. These Christian virtues need an object: we need to love and have faith in some-one outside ourselves, and we need to hope in something beyond us.

God did not create us to be independent beings; rather we were designed to be interdependent with each other, and each of us dependent upon him.

Prayer: Dear Lord, grant me your insight to gauge my actions according to your measure of love in your Word.

Purpose

Read: 2 Corinthians 5:1-10

[God] has made us for this very purpose and has given us the Spirit as a deposit, guaranteeing what is to come. 2 Corinthians 5:5.

We touched previously on the provision, protection and purpose that are required in all families. Today's reading focuses on the need for purpose.

Paul sets out God's purpose for us: that we might be with him in heaven. This parallels the purpose given to Israel: that they would be God's people, Exodus 6:7, and as God's people heaven is our final destiny.

At present, confined in this earthly body, we look forward to our final rest with him, for whom the Holy Spirit is our guarantee.

Thus, whether here or at our final destination, Paul reminds us that it is "our goal to please him," from love and not coercion. Paul reminds us we will give account of our time and actions while on earth.

For some of us the value of our work may count as straw, not valuable stones, 1 Corinthians 3:10–13. This may be a fearsome notion: have we fulfilled the task given to us? What if we have missed God's calling for us? But we can be sure of one task.

One reason for these meditations is to demonstrate that the home is the primary place to practice transparent faith and love. Our closest relationships, where we live moment by moment, are the major part of our pilgrimage.

This is attainable for everyone. Whatever we may feel called to, fulfilling God's requirements to our partners and family is the core of a life pleasing to God. In fact, to fail in this area may nullify all the other efforts we make to please him.

Prayer: Dear Lord, we want to please you. Thank you for the training ground—our family—you have provided for us. Help us to us to use that experience in all relationships to which you call us.

WEEK FORTY-NINE: THURSDAY

Equality

Read: Galatians 3:23–29

There is neither Jew nor Greek, slave nor free, male nor female, for you are all one in Christ Jesus. Galatians 3:28.

Today's reading shows how God's intervention in human history has begun to restore the equality of all human beings.

The short list given: Jew and Greek (Gentile), slave and free, male and female, is representative of all classes of people as a wider reading of the New Testament shows, see also Luke 14:7–14; James 2:1–4. Whatever was lost at the fall is now recovered in Jesus Christ, for we "are all sons (children) of God through faith in Christ Jesus."

It is lamentable that some faith communities base their conduct on the Bible yet deny full fellowship to some based on race. White supremacists come to mind, as do the South African churches that supported apartheid.

It is also true that within North American Christian churches, there are many that are all white or all black—less by design than by attitude. While many of us pay lip service to the idea of equality in Christ we are hesitant to associate with those different to us.

While the role of women in the Church is beyond our scope, restrictions placed upon the service of women often seriously undermine the equality of women in otherwise faithful churches.

This pales to insignificance alongside the attitude of some Christian husbands that their wives and family are simply adjuncts to themselves. Apart from the inequality this fosters, the greater tragedy is the loss of companionship and efficiency of the family unit when dictatorship is the basis of family life.

Prayer: O Lord, search our hearts for prejudices we may have built up during our lives. Please forgive us and grant us courage to overcome our fear of differences.

Submit to Each Other

Read: Ephesians 5:15–21

Submit to one another out of reverence for Christ. Ephesians 5:21.

The verses that follow today's reading (verses 22-33) are probably the most referred to in establishing a marriage relationship, yet are as frequently misapplied.

First, in those verses, it is significant that men have far more instructions than women, possibly because they are harder of hearing. Second, the standard set for men is far higher than that for women; men have no cause for superiority. But of greatest importance, today's passage—often ignored—sets the context for the marriage relationship.

Today's verses set a standard for relating to others in the Body of Christ. It is instructive to read these verses as though they refer specifically to husband and wife—avoid drunkenness, be filled with the Spirit, rejoice and be thankful to God for his goodness together.

The passage concludes with a simple charge to "submit to one another out of reverence to Christ," which then becomes the context for the following instructions on marriage. Both wives *and* husbands, as part of the Body of Christ, are to submit to each other.

So the following verses, Ephesians 5:22-33, seen in this context are a description of how each—both man and woman—submit to the other. Contrary to some views, it particularly means that a husband will submit to his wife as a sister in Christ.

This submission is obviously out of consideration for one another, but particularly "out of reverence for Christ." To submit to one another is a Christian duty, for it follows the example given by Christ, Philippians 2:6–8, part of the growing image of God in us.

Prayer: Thank you Lord, for making marriage a place of learning to serve. Help us learn what submission means in the context of our different roles as husband and wife.

295

WEEK FORTY-NINE: WEEKEND

Anger

Anger is like fire and as common and deadly. It harms those of us who harbour it as well as those at whom it is directed. As a motive for violence, it is the most destructive force on earth, but rarely dealt with as such. At the time, anger seems reasonable, for anger always has a reason, but seldom a good one.

Whether anger is justified is not the issue, but rather how we use it. Anger is not a sin in itself—God has anger—but it is the temptation to sin; the temptation to violent words or actions, often irrespective of justification.

Anger is like pain, an indicator that something is wrong. Avoid the cause of anger if possible, but we need to handle anger correctly when it arises. Anger is often triggered by failure to deal with a situation, a sense of helplessness or the meaninglessness of a situation.

We must not only evaluate our anger, but also *own* it. We are responsible for our *re*-actions as well as our actions. Provocation is a cause, not a justification.

Anger is like alcohol, a way of escape, of avoiding reality. Anger becomes comfortable, like a warm coat on a cold day and when continuously indulged, anger reinforces itself. How can we deal with it?

We have three choices. We may express it, and risk injuring others. Expression releases tension, but reinforces the anger and its justification. To repress anger risks injury to ourselves: it threatens depression or a later explosion.

Christians, have an alternate recourse: confess our anger to God, deal with its roots, and leave the issue that provoked it in his hands. It will help diffuse our anger and direct it into constructive channels.

Prayer: Lord, we thank you for giving us anger to help us recognize injustice. Guard us from letting our anger out indiscriminately and help us to channel our anger in constructive ways to ease tense situations and even change circumstances.

A Wife's Submission

Read: Ephesians 5:22–24

Now as the Church submits to Christ, so also wives should submit to their husbands in everything. Ephesians 5:24.

These instructions for the wife have been widely used to establish some sort of lordship of the husband over the wife so that she becomes a resource for the husband's own advancement.

The repetition of "submit" and the phrase, "for the husband is the head of the wife," enhance this idea. As the Church is obedient to Christ, so the wife must be obedient to the husband. Even when the husband has the best interests of his family at heart, he still assumes his wife's resources are for his direction.

How can this agree with the equality of the sexes we have already seen? Equating the husband with Christ does not take into account a man's imperfection and differences to Christ. Ann puts it concisely: "I submit to my husband as he loves me as Christ loves the Church."

But the greatest difficulty is relating this to the "submission" of the husband required in verse 21. That is totally out of keeping with the idea of subservience of the wife to the husband. How do we reconcile these two ideas?

The idea of submission in found in service. In recognizing the different God given roles for each sex, each serves the other within those roles. Thus the wife's submission is in love and respect for the husband, and the husband's submission is in loving her by setting her as his first priority.

Submission results, not by control of one over the other, but rather in showing mutual love and respect, Ephesians 5:33.

Prayer: O Lord, help us both understand how we remain equal yet with differing roles which you have assigned to us. Show us what mutual submission means in our respective roles, so our marriage reflects your truth to the world.

A Husband's Submission

Read: Ephesians 5:25–33

Each one of you also must love his wife as he loves himself.
Ephesians 5:33.

As we noted previously, the context for today's reading in husband and wife relationships is the charge to "submit to one another," verse 21. This necessarily includes the husband; but how does a husband submit to his wife?

Marriage is a partnership of equals. Our reading painstakingly describes a husband's submission which adds up to recognizing his wife as his first priority.

My wife's well-being and fulfillment come before anything else, based on an ultimate standard—for me to love her "just as Christ loved the Church." Here are three suggestions on how to fulfill our obligation as men to our wives, based on this passage.

First, we are responsible to provide for our wives in the same way that we look after ourselves, for everyone "feeds and cares" for his own body.

Second, we need to give our lives for our wives as Christ gave himself for the Church. As we previously suggested, it may not mean dying for our wives, but it certainly means living for them. Despite other legitimate calls on our time, their need of us outweighs them all, for their welfare is our first priority.

Last, we have opportunity to present our wives to Christ as he will present the Church to himself. It should be my supreme service and joy to present my wife to Christ complete in him.

The roles of husband and wife dovetail; each completes the other, which builds full potential for both.

Prayer: Thank you Lord, for giving us clear directions for maintaining a peaceful and constructive marriage.

Respect for Children

Read: Ephesians 6:1–9

Fathers, do not exasperate your children; instead, bring them up in the training and instruction of the Lord. Ephesians 6:5.

This is one of few passages giving specific instruction for the relationship between parents and children. Perhaps their scarcity points to the fact we find life's guidance in God's dealings with us, his children by creation, rather than by specific instruction.

Even in the detailed instructions regarding relationships between masters and slaves, the relationship between each rests on the relationship with Christ.

However, there is an interesting twist to the instruction to children. We know that for children, promise of reward can be a greater incentive to obedience than punishment; honouring parents is the one commandment that has a promise attached.

There is, of course, a practical application of this promise; a child that rejects a parent's advice is more likely to experience risk to life. On a more positive note, a child that learns respect for parents is more likely to carry that respect into life, and create a stable and safe society.

But there is a reciprocal requirement that parents also respect their children. Parents that treat children as commodities, or personal belongings, are also more likely to generate rebellion later.

A child learns respect for parents by the respect he or she receives. While this may seem obvious, the way many parents humiliate their children would suggest they believe they gain respect from intimidation like bullies the world over.

To bring children up "in the training and instruction of the Lord," is to treat them with the fairness and justice God grants us.

Prayer: Lord, we thank you for the children you gave us. Grant us the grace to treat them with fairness at all times, particularly during frustrating times.

WEEK FIFTY: THURSDAY

Here: Or With Him?

Read: Philippians 1:12–26

For to me, to live is Christ and to die is gain. Philippians 1:21.

As Christians, we commit our marriages and families to God and aim to serve him by serving them. When we finally reunite with our loved ones in the next life, we will clearly see Christ as the source of joy in those relationships.

Thus, being "married" to him will fulfill all the desires of our hearts we lacked on earth. The longing to be with an absent loved one is symptomatic of our desire for God; for him to fill the "God-shaped" void within us.

Paul was unmarried, but sensed the conflicting desires between being present with God and remaining on earth to continue his ministry.

Our relationship with our partner is a part fulfillment of our relationship with God, but our bond with God gives depth and stability to our marriage. Our desire to remain on earth is the wish to fulfill our responsibility to God by serving our partners, but it does not, and should not, preclude our desire to be with him.

Paul recognized both to be legitimate. We may often feel we enjoy our families or sense their need so much we are loath to leave them. Any desire to leave for our final rest may seem like a betrayal of our loved ones.

Paul resolved it by accepting that his staying would increase the joy in Christ of those who depended on him. In the end, the choice is not ours anyway.

God will decide when our work is done and take us at the appropriate time. We can rest in faith, without guilt, in the decision that he deems right for us.

Prayer: Heavenly Father, we rejoice in our salvation and our final destiny to be with you for eternity. Cause us to live joyfully here and now, while anticipating final joy in heaven with you.

Respect for Partners

Read: Philippians 2:1–8

Your attitude should be the same as that of Christ Jesus.
Philippians 2:5.

Given the equality of the sexes in creation, and the image of God in both, how does this work out in practice? What attitudes and conduct express these characteristics?

An attribute that is common in all relationship breakdowns is lack of respect—treating another as inferior, unworthy or inadequate and using words that degrade, insult, or injure. Lack of respect to some degree is common in all marriages, and we treat our partners too often in a casual and cavalier manner.

Verse 5 encourages us to mirror the servanthood of Jesus by actions listed in the previous four verses. As Jesus is the express image of the Father, Hebrews 1:3, our imitation of him will reflect the image of God in us.

Respect means treating each other with deference, esteem, and honour, and considering the other's views, concerns, and ideas all worthy of a conscious and deliberate hearing.

Respect for each means both partners agree on decisions. If there is disagreement on a course of action, this usually means compromise, but both will embrace the decision, even if either or both are somewhat dissatisfied.

Where disagreement is fundamental, it may mean making no decision or deferring it. When a decision is unavoidable, one may defer to the other, but consider the decision a joint one to deny future recriminations.

Showing respect and sharing decisions both reflect the equality God has built into the sexes, the image of God placed in both.

Prayer: Dear Lord, it is not always easy to determine the better course of action. We depend on you, Holy Spirit, to guide us to right decisions.

301

Agreeing Together

Equality in marriage means unanimous agreement on decisions taken that affect the marriage. This importance of agreeing together cannot be overemphasized. It means that each has a veto over the other, which you may consider unworkable.

But it has the clear advantage that neither partner can carry resentment over a decision that the other has made. Some examples may show ways in which constant agreement may work.

Ann and I attended an investment seminar together but I was skeptical of the excessive claims made for property investment. However, it was important to Ann and I thought it might work, so we went ahead.

But due to a downturn in the markets it caused us financial problems for years. But despite my misgivings, we had taken the decision together and we weathered the difficulties together.

During a period of time spent on the west coast of British Columbia, we searched for a house to buy. Our agreement to buy a house that we both liked meant that it took over a year to find the right one.

Each of us found places that we liked, but not to the taste of the other. The home we finally settled on was one of the best we owned.

When we moved back to the prairies, we needed to move quickly and Ann went ahead to find a place to live. I gave my agreement to her choice before she made it, on the assumption that her choice would be a good one.

She bought a house that was an ideal unit for us, and which turned out to be a good investment. I had finally learned to trust Ann as she had trusted me.

Prayer: Dear Lord, agreeing together may not always be easy, and we call on your grace for each of us when either of us may need to defer to the other.

Power and Suffering

Read: Philippians 3:1–11

I want to know Christ and the power of his resurrection and the fellowship of sharing in his sufferings, becoming like him in his death. Philippians 3:10.

Respect for others frequently hinges on the status that we accord ourselves. To be popular, influential, attaining a social or career position, or having recognizable gifts or other personal success, can lead us to disparage others less privileged.

Paul was a Jew of great intellect and status in the Jewish hierarchy of his time. He had all the qualifications: physical circumcision, a Hebrew of the tribe of Benjamin, a Pharisee, zealous and faultless before God.

Yet in this passage Paul recognized that all his personal, particularly religious, assets meant nothing apart from his relationship to Jesus Christ. He considered none of these had any value before God, only the righteousness of Christ in place of his own sin.

This drove Paul to participate in the risen life of Christ—to experience the power of his resurrection but also to share in his sufferings. He experienced some of the sacrifice that Jesus made to bring the change that only God's power could bring.

The relationship between achievement and suffering is not uncommon in the New Testament, Romans 8:17–18; 2 Corinthians 4:17. The Early Church as well as modern China, show the Church flourishes under persecution.

Personal achievement, ability, or knowledge alone will not promote success in relationships, especially with our partners. It is only as we recognize our need to seek God's direction for our knowledge and talents—perhaps calling for sacrifice on our part—that we will see the power of the risen Christ evident in our lives and marriages.

Prayer: O Lord, help us to understand it is only in identification with you—even in suffering—that we experience your power in our lives.

WEEK FIFTY-ONE: TUESDAY

Leadership

Read: 1 Timothy 3:1–5

He must manage his own family well and see that his children obey him with proper respect. 1 Timothy 3:4.

Here's a passage that we may assume does not apply to us. We do not seek a position of Church leadership, or are unlikely to assume one.

But the requirements listed are not exclusive to leadership, although necessary for it, but are required of all who profess to follow Christ. Most of us can probably comply with the faithfulness to one partner requirement, but may have more difficulty obtaining children's obedience. Thus, many are tempted to exempt themselves from leadership because of this requirement.

Does this really mean that disobedient children indicate unacceptable Christian behaviour of the parents? If this is so, then perhaps to some degree none of us fulfills this requirement in our parenthood so none of us is eligible for leadership.

What is more likely, when children are disobedient, parents deal with it in a way that garners respect from their peers and is also respectful to the children: "in a manner worthy of full respect." The emphasis is on good management of the household, not on attaining the perfect family.

For those currently in leadership, or considering it, recall that God, as the perfect parent, still encountered disobedience from his created "children." That episode, and the way God has interacted with mankind since, should be the pattern for our parenting.

Remember, leadership is not just a calling for directing the affairs of the Church on earth; it is a calling for all who have others, especially children, dependent on them.

Prayer: Heavenly Father, we know that we all have leadership responsibilities, at home or at work. Guide us to reflect you in our interactions with those dependent on us.

Caring for the Elderly

Read: 1 Timothy 5:4–8, 16

If a widow has children or grandchildren, these should learn first of
all to put their religion into practice by caring for their own family.
1 Timothy 5:4.

The relationship between parents and children is given clear attention in today's reading. There is an echo here of the fifth commandment to honour one's parents.

The divide between members of the same family was as prevalent in Paul's time as it is now, making this passage as relevant today. The need to care for others, but especially our parents, is part of our Christian duty.

The irony is that it is natural to love our children and parents, which should make the requirement unnecessary. But conditions in society betray our basic selfish instinct.

Many adult children often ignore their elderly folk, and increasing life expectancy makes some children seniors themselves, often less able to cope with sick and aging parents. This has created the "sandwich" generation: those trying to look after aged parents, while still raising their own family.

Scripture neither recognizes nor downplays the difficulties in looking after parents and grandparents, particularly those who are widowed. But it does require children to take responsibility for their aged forbears at a level they can manage.

This may mean taking steps unpopular with both parent and others—placing them into a senior's home is a particularly difficult decision—to ensure the elder's proper care. One who ignores an elderly family member "has denied the faith and is worse than an unbeliever."

Prayer: O Lord, you know the pain and frustration of trying to look after aging and failing parents. We thank you for them and their love for us. We seek your guidance for their well-being daily.

WEEK FIFTY-ONE: THURSDAY

Single Mothers

Read: 1 Timothy 5:11–15

I counsel younger widows to marry, to have children, to manage their homes and to give the enemy no opportunity for slander.
1 Timothy 5:14.

Paul would be in hot water today for the stereotyping apparent in this passage: to "counsel younger widows to marry, to have children, to manage their homes . . ."

Some may argue that he had a poor opinion of women who succumb to "their sensual desires," or who are "idle" and "busybodies." These characteristics are in opposition to "their dedication to Christ." However, this was at least partly Paul's experience, as some had "already turned away to follow Satan."

We should also recognize the culture of Paul's day. Then, widows may have had few options, whereas the opportunities for women in our culture are many.

Paul's main concern was that younger widows who had youth and health on their side should not consider themselves entitled to be wards of the Church. While Paul does not mention divorcees, divorce was common; particularly men divorcing their wives for frivolous reasons, so divorced women could also have been in view.

Today, with the high number of single mothers in society and in our churches, similar guidelines may well apply. I have great admiration for single mothers who under that handicap work, pursue professional goals, and raise their families alone.

I also applaud those parents of single women who, in an apt reversal of Paul's advice and despite their age, pitch in to assist in stabilizing their daughter's family and create an environment that will foster responsible citizens. I'm sure Paul would feel the same way.

Prayer: Dear Lord, strengthen us to assist those in our family who are single through little or no fault of their own.

306

A Faithful Son and Grandson

Read: 2 Timothy 1:1–5

I have been reminded of your sincere faith, which first lived in your grandmother Lois and in your mother Eunice and, I am persuaded, now lives in you also. 2 Timothy 1:5.

Timothy was a "son in the faith" to Paul. The amount of ministry that Paul left in Timothy's care reflected not only a close relationship, but also Timothy's clear understanding of the faith and its practical application.

From reading Paul's other letters, he had many whom he commended in the faith, but Timothy stands out because of his administrative qualities which Paul used extensively.

What is noticeable in this passage is Timothy's genealogy as listed by Paul. Remember this letter was only written about thirty-six years after the crucifixion.

Timothy was young, 1 Timothy 4:12, and his mother Eunice and his grandmother Lois must have been converted to Christianity during those years. So Timothy probably grew up from early childhood in a Christian household, where his mother and grandmother expressed their faith.

This records a transmission of the faith through generations. Timothy was perhaps a compliant child and he easily adopted his mother's faith, but eventually making the faith firmly his own.

The ability to carry out the tasks allotted to him, especially during a time of persecution of the Church, would be impossible through a second-hand faith.

Lois and Eunice's faithfulness to God had their outcome in Timothy; his work for the New Testament Church is a continuing legacy for us today. This example from Timothy should be an example to us that faithfulness to God will produce children of similar influence.

Prayer: Dear Lord, thank you for this encouraging example of what our children and grandchildren could be.

Raising Children: Then and Now

Most parents need all the help they can get. Raising children today is a hazardous venture with so many dangers to which they can fall prey.

During my teen years in England in the fifties I watched a television program showing a person admitted to hospital with injuries, but feeling no pain. It turned out that he was addicted to heroin, a so-called "dangerous drug." That was my first introduction to recreational drugs—they were unheard of in my childhood. Life is different in the brave new millennium.

That is one example of the difference between now and then. Although Ann and I spent our young childhood during World War Two, we always knew who and where the enemy was.

The England of our childhood was a Christian society. Not that all were Christians, we were a similar minority as today, but Christian values were universal: sex was for marriage, children obeyed their parents, infractions were stigmatized and restrained, and divorce and children out of wedlock were almost unheard of.

I have great concern and admiration for those raising children at the beginning of this century, facing challenges we escaped in our era. Some refrain from having children at all because they consider the world an awful place for child-rearing. Understandable.

But those of us with children have already found some of the greatest joys as well as heartaches accrue to us from family. We have learned that closeness to God and prayer for our children are not optional but a necessity.

Raising children *is* a challenging calling, but perhaps your child will lead the way to a better world.

Prayer: We love our children, Lord, and often fear for their future. But your love, O Lord, casts out fear. Life with you is an adventure.

Self - Control and Integrity

Read: Titus 2:1–8

Be self-controlled. In everything set them an example by doing what is good. In your teaching show integrity, seriousness and soundness of speech. Titus 2:6-8.

Titus, like Timothy, was a "son in the faith" to Paul and was committed to similar work, Titus 1:5. Much of the letter to Titus contains similarities to Paul's first letter to Timothy, including potential criticism we noted against the previous passage, 1 Timothy 5:11–15.

A similar defence against stereotyping, particularly of female roles, is the culture of Paul's time that had few options for women. Most would fall into the "wife and mother" category.

However, we must note Paul's purpose in this passage. He is not defining roles, but the behaviour expressed within them. For today's men and women, the message is the same irrespective of their function in society: behave in a way that does not malign the Gospel.

We identify best with encouragement for young men to be self-controlled, for the older women to be mentors for the younger, and the older men to be of sound faith. Moderation and faithfulness to others are the keys Paul requires to reflect the truth of what they believe.

Note two words in this text. First, "self-controlled," used three times in the admonition teaching the older men and both younger men and women. The Greek word suggests sober, clear-headedness which reflects a trust in God's control of life's situations. The second word is "integrity," which simply requires both belief and practical life to be integrated.

These two passions are symbiotic, they reinforce each other to strengthen our faith and witness to those whose lives we touch.

Prayer: O Lord, we want to glorify you in the roles you have designed for us. Grant us grace to maintain self-control and integrity in whatever situations we find ourselves.

WEEK FIFTY-TWO: TUESDAY

Jesus: Our Perfection

Read: Hebrews 5:5–10

He learned obedience from what he suffered and, once made perfect, he became the source of eternal salvation for all who obey him. Hebrews 5:8-9.

This is a difficult passage to understand; particularly that Christ *learned* obedience though suffering. As the perfect Son of God, why would he have to learn obedience? Surely, obedience was in his perfection.

The answer lies mainly in the fact that he was a Son with a responsibility to his Father. He could not fulfill his mission on earth without complete earthly obedience. Whatever plans the Trinity had made together depended on Jesus becoming a man and obeying his Father.

This meant he had to succeed where Adam did not; to be tested where Adam failed and he would not. Only this way could he be the perfect substitute for humankind.

His earthly ministry began with being "led by the Spirit" to a place of temptation, Matthew 4:1. Where Adam succumbed to the desire to "be like God," Genesis 3:5, Jesus, despite great need, refused to use his divine powers for his own benefit. Adam could not be like God, whereas Jesus became the perfect man.

Obedience to parents is not easy, particularly during puberty when questions about life and peer pressure create an environment of challenge. Of course, parents are not perfect and subject to errors and subjective decisions.

Perhaps this is the basis of *our* suffering in learning obedience. Our obedience to instructions that appear incorrect, mistaken, or unjust, reflects the obedience of Jesus to his Father's instructions. For Jesus, those instructions were unnecessary and unjust for him, but he obeyed so that he could be our perfect sacrifice.

Prayer: Dear Father, Jesus was obedient to you for our sakes. May we be obedient to you for the sake of your Gospel and your desire to establish your Kingdom on earth.

Discipline

Read: Hebrews 12:4-13

"The Lord disciplines those he loves, and he punishes everyone he accepts as a son." Hebrews 12:6.

The writer to the Hebrews presses home the necessity of discipline. For the Hebrews in their time, the writer is thinking of persecution, as he tells them, "you have not yet resisted to the point of shedding your blood."

Thus in verse 7, he equates hardship with discipline from God, a concept our soft western culture would find hard to accept. Surely, if all good things come from God, how can we expect pain and suffering from him also?

The New Testament teaches that adversity often accompanies our faith, whether by persecution, sacrifice, or just living in a broken world. That adversity is a form of discipline.

Discipline falls into two categories: punishment from others for a wrong committed or a self imposed routine of training for some endeavour. Paul indicates both are included in the adversity that we experience, a discipline that later "produces a harvest of righteousness and peace."

But Paul emphasizes discipline is a product of love; without discipline there is no love. Apart from some misguided individuals who think "free expression" is the ideal for raising children, most parents see the need for shaping a child's behaviour.

Most discipline is born of the parents' desire to prepare their child for life in the real world. Children who learn that there is conduct unacceptable in both the family and society will develop a well adjusted and happier life for themselves and those around them.

Prayer: Dear Lord, few of us like discipline, but we know from our own childhood and children it is necessary. Help us to rest in your love during times of testing.

ANN AND BRYAN NORFORD

Death and Persecution
Read: Revelation 12:1–17

Then the dragon was enraged at the woman and went off to make war against the rest of her offspring — those who obey God's commandments and hold to the testimony of Jesus.
Revelation 12:17.

The symbolism in this reading is generally clear. The woman about to give birth is the nation of Israel; the sun, moon and stars refer back to Jacob—renamed Israel—his wife and twelve sons, Genesis 37:9. The dragon is "that ancient serpent called the devil, or Satan, who leads the whole world astray."

The son born is Jesus, whom Herod sought to kill at birth. He acted for Satan who knew the coming King would be the one to destroy him. Evil men thought they had triumphed at the crucifixion, but the resurrection changed it all; Jesus "was snatched up to God and his throne," see Acts 1:9–11.

This passage also sets the basis for the persecution of the Christian Church. It is not one ideology pitted against another, it is a spiritual battle, won by the King himself, but now waged against those who follow him—the woman's offspring: "those who keep God's commands and hold fast their testimony about Jesus."

Satan is non-discriminatory. His campaign against the unborn, newly born and children is an attempt by him to kill off any who might form allegiance to Christ. Herod set the pattern, killing off a generation of infants trying to ensure the death of one.

Likewise, by infanticide in China and India, by abortion worldwide, by suicide, and indiscriminate bombing of women and children, the enemy of God tries to eliminate children who may turn to Christ.

Prayer: O Lord, help us see the tragedies of this world are the result of Satan's work in trying to depose you. Show us our own adversity is part of the spiritual warfare that engages us.

The Ultimate Wedding

Read: Revelation 21:1–10

I saw the Holy City, the New Jerusalem, coming down out of heaven from God, prepared as a bride beautifully dressed for her husband. Revelation 21:2.

This passage meditates on the final marriage that earthly marriage illustrates, however poorly. The Holy City of Jerusalem adorned as the "Bride of Christ," represents all those who have entered that symbolic city by their allegiance to Jesus Christ, Revelation 19:7–9.

Christ will present to the Father as his bride, those that he has drawn to himself by his work on Calvary, Ephesians 5:27. That final marriage will contain within itself all marriages we have known, and will surpass any union we may have known on earth.

Entry into that marriage will be the desire of both partners for union, not based on the purity of the bride, but the beauty the groom sees in her, and his willingness to provide her with new clothing, Revelation 7:13–14.

But the work of the bride does not go unrewarded; her clothing also represents the fulfillment of her commitment to the Groom during her engagement, Revelation 19:8.

Perhaps our earthly marriages would improve if we would see them through the image of that final wedding. Christ displays his love for the bride, but acknowledges her failures.

While that is the position of Christ for us, it should be the attitude of both partners in an earthly marriage. Men have no advantage over women when it comes to sin and also need acceptance of frailty from their wives.

But will we have the same pride in presenting our wives complete in Christ as he will have in presenting his bride to the Father? Ephesians 5:27.

Prayer: O Lord, how we look forward to that final reunion with you. Teach and guide us to be partners more like you in our earthy marriage.

313

WEEK FIFTY-TWO: WEEKEND

That Final Reunion

W hen our youngest daughter and her husband put their house up for sale, they had a number of people view it. There was one couple from an eastern background who believed artifacts had meaning rather that just being ornamental.

Passing the dining room table, the wife noticed a centre piece with three candles, and asked if there was some meaning for that display. For most in western culture the answer would probably have been: "It's just an ornament"

In this case that answer would have been wrong. Alexandra's previous three pregnancies had resulted in miscarriages. Most would have put these behind them as part of life's misfortune; after all, our culture considers the unborn child a non-person.

However, Alex kept these three candles as a reminder of three children that she had lost, although they had not been born. Apart from giving honour and respect to the unborn, they kept alive another Christian belief—that of final reunion.

Those three children that God took home to be with himself for reasons best known to him, had not been lost; they will be there to greet their parents in the place where all tears will be wiped away.

All who have lost children or other loved ones in the Lord will have a final, complete, and eternal fellowship with them. We "do not grieve like the rest who have no hope," 1 Thessalonians 4:13.

That reunion with Christ and loved ones who have gone before is one of the most precious expectations of all Christians. We may look back at events in life with sorrow, but we look forward to that final reunion with joy.

Prayer: Dear Heavenly Father, we continue to mourn those who have left us, many prematurely. But we rejoice now in the certain hope you have given us for our final reunion with them and to that final marriage union with you.

314

Indexes

Old Testament Index

New Testament Index

Subject Index

Note: the articles "A" and An" and "The" are placed at the end of titles in this index.

329

Comfort

Destructive Emotions

Faith

Families

Infidelity

Maintaining Marriage